12.99

JUL   2016

All But Normal

life on victory road

a memoir

SHAWN THORNTON

with JOEL KILPATRICK

Tyndale House Publishers, Inc.
Carol Stream, Illinois

Library of Congress Cataloging-in-Publication Data

Names: Thornton, Shawn, author.
Title: All but normal : life on Victory Road / Shawn Thornton, with Joel
  Kilpatrick.
Description: Carol Stream, IL : Tyndale House Publishers, Inc., 2016.
Identifiers: LCCN 2016003194| ISBN 9781496413932 (hc) | ISBN 9781496411723
  (sc)
Subjects: LCSH: Mental illness—Religious aspects—Christianity. | Families
  of the mentally ill—Biography. | Families—Religious life. | Thornton,
  Shawn. | Thornton, Beverly.
Classification: LCC BT732.4 .T56 2016 | DDC 248.8/62092—dc23 LC record
available at http://lccn.loc.gov/2016003194

This book is dedicated to my mother, Beverly Mae Thornton. She introduced me to Jesus and showed me in the midst of all her struggles what it looks like to live and love like Jesus. Thank you, Mom.

Publisher's Note

DEAR READER:

The story you are about to read is true. The events depicted include vulgar language of a kind that typically doesn't appear in books we publish. But after careful consideration, we decided to include some dialogue that, though potentially offensive, is accurate, helps to capture in an authentic way the intensity of the events, and gives a truthful illustration of the human condition.

Author's Note

THIS MEMOIR is based on events that happened across nearly five decades, including events that occurred before I was born. I have done my best to tell these stories accurately. In some places, I have used composite events, dialogue, and chronology for the sake of clarity, and I have changed some names and details to protect the privacy of individuals. I understand and respect that others may have different perspectives on the events and stories I have included in this book. As with any memoir, this version of my story is uniquely mine.

Foreword

SOMETIMES BEFORE I SPEAK, when I'm in the wings peering at the crowd, I'll wonder, *How did I get here?* I don't mean "here" in the sense of directions; I mean, how does the least likely candidate to speak at a Billy Graham crusade, or to write books that people actually read; how does a person who takes the gospel to disabled people around the world; how did the strange and twisted circumstances of my life bring me to this point?

I bet on Sunday mornings Shawn Thornton wonders the same. When he's standing in the wings at Calvary Community Church, ready to give the sermon, perhaps he glances at the crowd and thinks, *How did I get here?*

Shawn is an effective, godly leader who does not appear to bear the emotional wounds of a shattered and chaotic childhood. Where did he get such a glad disposition and easy manner? Knowing his background, if I were him, I'd be a basket case. Yet he is easily one of the kindest and most influential Christian leaders I've ever met.

I have only recently heard Shawn's whole story—it was a few years ago, when I asked him to speak at one of our conferences for Joni and Friends. I asked because his church has one of the largest, most successful disability ministry programs in the country. However, I had no idea he was actually *raised* in a special-needs family (a very polite way of putting it). Disability in any family is never easy, but in Shawn's case, it nearly ripped his childhood to shreds.

Growing up under a parent with a serious mental illness? Being raised by someone who'd scream every name in the book at you? How does a kid survive that? In the sixties and seventies, a psychiatric disorder was just not talked about, let alone treated effectively. It was a tragedy you would try to forget when you packed yourself a bag lunch and headed to school in the morning. But family tragedies have a way of catching up with you. And so it did for Shawn.

But please do not think that *All But Normal* is a scathing tell-all against a crazy mother. Shawn loved her then, and it's obvious in every chapter that he loves her now. Like any good family member, he has taken the high road when it comes to dealing with disability. Rather than scorning his mother, he clung to those moments when he felt her love. As broken and bewildering as their relationship was, Shawn's bruised heart was filled with compassion for her.

And as I read Shawn's story, I learned to love her too. There is a secret why, but I won't share it here—after you read a few chapters, you'll understand my special affection for Mrs. Thornton.

One more thing about *All But Normal*. Shawn's story will force you to forget everything you've ever been taught about personal power leading to effective leadership—confidence, charisma, and chutzpah count for little over the long haul. As a psychologist friend once told me, the leaders God chooses are often more broken than strong, more damaged than whole, more troubled than secure. God's most effective leaders don't rise to power in spite of their weakness; they lead with power *because* of their weakness. By the last page of this book, you'll be convinced that God's greatest leaders seem to rise up from beds of nails, not roses.

This is the fascinating story you hold in your hands. It is laced with horror yet softened by humor. It has lots of jagged edges yet is honed and polished by the tender traces of God's love. There are dark, hellish storms, but you learn to see silver linings gracing most of the clouds on Shawn's horizon.

No one can describe it better, though, than the man himself. One of his most touching reflections in *All But Normal* reads, "I realized our family possessed something in our little house on Victory Road that many people simply didn't have: the love and the purpose of God in the midst of seeming chaos."

There you have it. This remarkable autobiography is filled with hope and redemption, revealing how God used unimaginable turmoil in one little boy's life to ultimately rescue him, hone him for leadership, and fill his heart with compassion for the poor and needy, for the broken and damaged.

It's why I don't think Shawn would trade his abnormal childhood for any amount of normal.

Joni Eareckson Tada
Joni and Friends International Disability Center
Agoura Hills, California

IT HAD BEEN a night of hell like no other.

Red and blue police lights flashed against our house. From my bedroom window, I could see the front yard where the officer's car was parked. It looked so unusual sitting there, like something out of a TV crime show that my family, on more peaceful nights, might watch together. But the tears on my face, the pit in my stomach, and the sound of hateful words and shattering glass ringing in my ears reminded me that this was not a scene I could switch off by pushing a button. Tonight, it was real, and it was happening to the Thornton family.

I wasn't even sure how it had started, but I realize now that everyone in our family had seen it coming for months. Although few outside our home knew it, Mom's deteriorating capacity to manage life, to even walk safely, and her utter frustration with her limitations had brought her and Dad to a point of total exasperation. Dad or one of us boys must have said something to set her off—something small, not worth noticing under normal conditions, when grace flows more freely. But tonight it pierced and wounded, and Mom escalated into one of her outbursts, the terrifying rages that had begun to grip her with ever-greater frequency. Her sudden flare-ups seemed to have otherworldly power and put her under the influence of something we didn't understand. Whatever it was, it transformed her from a kind, loving mother to a volatile tempest of emotions. Our home could become a battlefield in seconds.

"I'm tired of this s—!" Mom yelled. "I'm not living like this anymore. I'm going to divorce your a—!"

"Go ahead. What do I care?" Dad responded.

Dad seemed worn out from a long day at the factory—more fatigued and irritable than usual. Sometimes he could bear her flare-ups. Not tonight.

"I will!" she promised. "Tomorrow I'm leaving you. It's over!"

Most of these battles died out after a little while, but thirty minutes later, this one was still going strong. My brother, Troy, and I glanced at each other. This was getting bigger, scarier, and more violent, like a river rising beyond its banks, unpredictable and wild. Mom grabbed something and threw it from across the room at Dad, hitting the cabinets near his head. In anger, Dad whirled around and threw something back at her, not full force but enough to warn her not to do it again.

"I hate you!" she screamed. "It's all your fault! If it wasn't for you, I wouldn't be this way!"

"Shut up, Bev!" Dad yelled back. In response, Mom held out her stiff arms and bent fingers for inspection.

"Look how I am! Look at you! You don't have to live like this!" she cried.

He turned away.

Crash!

She had hurled another item at him, something randomly snatched from a counter nearby.

"Boys, go to your rooms," Dad said.

Troy and I didn't hesitate. We wanted out of there as much as our parents wanted us gone. Usually their arguments held to a pattern. One of them would eventually calm down, and the violence and recriminations would stop. Now they were squaring off for extended battle. This was something we had rarely seen.

In my bedroom, I huddled on the bed and listened to the sound of objects crashing in the kitchen. Something shattered—a glass? A vase? A picture frame? Something else hit the wall so hard I knew it had made a hole. Something shattered and knocked down other items around it. Would anything be left in the morning?

Their voices sounded different—more raw, more capable of hatred and wounding power. Dad's yells were a throaty roar, sharper than usual, full of anger. Mom's voice was simply terrifying—shrieking, spiteful, unrestrained. More hurtful than Dad's. Tears flowed down my cheeks in wide channels, and I wondered how long I had been crying.

Is this the end? Is this where our family rips apart forever?

With hardly a pause, the raging went on for hours, walls pummeled by unseen objects, glass shattering, accusations of the most penetrating kind wielded like daggers. Lady, the mutt who had joined herself to our family, lay patiently against my chest and endured as I squeezed her tightly, as if I could transfer my mounting sadness and grief into her little body. I had never known such a friend. She was with me when even God seemed absent. Like now.

Lady looked up sympathetically at me. *Why, God?* I asked. *Why did you let this happen to us? Can't you just take me away from here? I don't even want to live if this is the way life is going to be.*

Just when I thought the house might come down with all the shouting and violence, I heard a car pull into our front yard. A strong knock sounded at the front door, and Dad answered it. The officer came in, his radio crackling and chattering in the car outside. The police had never been to our house before. The fight must have alarmed the neighbors.

Mom and Dad's voices de-escalated as they told the officer what was happening. Mom still spoke through tears and with heightened emotion. Her words ran together in seething incoherence.

"To hell with him!" she said. "I can't stay here anymore!"

There were spans of silence when I imagined that the officer was inspecting the ruined house. How could he know that even in normal circumstances our house looked like a total wreck? How could he tell the busted plates and glasses from the rest of the junk that normally littered our floors?

Sinking further into my bed, I held Lady close. If nothing else, I was thankful the yelling and throwing had stopped. Mom was still obviously simmering, agitated, out of control.

Dad and the officer were speaking. His voice had returned more or less to normal. My ears rang in the relative silence.

Then out my window I saw something that wrenched my heart apart, something I never thought I would see: my mother, her body so stiff she could barely walk, her voice issuing long moans through gritted teeth, walking with the police officer, slowly making her way through the yard. The rotating red and blue lights from the police car painted her in a surreal portrait of sadness and futility. I watched as the officer gently helped my mother into the back of his squad car.

It was the night my mother was taken to the mental ward.

CHAPTER I

"Mom, can I go with John to the department store?" Beverly asked, holding up a blouse on a hanger. "I want to exchange this blouse before our trip tomorrow."

She stood in the doorway of the girls' bedroom in their 900-square-foot house in Mishawaka, Indiana. The seven-member Gilvin family was getting ready to head "down home to Kentucky," as they put it, to visit relatives on Aunt Beulah's farm.

"Oh, Bevie, don't do that now," Bev's mom, Betty, said. "We're getting everything ready. You don't need a new blouse anyway."

"But I don't want to wear this white one down at the farm," Bev said with a level of concern only a ninth-grade girl could attach to her wardrobe. Little sisters Connie and Gail, twelve and ten years old, respectively, listened from the doorway. "She just wants to go driving with that boy," Connie whispered. Gail nodded.

"Well, you've got plenty of clothes," their mother said.

"Can't I trade this for something new?" Bev pressed. "It's our vacation. I want to wear the right thing."

The day had been full of rushing around. Betty had packed for all five daughters, of whom Bev was second oldest. Darkness had fallen over the leafy northern Indiana city, and suitcases lined the walls of the tiny home, ready to be shoehorned into the wood-paneled family station wagon for the next day's journey. From the living room, sounds of voices on television drifted in as their father, Russell, finally got off his feet for a bit.

"Are you all packed up?" Betty asked.

"I think so. Yes." Bev could sense a weakening in her mother's resistance.

"Then go ask Daddy."

Bev's eyes gleamed. She paused before walking toward the living room, gathering her thoughts, her eyes reflecting the words she was about to say.

Everyone knew Bev was clever and highly intelligent and not a schemer. Her sisters considered her the kindest and most playful sister. Her giggle was infectious and smart, not silly. It emanated from a warm heart that loved to laugh. She spent a lot of time with her younger sisters—playing make-believe school in the basement and volleyball in the park, and rollerskating and bike riding on the sidewalks around their house.

Measured in birthday invitations, Bev was the most popular outside the home as well. On Valentine's Day a month earlier, she had received flowers from a number of boys at school. Few were brave enough to come calling to the house, but Bev's sisters knew she was the focus of special attention from boys.

Bev was at the head of her class academically as well, her report card a tribute to the first letter of the alphabet. When not socializing or playing, she sat in the house and read dense books with no pictures in them and sometimes Latin primers. She had recently won the highest honor given in eighth grade, the Daughters of the American Revolution award, for being the student with the best academic performance, best citizenship, and most well-rounded personality. The family had gathered at the school to watch the presentation, her sisters giddy with excitement, Russell and Betty taking lots of pictures. Nobody in the family had received such an award before, but it seemed obvious that it would go to Bev.

Bev also served as crossing guard at the school, a conspicuous honor given to only the most responsible students. Every day, she left class early, put on her patrol belt, and helped children safely cross the street after school. It made her proud that she had been entrusted with the lives of her younger schoolmates.

Tonight, Bev's well-known tenacity was on display. Her sisters were right. She was indeed hoping to spend a few moments with John Thornton before heading to Kentucky for spring break. She barely knew him—he was seventeen and a senior in high school, and she was fourteen. John had asked her to a dance, prodded by his best friend, Chuck, who was dating Bev's older sister, Sue. Bev's parents agreed she could go to the dance, and John began dropping by the house to get to know her. In truth, Chuck had pressured him into it.

"You can't ask a girl to a dance and then ignore her for two months," Chuck scolded John. That made sense to John. If he didn't get to know Bev, what would they talk about at the dance?

Normally, the Gilvin and Thornton families would never have associated. They shared no friends, no church, no clubs, and little cultural background. The Gilvins were transplanted Southerners. Russell had moved the family from Kentucky to Indiana after World War II in search of a better job and now drove a truck for one of the factories that had sprung up in the Midwest after the war. The Gilvins' modest home, with a simple porch out back and a tiny awning over the front door, could barely contain their growing family. Four girls shared one bedroom. Three-year-old April slept in her parents' room. If someone sneezed at night, everyone said, "Bless you."

The Thorntons resided on the opposite side of town—and on the opposite side of the social spectrum. Their two-story home faced the St. Joseph River on a new, well-to-do street in Mishawaka. John's dad was a proud Notre Dame graduate, a politician and businessman who partnered with the Chicago mafia and ran an illegal casino behind a false wall in Mishawaka's most upscale restaurant, the Lincoln Highway Inn. When his political party was in office, he wielded great power locally, running the license bureau. Political cartoons of him appeared in the local newspaper's opinion pages, and reporters knew better than to dig too deeply into his affairs. The Thorntons were big fish in a small pond and often made the ninety-minute trip to socialize with Chicago's elite. Mrs. Thornton kept weekly appointments at the bridge club and beauty parlor. Their calendar was full and so was their bank account.

When John turned sixteen, his father took him to the auto dealership on Highway 31 in nearby Niles, Michigan.

"Pick out a car," he said, waving his hand toward the lot.

John, newly licensed, chose a sporty, cream-colored '62 Corvair, and his father purchased it outright.

Russell and Betty naturally had not allowed Bev and John to go out alone, protective as they were of their daughters. Russell was gentle and gregarious, a natural salesman and an easy friend, but he was not so friendly to teenage boys interested in taking his daughters around town without supervision. John and Bev had already failed to get his permission to go for ice cream without Chuck and Sue. In John's first visit to the Gilvin house, Russell had seemed standoffish, powerful, and mysterious. It didn't hurt that he had the muscles of a dock worker from driving heavy trucks before the advent of power steering. John got the distinct impression that if he caught him crossways, Russell might chase him around the side of the house with a baseball bat or maybe one of those Kentucky long-barrel shotguns.

Still, John had been courageous enough to call on Bev again, and even with limited interactions, puppy love was blooming between them like the dogwood trees along the boulevard. Now, on the night before the family's spring break trip, Bev approached her father in the living room, heart more hopeful than when she began. Blue television light radiated against the drapes and against his hands, resting on the arms of his chair.

"Daddy?" Bev said. She never faked sincerity. Even when asking with a purpose, she could only come across as sweet and believable. They were kindred spirits, she and her father—witty and sociable but gentle and kind.

"Mm-hm," Russell replied.

"I wanted to go exchange this blouse at Goldblatt's. I'd like to get a better one for our vacation."

"You're running out of time. Goldblatt's closes at nine."

"If I go soon, I can make it."

"Did you ask your mother?"

"She said to ask you." Bev paused. "If it's easier, John can take me."

Russell didn't respond immediately.

"He's got his license," Bev added helpfully.

Her father's thoughts seemed set on the next day and the long drive, not on the television show that continued before him. Connie and Gail stood behind Bev and awaited the verdict.

"I hope they let her go," Gail said softly, thinking of her brand-new roller skates. Bev was the hero among the girls that Christmas because she had prevailed on their parents to buy them all new roller skates—not the clip-on kind but roller skates with real boots.

"I hope they say no," Connie whispered back. "That boy's too old for her."

Russell seemed ready for bed and tired of making decisions. He heaved the air from his lungs.

"Whatever your mother says."

"Okay. Thank you." Bev went quickly to see her mother, her goal coming to unlikely fruition. "Daddy says it's okay with him if it's okay with you."

Betty looked up from packing a bag for April and shook her head a few times slowly, unconvinced but worn down. Bev wasn't usually *this* insistent, and the other girls needed help getting to bed. Tomorrow would be long, and she didn't want cranky kids stuck in the car together.

"Fine," Betty said. "Go ahead and go. Just don't be late. And come right back."

"Yes, Mom," Bev said and disappeared to call John before her parents' decision could change. Gail beamed at Connie. Connie bunched up her lips.

"He's still too old for her," she said. Gail shrugged and hopped off to make sure she had gathered all the toys she wanted to take.

Lately, Bev's sisters admired not just her grace and gentleness but her deepening faith. The Gilvins were regular church attenders but not overly religious. Russell often worked second jobs on Sundays or went to car shows. Betty took the girls to Twin Branch Bible Church, a congregation that met in a three-hundred-seat A-frame building twelve doors down from their home. Bev had always embraced faith more passionately than the others in her family. She worked with Child Evangelism Fellowship to conduct backyard Bible clubs and summer 5-Day Clubs for children. She also began attending Youth for Christ meetings led by a committed young couple, George and Pat Phillips. Their zeal for the Bible and prayer inspired Bev, and in recent weeks, her prayers took on an urgency that caught the attention of the Phillipses and her friends.

"Pray for this boy I like, that he'll come to Jesus," Bev asked repeatedly at Youth for Christ meetings. "And for my dad to come to Jesus too."

That prayer became the focus of her life, and friends heard her pray with startling passion, "God, use me in any way that you want to see John and my dad come to know Christ."

John had attended church with Bev's family a couple of times, though he would have rather spent time alone with Bev, enjoying conversation outside the presence of spying sisters and Bev's parents. That kind of opportunity had not come until now, the evening of March 30, 1962.

At around eight o'clock, John pulled up outside the Gilvin home in his Corvair. The quad headlights lit up the street, and the Chevy bow-tie badge seemed to glow with inner warmth. Without making a scene, Bev traipsed out the back door and hopped into the passenger seat. John's lanky frame and goofy smile were visible in the darkness.

"Hey," he said.

"Hi," Bev responded, grinning across the divided bench seat. He thought she was vivacious and beautiful, good-hearted and mischievous, all in right measure.

"Well, here we go."

John took the long way to Goldblatt's, making a circle

around town. Otherwise it was too quick, and there was no time to be together.

"Isn't the dance going to be fun?" Bev said.

John shrugged. "I don't dance much. I guess we'll watch Chuck and Sue."

"I think we could try," Bev offered.

He nodded. There was a silence. "Kentucky, huh?"

"My Aunt Beulah's farm. It's always so much fun. They have farm animals, and my cousins will be there."

"Pretty far away."

"A day's worth, I guess. But it's a pretty drive."

John drove on in silence.

"Guess I'll see you when I get back," Bev said.

"That'd be nice."

John was often at a loss for words with Bev. She struck him as so smart and genuine and promising. John, by contrast, was disappointing his family's academic expectations. Classrooms didn't fit him well. As a boy, he stared out the windows at passing airplanes, wondering where the passengers were going and wishing he could join them. When teachers called on him, especially in math class, he usually had no answer. Equations made no sense to him. This surprised his parents because Wilson Thornton, John's grandfather, was known for a geometric algorithm he created in 1951, which was lauded among mathematicians across the country. Wilson's name even appeared in popular geometry textbooks.

John was a different bird. In grade school when the teacher taught two plus two is four, John's immediate response was, "Why? Who says it's got to be four? Let's make it five. How about twenty?" It seemed to him that teachers were assigning arbitrary numbers to arrive at easy solutions. John questioned everything in the same independently minded way. It didn't help his grades.

His parents put him in college prep classes in high school, clinging to their dream of another generation of Fighting Irish. Many family members—cousins, uncles, grandparents—were college-bound or had their degrees framed and hanging on the wall. The plan was for John to attend college and become a teacher. But reality was going another direction.

Finally, the high school principal sat the Thorntons down.

"John won't be following in your footsteps to Notre Dame, Mr. Thornton," he said bluntly. "He hasn't performed well enough. He's had to take extra classes to make up for the ones he failed. Right now, he's struggling in all his college preparatory classes. My question is, do you want him to graduate from high school at all? If so, I recommend he switch to classes he can pass and enroll in summer school so he can at least earn a diploma."

It was bitter news for the Thorntons, but not much more could be done. They had given him the best they could with their money, influence, and encouragement. Now, with an uncertain future ahead of him, John would have to make his own path.

"Say, how do you drive a car like this?" Bev asked as they glided through the night. A light spring snow still graced the sidewalks, though the streets were clear of it.

"You mean shifting gears?"

"Yes. Daddy's trucks always have a gear shifter coming up from the floor."

"This one's very much the same. You just—well, here. Put your hand here."

He pointed to the gear shift protruding from the floor.

"I'll speed up. You move that thing when I say so."

John stepped on the gas as they traveled down the four-lane road.

"Okay—now," he said. Bev switched the gearshift lever. The car smoothly settled into a higher gear and a lower rev. "Good job, Bev!"

Bev smiled. "I drove a car! I can't wait to get my license someday. Then I could drive us places."

John smiled back in spite of himself. He was drawn to the liveliness and affection of the Gilvin family. Home life at the Thorntons' was good but staid. They showed love through duty and commitment, not gauche displays of emotion or bantering conversation. Something about this Southern family and this girl sitting an arm's length from him struck him as fresh and exciting.

"Coming up to Goldblatt's," he announced with a trace of new-driver's pride.

Goldblatt's was in the town's new shopping plaza on Miracle Lane. Bethel College, a small Christian school, sat opposite the mall. They had named the street, deeming it a miracle they had been able to buy the campus. Bev, her hands folded on the white blouse in her lap, sighed contentedly and pondered what she would exchange it for. She was thinking of a pair of blue jeans.

John signaled and arced left into the intersection.

The impact was so sudden and jarring that neither John nor Bev knew what had happened. Coming the opposite way across Miracle Lane, a pickup truck banged the Corvair's passenger side bumper, sending John's car spinning backward and sideways. Another car collided with the back of it. John's head smacked the window and driver's side door. Bev's head came down squarely on the dashboard. For both of them, everything went black.

The three damaged cars sat silently, waiting for help. Bystanders rushed over, alerting other drivers and peering into car windows.

"What happened?"

"That sports car turned into the intersection. He must not have seen the oncoming traffic."

"Who hit him?"

"That truck. It can't have been going more than thirty, forty miles an hour."

"Nobody looks too badly hurt."

The pickup driver got out of his banged-up vehicle and walked over.

"You okay?" someone asked.

"I think I'm fine," he said. "He turned right in front of me. I couldn't stop."

He sat on the curb and waited. Within minutes, emergency personnel arrived and helped John from the car.

"Can you stand up?" a medic asked.

"Yeah," he said, feeling woozy and not completely aware of what had just happened.

"Can you walk over here and sit down?"

John did.

"Does it hurt anywhere?"

John held up his hand. There was a small cut on the back of it. The medic looked him over before ushering him to the ambulance.

"You're a lucky boy," he said. "They'll stitch that hand up for you at the hospital."

"This one's not awake yet," said another medic, examining Bev in the passenger seat.

"How's she doing? She alive?" one medic asked.

"She's alive. Doesn't look too banged up, but she's unconscious."

"What about her head?"

"Nothing there, really. Just a cut under her chin. And on her knee. That's all I see."

"But she's not conscious?"

"I don't think so. Miss? I'm a medic. Are you all right?"

Bev did not respond.

"Miss? Are you all right? Can you hear me?" He shook his head. "No, she's out."

They carefully pulled her from the car and put her on a gurney. Her body convulsed several times.

"Whoa, whoa, watch out!" one medic said to another.

"Did she wake up?"

"I don't think so."

"Probably just knocked out for a while. I've seen worse."

At the hospital a little while later, John's brain seemed to refocus. He found himself in a small room. Looking down, he saw a bandage on his hand. An ER nurse came in.

"You're okay to leave. Your parents are here to take you home."

John followed his parents to the car, to their home, and to his bed.

At the Gilvin house, the phone rang just before nine o'clock. The girls were almost in bed, their thoughts full of the cows, horses, and cousins they would play with at Aunt Beulah's farm.

"Mrs. Gilvin?" the voice said. "There's been an accident. Beverly's at the hospital. It looks to the doctors like she has a blood clot in her brain. She's sleeping right now."

"Oh, God, please," Betty said, and she and Russell rushed to the station wagon.

The packed suitcases and their owners would not be going to Kentucky.

Bev lay in a bed in the intensive care unit looking like her normal self except for an abrasion on her forehead and a cut under her chin. An IV protruded from her arm, and the doctors had given her a tracheotomy. Otherwise she simply appeared to be asleep—not bruised, not broken, not seriously harmed.

"It looks like she's just knocked out," the doctor said, somewhat unhelpfully. "We should know more in three days."

A specialist was brought in, but in the hours and days that followed, everyone seemed mystified by her condition. Several times the dire phone call came.

"Mr. Gilvin, you should probably bring the family in. Bev may have a short time to live."

Each time, the family stood around the bed as Bev slept as if nothing could wake her.

A somber feeling pervaded the house as days blurred into weeks and weeks blurred into months. The girls saw little of their mother, who stayed at the hospital all day. The family summoned their financial resources to pay for a registered nurse to stay all night with Bev. Betty and Russell's conversations bled through the bedroom walls, full of sadness, self-recrimination, and occasional blame.

"Why did he have to turn in front of that pickup?" came Russell's voice, exasperated.

"I don't know, Russell. It breaks my heart."

"Ah! We should never have let her go. I can't believe that boy did this to her."

The sisters were never part of these conversations, but one night, Connie began crying in her bed.

"Why are you crying, Connie?" Gail asked in the darkness.

"'Cause Bevie's going to die."

"No, she's not. Don't say that."

"Then why isn't she awake yet?"

"I don't know. She needs rest. Sleep is good. She was in an accident." Gail paused, then added, "Everybody at church prayed for her this Sunday. And three people called the house today to ask how she was."

"But she's unconscious."

"I know that. She's sleeping," Gail countered.

"Shush! It'll be all right," Sue said. "Whatever happens, it'll be all right."

• • •

On the night of the accident, John started vomiting and experiencing an intense headache while lying in bed at home. He returned to the hospital. The doctors diagnosed him with a concussion and kept him for three days. After that he returned home and suffered no further obvious effects.

His senior year, with all its excitement and anticipation, was winding up, but John's mind was on Bev, lying unconscious in a hospital because of the accident he had caused. He tried to visit her, but the Gilvins had denied him access. Their pain was still too fresh. On the other side of town, Mr. and Mrs. Thornton were deeply unsettled that their son was now mixed up with a family so unlike them. At the same time, they, like John, wanted to help the Gilvins if possible.

The problem for John was that no one seemed interested in his feelings about the situation or offered to help him sort out his responsibility—not his parents, not the Gilvins, not anyone. As Bev slept on, John sought counsel from Chuck one night while they drove John's newly repaired Corvair to a bank overlooking the St. Joseph River.

"I hear what you're saying," Chuck said. "So, what do you think you're going to do?"

They both leaned against the hood of the car, watching the river flow by like liquid time.

"How do I know?" John almost shouted with frustration. "Nobody's telling me anything! The adults are handling everything. I'm not involved. It's like they don't even care that I was there!"

He paused to hurl a rock into the void. It landed too far away to register a splash.

"My life has always been confusion," John went on. "I don't even know which end is up. I'm just bouncing around. One day this happens; another day that happens. It's all just random. So now this accident. What do I do? Stick around? Slowly move out of the picture?"

He shook his head, unsatisfied with every option.

Chuck thought for a moment. "You ought to go visit her," he said, leveraging himself up and looking back toward the city center.

"I tried."

"You should try again."

John knew in his gut it was the right thing to do.

A few days later, he ventured back to the hospital, feeling horribly awkward and conspicuous. *Does everyone know I'm the one who was at the wheel of the car that injured this innocent girl?* This time the nursing staff let him through—with or without the family's permission, he didn't know. He walked quietly into Bev's darkened room. She lay there alone, several medical machines standing cold sentry around her. The vivacity that had drawn him to her seemed to have drained away. She was sleeping, empty, gone. He opened his mouth to say something, but speaking didn't make sense—she was unconscious. She still looked so young.

A nurse slipped in. John turned.

"I brought her something," he said and handed the nurse his gift: a stuffed white dog.

"That's very sweet," she said and laid it beside Bev. It

seemed to enliven the scene just a little, as if some part of Bev's personality had returned in the silly expression of the animal.

"I'll see you later, Beverly," John said haltingly. Then he walked out. A deep weight of responsibility went with him to his car and back home.

•   •   •

The Gilvin girls visited their sister on occasion, gathering soberly around the foot of her bed. Nobody had scripted their interactions with an unconscious sister, so Betty coached them. "She can hear you. Talk to her."

"Hi, Bev," Sue said bravely.

"You look really good, Bevie," Connie added.

"Hi, Bev," Gail said, not feeling very creative.

"You're safe here," Sue continued. "Someone's always here with you. You're gonna be all right."

Connie turned to their mother. "I'm scared." It was the sight of Bev's eyes, slightly open at the time, and of the rolled-up towel placed in her tightly clenched fist to keep her fingernails from embedding in her palm. The scene frightened her.

"It's okay," Betty said. "This was a nice visit. They'll see you later, Bevie. Say good-bye, girls."

"Good-bye, Bevie. See you soon," Sue said.

"Bye, Bevie," the others said and filed out as silently and respectfully as they could.

Back home, the girls heard their parents praying in their bedroom.

"Dear Lord, please bring Beverly back to us," came their father's muffled voice through the wall. "Please don't let her die. We want to see her. Let her be part of this family again."

Their mother's weeping flowed under his words like a stream of grief.

In the small home of George and Pat Phillips, the Youth for Christ group also prayed earnestly for their friend Bev and felt gripped to pray with urgency for John Thornton and Russell Gilvin, just as Bev had been asking them to do. Together in the modest living room, they cried out, lifting up the request Bev had asked them to pray in the months before the accident: "Lord, use Bev in any way you see fit so that John and Mr. Gilvin will come to you."

One Sunday not long after the accident, John, who had started to attend church occasionally, listened intently to the sermon at Twin Branch Bible Church. When the pastor invited the congregation to come forward for prayer, John stood up and walked to the front. The situation surrounding the accident had opened his eyes. Awareness of his own failure and inadequacy had led him to recognize his need for a Savior—or for something to guide him out of his brokenness. On a different Sunday, Russell did the same thing. On his previous visits to church, he had jangled the change in his pocket with nervous energy, to the point of distracting people nearby. Now he was baptized, and he attended Sunday school so faithfully that in the years to come he would win medals for attendance.

John's quiet journey of faith helped him formulate a way to respond to Bev's new reality—and the future staring so blankly at him.

• • •

"Good morning, Bevie. It sure is a nice day."

The nurses always talked to Bev as they did their rounds. As usual, the only response was the hiss of air flowing into her neck through the tracheotomy tube. A small black-and-white television droned on from the desk across from the bed. Russell had picked it up somewhere on his truck-driving journeys. The nurses left it on permanently, on the doctor's theory that it would stimulate Bev's brain.

"July Fourth was nice," the nurse continued. "Kind of hot. The fireworks were spectacular. You could see their reflection in the river. It was gorgeous."

Suddenly something hit the nurse's back and fell to the floor. She looked down—a white stuffed dog rested at her feet. She turned. Bev's eyes were open, and her glare indicated she was seriously annoyed. The nurse had been standing between Bev and the television, and Bev had thrown the dog to get her to move. The nurse gasped, dropped her tray, and rushed from the room.

The call to the Gilvin house was triumphant, joyful, and unexpected.

"I'm happy to tell you that Bev woke up today," the doctor said. "She's going to live."

Russell hugged Betty tightly, both of them feeling waves of victory and relief. Betty cried. A miracle, it seemed, had been granted as a result of the prayers of friends and family. After three months, few people were expecting Bev to live.

The Gilvin sisters were beside themselves.

"Bev's back!" Gail yelled, running around the house before being herded to the car to visit her. April clapped her hands in celebration. If everyone else was happy, she was happy too.

Bev's eyes were open, and she was looking around, but as was to be expected for someone who had lain motionless in bed for three months, she had lost some of her body's functions. She could not speak, sit up, walk, or use her arms or hands in any consistent way. She had partial amnesia and had forgotten the three days preceding the accident and the accident itself.

"Sit up now, Bev," the nurses said as they led her through her first rounds of physical therapy. Carefully, they placed hands behind her back and brought her forward. Bev's eyes registered that it was happening, but her response was wordless.

"We're going to put your legs over the bed for a few minutes before laying you back down again, okay?"

Bev gave approval with a look.

Within a few days, they were standing her up between two strong nurses who held her arms like fence posts so she wouldn't pitch forward. They trained her hands so she could feed herself and handle her own hygiene. She did these tasks roughly. Her fine motor skills appeared to be gone. She could not pick up an object without long moments of mental determination and a slow, clumsy physical response. Her joints seemed locked in place and no longer moved with the fluidity of normal human motion.

"These things will come back," the doctors told her family encouragingly. "Just keep working with her on them."

John heard that Bev was conscious and waited a few days before coming to the hospital to visit. As he stepped into the second floor hallway, he saw Bev standing there between two nurses, struggling to take a step. Her body was bent unnaturally, and she was still wearing a hospital gown. To John she appeared elderly, broken, even forlorn. She looked up at him slowly, still unable to speak, and their eyes met. John wasn't sure if she even recognized him. Her mind appeared entirely focused on regaining control of her legs. Shocked, unable to imagine a conversation, and not wanting to interrupt her therapy, he turned and walked briskly out.

The tracheotomy had left Bev's throat scratchy and injured. One day she spoke her first word since the accident: "Daddy." It came as a low croak, so frightening to Connie and Gail that they secretly hoped she would not speak again until her voice returned to normal.

After a couple of weeks, doctors were satisfied that she was making enough progress to go home and continue her recovery there. She still could not walk on her own and spoke only in an unnerving baritone rasp.

"Her motor skills will return over time," doctors said. "Just keep working with her."

A hospital bed, quietly donated by the Thorntons, was waiting for Bev at the Gilvin residence. It was placed in the girls' bedroom, then later in the tiny, centrally located dining room, which would become Bev's room for two years.

A day or two after Bev's return, Connie and Gail lowered the rails and helped their sister down from the bed.

"The doctors said you should crawl because it will help you get your coordination and flexibility back," Connie said. Bev looked at her wide-eyed, partially comprehending.

"Come on," Connie coaxed. "Let's get down on the floor." Carefully and slowly they helped her to her knees, then laid her flat on her stomach. They got on either side of her, took her same face-down position, and began the exercise.

"Now pull your knees under you and push up with your hands," Connie said. Bev slowly followed their example with moderate success. She seemed taxed to her limit. She awkwardly pushed her chest a couple of inches off the ground.

"That's good, Bevie!" Gail said as Bev sank back to the floor, unable to hold the pose or to complete the desired movement. "Let's do it again. This is fun!"

Gail enjoyed playing teacher in the mock schoolroom in their basement, and now she was able to teach a real, live pupil. Hopes of a full recovery filled everyone's minds.

Bev rested a moment, then tried to push herself up again. This time she got farther.

"Good, Bevie!" Connie said. "Now let's crawl forward, just one step."

"I . . . can do . . . this," Bev said. To their relief, the scratchy, deep voice had gradually gone away. But her speaking cadence still sounded off, as if she were drugged. Gail reached over to move Bev's free arm forward.

"Don't . . . help . . . me! I . . . can do . . . this," Bev said gruffly.

She seemed upset, humiliated. Older than both Connie and Gail, she was now groveling painfully on the floor. Her sisters could get up and walk around at whim, but Bev was stuck.

"Here—come this far," Gail said, sitting a few feet in front of her. Bev grunted and willed her limbs to move.

"Like this," Connie said.

"I . . . can . . . *do* . . . it!" Bev snapped back. "Don't . . . help . . . me!"

"But Mom said to help you," Connie said. "She wants us to help you."

Bev collapsed on the floor.

"I . . . can do . . . it," she said, voice muffled by the carpet, where her face was now half-buried. "Stop . . . helping . . . me."

The next morning, Connie, Gail, and April came into the bedroom holding a plate of runny eggs, a glass of juice, utensils, and a dish towel. Bev stared at them, leery and confused.

"What . . . happened?" she said.

"It's breakfast time!" April announced. Bev shook her head and repeated, "What . . . happened?" They knew what she meant.

"You were in an accident," Gail said plainly. "You don't have to think about it."

"I don't . . . remember." Bev's face held unspoken questions. *Why am I in this room? Why am I in this bed? Why can't I move or speak normally? What happened to me?*

"Everything'll be fine, Bevie," Gail said. "Look, we brought you some eggs!"

April approached and set the eggs on Bev's lap. Connie gently put a fork in Bev's left hand and helped her poke some eggs, dribbling with yolk just like their mother always made them. She guided the fork to her mouth, and Bev took them in and began chewing. She was right-handed, but the effects of the accident had caused the whole right side of her body to remain stiff.

"After a while, you'll be doing this on your own," Connie assured her.

"I've got juice when you want some," Gail volunteered.

Connie turned for a moment to April, who was standing by the fan they called "big blue" because of its size and color. It was the only thing that kept them from madness during sweltering summers. "April, would you get the salt and pepper from the table?" she asked.

Just then, April's eyes went wide and she ducked. A plate full of eggs zoomed by her and into the fan. Yolk flecks spattered around the room in an explosion of yellow stickiness. The girls looked toward the bed. Bev's left hand was wavering in midair, her face a picture of rage. Connie and Gail looked at her as if to question why. April sobbed and ran from the room to find Betty, then threw herself into her mother's arms.

"I can't help with Bevie anymore," she said. Connie and Gail came behind her.

"Bev threw a plate of eggs at her," Connie said in a confused whisper.

Betty's expression clouded, but just for a moment.

"April, we can do this. We can all do this. We need to help your sister. Now Gail and Connie, why don't you clean up the egg before it dries all over the place?"

Betty held April until she stopped crying.

A few days later, Connie came in to bathe her sister the

way the nurses had taught them, using a basin filled with warm water. Afterward, she began brushing Bev's hair.

"You're getting much better at walking," Connie said with a mother's assurance. "It won't be long before we're all back at school. Everything'll be fun. Ooh, your hair looks nice, too. I'm glad we washed it—"

Without warning, Bev swung her elbow around angrily, smacking Connie's arm and sending the hairbrush flying across the room. Connie jumped back, unable to mask her emotions. The hairbrush clattered to a rest. Bev's eyes flashed with ire, and she settled into an angry, unexplained silence. Connie quietly picked up the basin and walked out of the room.

Questions poured out when the girls were riding in the car with their mother.

"Why is Bevie different now?" April asked.

"Because of the accident," Betty said.

"But why?"

"April, that's enough."

"Is she going to be normal again?"

Betty paused. "She's going to be just fine."

Connie and Gail looked at each other, wondering how much hope to set on her words.

• • •

After two months, Bev was walking and talking well enough to enroll for her sophomore year in the fall. The high school had passed her through ninth grade, due to her academic strength. Now it was time to return to normal life.

While Bev was unconscious, John had graduated and taken a job with Everett-Ballard Funeral Home. His goal: to become a mortician. They put him to work cleaning the place, doing routine maintenance, and driving an ambulance—mostly to pick up drunks and vagrants. At the time, the mortuary business operated ambulances that offered no service except a fast ride to the hospital. After a year of apprenticeship, John could attend mortician school, then get his license and perhaps one day own a funeral home or become an embalmer on staff.

He had chosen not to fade away from the Gilvin family and instead was quietly allowed to see Bev again. Betty and Russell even gave him permission to drive Bev to school occasionally.

But school was proving difficult for Bev. Her natural intelligence seemed bottled up inside her, tangled at times. Connie was tagged to help her with her homework. One day she brought in the geometry book for a quick lesson before the next day's exam.

"Triangles are very predictable," Connie instructed, reading from the book lying open on Bev's lap while she sat in a chair in the living room. "They have three angles, and the angles always add up to one hundred and eighty."

Bev listened and processed.

"So if this angle is forty-five degrees and this one is fifty-five, what is this third one?" Connie asked. The question hung there as Bev pressed her brain into the problem.

"Forty-five plus fifty-five would be . . ." Connie said.

Bev's face flushed. She clearly didn't like being prompted

or patronized. Her right fist, clenched tighter than normal, pressed hard against her body. An expression of pure fury tugged at her lips and lit a flame behind her eyes.

"I know!" she said. "I get it! I just—"

She was sputtering frustration.

"I'm a little thirsty," Connie said. "I'll go get us some iced tea and we can move on to another problem. Be right back."

She stepped away. The sisters were learning how to manage Bev's condition.

One day in the middle of September, John pulled up to the high school. Bev could no longer ride the bus—she was too stiff and slow; boarding and riding presented too many hazards. She walked over to his car. He pushed open her door from the inside in anticipation. With an awkward motion, she flung her pack in and sat down roughly. Pain emanated from her eyes so much that John didn't know how to greet her. He pulled away from the curb and began to drive her home.

"I can't do anything," she said after a time of silence. "The stairs—I can't get up them fast enough. I'm late for class. The teachers are marking me late. When I get there, I can't open my book to the right page or write anything down fast enough. It's like—like I'm in slow motion, or everyone is in fast motion. I don't know how to keep up anymore."

John listened.

"People—people make fun of me for the way I do things," she said. "Everyone's too busy. Everyone's . . . *normal*. Like I used to be."

John's heart was burning now, his gut screaming with indignation. His words burst out almost unwillingly.

"Who are these kids?" he nearly shouted. "Who are these teachers? Who is this principal that lets someone get treated like this?"

He looked over at Bev in the passenger seat. Once a shining, spunky, school leader, she was now an afterthought to most people, an unsolvable equation. She was trapped, body and soul.

"You're not going back there," he announced simply, as if he had the authority to make it so. Minutes later at the Gilvin house, John parked the Corvair in front and walked in with greater resolve than he had ever shown in anything. Betty and Russell were both in the kitchen. They looked up at him, sensing he had something to say. Bev stood behind him, clutching her book bag, not knowing what would happen.

"Mr. and Mrs. Gilvin, I don't know if Bev has told you what's happening at school," John said.

They looked at him and waited.

"Things aren't working. She can't get around. People are making fun of her. The teachers aren't helping her. Nobody's helping her!"

He reined in his frustration and continued evenly.

"I don't think she should go back. Not in her condition, not the way she is right now. It's not helping her. It's not helping anybody."

He was surprised at his own boldness. Their response surprised him even more.

"We've been thinking about that too," Russell said. Betty sighed. John and Bev didn't know her parents had met with

the principal, who concluded that because Bev could no longer navigate the hallways and stairways fast enough to make
classes on time, it was impossible for her to function as a
student anymore.

"We think this is probably the end," Russell said. "We'll
have to do something else."

The four of them took the decision in somberly, minds
full of unspoken questions about the future. So Bev's academic career ended. The straight-A student became, by force
of circumstance and lack of viable options, a high school
dropout.

• • •

Life went on around her. Bev sat at home and read for hours, a
pleasure still available to her. Her sisters played volleyball and
roller-skated in the skates Bev had won them. Betty cooked and
managed the house; Russell drove the truck; April got bigger;
Chuck and Sue got serious and married that fall. Perplexed by
Bev's condition, everyone quietly hoped she would get better
over time. Doctors told them—more hope than prognosis—
that she would improve. After all, there were no obvious injuries, no broken bones, not even a notable scratch or bruise left.
But Bev was a different person, and everybody knew it.

Meanwhile, John's stint at the mortuary wasn't going
well. Maybe it was the monotony, maybe the dead people.
He just knew he wanted to go in a different direction.
Serving in the US Army for four years seemed to offer pro-
ductive work and extra time to plan his life. He told Bev
of his decision, and though they were still only shallowly

acquainted, they spoke tentatively of a shared future. One day in December before heading off to Korea, John went to Will's Jewelry in downtown Mishawaka, with its big, landmark clock out front, and bought three matching rings, one for him and two for Bev. He surprised her with them on Christmas 1963. They weren't exactly engagement rings. After all, she was just sixteen. But they were a statement of commitment, his way of saying, "I'm not walking away from this." What that meant, he wasn't sure. He still saw her as the pretty, mischievous, vibrant girl on whom he had developed a teenage crush. But now their situation bore the weight of adult decisions.

In Korea's demilitarized zone, his head was full of its own battles. *I've got to be a man. I'm the one who turned in front of that truck on Miracle Lane. I liked her before the accident, didn't I? Does that mean I love her now? Should I marry her because of the accident? What's my responsibility? Am I doing this out of guilt? If the accident hadn't happened, would I still be interested in her?*

Letters went back and forth over the ocean. John sent gifts of beautiful Korean fans to the Gilvin sisters, and they wrote back with thanks. The sisters spied on Bev as she wrote letters to John at the kitchen table. Writing was so laborious for her that it took hours to commit enough words to paper to merit the stamp. Soon their frequent letters circled around the idea of actually getting married and setting a date. Following his gut and settling the storm inside his conscience, John confirmed he would like to marry Bev. She received her parents' approval. They thought Bev was young, but John was trying to do the right thing, and what other future would a daughter in her condition have?

The wedding was planned while John was in Korea. He came home on leave, stepped into a nice suit, and put a ring on Bev's finger in a ceremony at Twin Branch Bible Church. She wore a borrowed dress and gripped her father's arm like a vise to keep from falling as she walked down the aisle. Her sisters wore pillbox hats and "rainbow dresses"—April in yellow, Connie in blue, Gail in pink, Sue in mint green, and John's sister, Donna, in purple. Each dress had ruffles around the bottom. April carried a little white basket. John's best man was a guy he had never met, because Chuck was Roman Catholic, and in 1966 Catholics and Protestants in that area didn't generally participate in each other's weddings. The reception was held in the basement with cake, punch, and pastel mints. Bev shone like the sun with joy.

As excited as the Gilvin sisters were to be in a wedding, their opinions of John were mixed. Bev insisted to Connie that she loved John, but Connie still felt Bev was too young to get married. And Sue openly disliked him at first. Gail and April were younger and more sanguine about the future.

The Thorntons hosted everyone for a rehearsal dinner at the Lincoln Highway Inn. The girls had concluded by now that John's family was rich.

"I bet the girls who eat here have their own bedrooms," Gail whispered as they admired the elaborate interior of the inn.

"I bet they have their own dressers," Connie said.

"I bet they have their own closets," Gail said.

"And lots of shoes," Connie added before their mother hushed them.

As Betty put it, the Thorntons were "not the kind of people we would normally have picnics with," but they were nice enough. The Thorntons paid for John and Bev's honeymoon—three nights in a classy Chicago hotel overlooking Lake Michigan—but the honeymooners didn't get that far. Twenty miles out of town after the wedding reception, John spotted a motel and took an early exit.

"That looks like a nice place," he said.

Bev eyed him with good-natured suspicion. John shrugged.

"Chicago's a long drive. We wouldn't be there for another hour and a half."

Five nights later, they reported to Fort Sill in Oklahoma, where John entered a new round of training. Then the army deployed him to an emerging global hot spot—Vietnam. There he worked the radio with a couple of officers, scrambling and unscrambling coded messages that came in. One day he got a message from his dad, delivered by the Red Cross: a son, Shawn, was born December 20, 1966.

John was now a father, and I was his son.

Mom sent reel-to-reel tapes of me crying, and the guys in Dad's unit lay on their beds and listened to those tapes for hours. They hadn't seen or heard their own children for so long that even my squalling sounded sweet.

Mom and I lived with Grandma and Grandpa Thornton in their large home until Dad got home in June 1967. He had avoided, by just a few weeks, the bloodiest months of that war. He got a job at Dodge Manufacturing—an iron foundry that made parts for large machinery makers such as Caterpillar. Soon after that, he and Mom found a home on the outskirts of Mishawaka on a dead-end cinder road with three homes. Ours was the smallest—handmade and less than a thousand square feet. But it was the house I grew up in.

It sat on Victory Road.

CHAPTER 2

"RACE YOU TO THE END OF THE ROAD!" Lance challenged.

Lance was our neighbor and my best friend. We we both in the second grade. Lance and I leaned on our bike handles and looked down Victory Road—our universe and, at this moment, a racetrack for our epic bike-riding competitions.

"Ready, set, go!" I said, and we both stood up and stomped on our bicycle pedals, pumping fast to be the first to reach the abrupt end of the road.

"I'm Superman!" Lance yelled, hunching over his handle-bars for maximum aerodynamics.

"I'm Batman!" I responded.

"I'm Spiderman!" he said.

"I'm Scooby Doo!" I replied.

Lance pulled a few feet ahead of me—he was naturally athletic even at a young age. If I beat him, it was usually only if I could cut in and around him to take the lead. He brought his bike to a skidding stop in front of my driveway.

"I win!" he announced.

"Let's do the Indy 500," I said, ignoring my loss and already imagining doing laps around the street.

We pumped back toward the starting line. As my knees bobbed under my wrists, I caught glimpses of several black cinder shards embedded in them from falls I'd taken on the bike. Victory Road was paved with porous black rock, a by-product of coal-burning power plants. This cinder was useless in most respects, but in places like Indiana with harsh winters, it was sometimes packed into the ground like a loose layer of concrete to keep the roads from washing away during storms. Cinders also gave boys like me, who insisted on wearing shorts and riding around like race car drivers, plenty of painful mementos. Every spill I took seemed to plant another shard in my knee, like a notch in my belt for some kind of war achievement.

Before we got going on our next race, I saw Dad turn our used sedan onto Victory Road. The Corvair was gone, known to me only in photographs. Dad had traded it for something sensible several years earlier. As he eased down our road, I stood on the pedals and started to ride alongside him, imagining I could keep up by sheer willpower.

"I gotta go in," I yelled at Lance. "My parents are going to Awana."

"Awana?" Lance said and shrugged. This was where our

routines parted ways. He pedaled back to his house, dumped his bike on the lawn, and ran inside.

Dad opened the driver's door. He smelled like burnt steel and looked like someone had blasted him with chimney dust, probably like the other three thousand United Steelworkers who worked at Dodge's. His work outfit didn't vary: blue jeans, boots, and a dark crewneck T-shirt. A blue handkerchief squirmed out of his back pocket, wrinkled and limp with a full day's sweat. For the past ten hours, he'd been laboring among massive hanging ladles, white-hot furnaces, overhead cranes, and conveyor lines clattering with metal parts. Dodge's was smoky, hot, and noisy, and the men probably should have gotten combat pay, given how some got burned. Earplugs and safety glasses were a thing of the future.

"Hi, Dad!"

"Hey."

He got out of the car, his lanky frame opening like a jack-knife. He squinted and pulled at his eye.

"What's the matter?" I asked.

"Got something in there."

I sat on my bike watching him. Sometimes he and other workers got metal shavings in their eyes. Other times the sand and dust would rise and swirl in the heat. An on-site nurse treated more scratched eyeballs than burns.

Dad opened his watering eyes wide, then shut them and opened them again.

"I'll go to the nurse tomorrow and get it checked," he concluded and walked into the house. I dropped my bike away from the car and followed him inside. Dad's work schedule regularly bounced back and forth from first shift to third, then back to second as he "bumped" for new jobs and pay increases. I liked it when he got home in the afternoons.

"Bev, we've got to go!" he yelled inside.

"I know!" she hollered from their bedroom. "I'm getting ready."

"You should be ready already! That's what you're supposed to do."

"I am ready!"

"Then let's go!"

Mom shuffled from the kitchen to the living room. She was still young and, I thought, beautiful. But her gait, ten years after the accident, was stiff, and her arms hung awkwardly at her sides. She checked under various piles for whatever she was looking for.

"Hold on. I've got to find that little book I bought at a garage sale for Sheryl."

"What little book?" Dad said. Even when he didn't mean to, he sounded exasperated.

"The one about the little girl and the baby duckling. It's very cute."

"What are you talking about? We're going to be late."

"I've got to find it. It's going to encourage her in what she's going through with her daughter. They're in a lot of pain right now. She asked me to pray for that and for her cousin's son who got hit with a baseball and is not healing right. They don't know why."

"How can you find anything in this mess?" Dad said.

"Oh, here it is." Mom giggled as if surprised and then

clumsily leaned over to take the book from an overloaded shelf. Wordlessly, Dad and I watched to see whether she would tip over and need catching. She managed it without falling.

"Now can we go?" Dad said, looking out the window. Grandma Thornton had pulled into the driveway, as proper and put-together as anyone in Mishawaka and the perfect contrast to the scene in our home.

"Just hold on, hold on," Mom said, working her way to her recliner—her domestic throne surrounded by piles of *Redbook*, *Woman's Day*, and *Good Housekeeping* magazines, Bibles, devotionals, romance novels, and used bags of potato chips and plates crusted with food. A TV tray held several glasses of iced-tea dregs and mugs with coffee stains in the bottom. Mom drank iced tea endlessly in the summer and coffee year-round. Around her chair bloomed a garden of used Kleenex. This chair, the bathroom, and the kitchen formed a small triangle in which Mom stayed pretty much all day.

She grabbed her most-used Bible, the one whose cover was overflowing with notes and church bulletins.

"Okay, I'm coming."

"Come on, then," Dad said.

"Oh! I forgot my sweater."

"You don't need your sweater!" Dad barked.

"But what if it gets cold?"

"It's hot out!"

"All right," Mom consented and took his arm. He led her down the front steps as she clung to him for stability.

Grandma Thornton, walking to the door, stepped back to let them pass. Tuesday nights were the only time Mom and Dad went to church without me and Troy, my younger brother by three years and my only sibling. He and I were still too young to attend Awana.

"We'll see ya at nine," Dad said to us over his shoulder, helping Mom into the car. Then he added, "Don't let those boys stay up."

• • •

Dad had come back from Vietnam to settle down and build a life with Mom, but the war had knocked the earlier commitment he had made at Twin Branch Bible Church off course. Though silent about his time in the military, it seemed to have made him apathetic toward faith. When I was still in diapers, my parents spent time playing cards with friends and distant relatives, and for Dad this included smoking and drinking. While these parties weren't terribly rowdy, they distracted Dad from the Christian life he had embraced years earlier.

One day a woman from Twin Branch Bible Church called.

"Hello, John. I saw you and Bev at church last week, and it hit me. We could really use your help in the two- to three-year-old class. Is that something you and Bev would consider doing?"

"Me?" said Dad, as if someone had asked him to be the pope. "Uh, I don't really know. Why do you want us? I'm not really the best person for that. I don't know anything . . ."

She laughed.

"You don't have to know anything, really," she said. "You only have to help out. Just being there would be helpful."

"Well, I'll think about it," Dad said, buying time.

He hung up, but the call caused him to reflect on how far he had drifted from his solemn commitment to God. Bothered, he did something highly uncharacteristic: he arranged to chat with Pastor Bryan Jones after service at Twin Branch.

Dad wasn't accustomed to talking about abstract things like inner turmoil and spiritual need. He almost didn't know where to start. "I think I'm a Christian, but I feel like I'm not really getting it," he blurted out.

Dad went on to explain his predicament—how his time in Vietnam saw him drift away from God and how he wasn't sure he had believed in the first place. His life, he said, didn't seem all that different from the way it was before.

"John, if I can be blunt with you," Pastor Jones broke in, "you get out what you put in. If you're not as committed as you should be, then new life in Christ is not going to be as evident in you."

"I think that's it, right there," Dad concluded. "If I'm going to do this, then I'm going to do it. That's the way it should be."

Pastor Jones nodded. Dad thanked him and left.

From that moment on, Dad was determined. He quit smoking and drinking entirely after that. Friends and relatives who had been a distraction stopped coming around. He and Mom accepted the offer to teach Sunday school, and soon they were helping in Awana as well. Inside his black lunch bucket, he began putting an *Our Daily Bread* devotional, wrapped around his Thermos and held fast with a wire clip. On lunch breaks, while many other guys wasted their time with filthy stories and off-color jokes, Dad often spent time reading the little devotional or chatting about better things.

Dad was as stubborn about his Christian commitment as he was with every other serious commitment he made.

One Sunday while we were driving to church, Dad announced, "We forgot the check for the offering basket."

"Oh, we can bring it next week," Mom said. We were just a few blocks from church. We could practically hear the music.

Without a word, Dad spun the car around and headed home. He walked into the house and retrieved the check, and we drove back to church, now twenty minutes late.

A few times he woke up late from his Sunday afternoon nap—sometimes because Troy and I turned off the alarm Dad had set to wake him up for the evening service. We weren't always enthusiastic about returning to church.

"Ah! We're late! Why didn't anyone wake me? Get ready, everybody!" he said.

Mom began pushing herself out of her recliner, a process that always took some time.

"But Dad," I protested, "the service will be more than half over by the time we get there!"

"Doesn't matter," he said, and within a few harried minutes, we were out the door. It was almost worse than being there on time.

Dad's renewed commitment kept all of us more involved in the church. Around the time of his meeting with Pastor Jones, when I was three or four, Mom hosted a birthday party for Jesus at our house. She was involved with Child Evangelism Fellowship again, as she had been in her teenage years. CEF helped volunteers host birthday parties for Jesus as a way of teaching the Christmas story to neighborhood kids who wouldn't normally go to church. The organization provided invitations, and kids came to the house to play games, eat cookies, sing songs, and hear a lesson based on Jesus' birth. The party culminated with a birthday cake for Jesus.

Mrs. McAtee, the local CEF representative, knocked on our door an hour before the party began and came in to set everything up—cookies and punch on the table, games in the living room, cake in the kitchen. Soon kids arrived and filled the house with lively play. Then the whole group sat and listened to Mrs. McAtee tell the Christmas story, focusing on what Jesus' coming meant to kids like us. For a young boy like me, it was an intoxicating blur of fun, laughter, and cake. Something also touched my spirit in the most gentle and attractive way. I decided then that I wanted what Mrs. McAtee had talked about—Jesus in my heart.

Kids were saying good-bye and walking out with their mothers. "We'll see you later! Thank you, Mrs. McAtee! Thank you, Mrs. Thornton!"

"Good-bye!" Mrs. McAtee said on her way out. "See you later."

Mom was sitting in the kitchen looking slightly fatigued but as content and full of life as I ever remember her.

"Mom," I said, tugging at her clothes, "I want to have Jesus in my heart."

Her face brightened even more.

"Oh, Shawn! Let's pray right now."

There was no waiting around. She clasped my hands in hers, we shut our eyes, and we prayed.

When we had finished, she cheered, clapping her hands and hugging me tightly to her chest.

•   •   •

Grandma Thornton looked out of place in our messy living room. Her hair was done up, as it always was. She was protective of her hair, and we had to hug her in such a way that we didn't mess it up. She even slept with a foam wrap around it.

She surveyed the scene before her without much visible reaction. Our house looked like it usually did—as if a category-five tornado had just blown through.

"All right," Grandma said, her voice as buttoned up as her dress. "Let's tidy up."

Mom's lingering condition kept her from consistently carrying out normal homemaking tasks. Our house displayed no order, no arrangement, no cleanliness. Floors were scattered mounds of clothes, garbage, books, toys, and random household items we forgot we owned. It looked like a hoarder's house, except we weren't hoarding anything, at least not on purpose. Stuff just accumulated over time and created strata that you could almost study as an archaeological record of our activity over the past several months. An item casually set on a table or shelf might collect dust there forever. Trash, food, and discarded odds and ends became semipermanent in our world. Dad rallied us to clean the house maybe twice a year, but it usually fell apart again within hours. Our carpets were truly vacuumed three or four times a year and then only in a haphazard way between mountains of stuff. My bed sheets were changed perhaps three times a year—at times not even that.

I bent down to pick up some obvious things and take them to my room. Troy stood there in his sagging cloth diaper, watching us work. Mom was still adroit enough to pin diapers onto him, though both of us bore marks on our hips where she had overshot the diaper.

"Shawn, where does this go?" Grandma asked, holding up a small green frog that looked like it might be a pincushion, a paperweight, or a stuffed toy.

"I don't know, Grandma."

She turned to the countertop as a possible place to set it. She was confronted with multilevel villages of used plates, pots and pans, cups with dirty silverware sticking out of them like grimy limbs, cracker boxes and vegetable cans we hadn't managed to put in the cupboard, dark brown vitamin bottles, and whatever else we had used in the past six months but not thought to put away.

The dinner table, too, presented an impossible, edge-to-edge mass of half-forgotten junk, the kind that invited thoughts of a shovel and a large trash can. Finding a place to eat dinner was our nightly challenge. Each night, we would clear a space large enough for our plates and cups to fit. I had seen other families pull clean plates and silverware out of the cupboard; our routine was to pull dirty plates and utensils from the stacks and wash them. We didn't wash dishes after we ate; we usually washed them in order to eat.

"Well." Grandma sighed with her lips closed, more out of pity than disapproval. She set the frog on Mom's TV tray to let Mom decide where to put it.

To me, the mess was completely normal. When Mom and Dad were first married, Mom's father would send Connie or Sue on a bus to the house every Friday to help Mom clean up. This was helpful on a practical level but upset Mom because she felt less capable than her sisters. As her sisters' lives progressed, they got busier with their own growing families and came over less frequently. We saw them mostly at Nana and Papaw Gilvin's house, where their families seemed shinier, newer, and happier than ours. Most of our cousins wore new clothes, a feeling I was rarely familiar with. Most of my shirts and pants were worn soft by previous owners, and my shoes got holes in them and pressed against my toes before Dad would consider taking me to get new ones.

Even their homes were nicer. Our house was built in the 1930s. It was almost perfectly square and sat on half an acre with a detached garage and a shed that had once been a chicken coop. The house was so small and its walls so thin that you constantly knew where everyone was and what they were up to. Our telephone, wall-mounted with a long curly cord, could reach into every room. My bedroom was ten feet square. The hallway, such as it was, barely separated the bedrooms from the kitchen or the bathroom. The roomiest space was a twelve-foot square living room addition to the main house. The all-important television sat there like a presiding guru, and there we hosted our rare guests.

"All right," Grandma said with quiet finality after some time. We had successfully sorted wearable clothing from the general piles of things, swept the kitchen, washed some dishes, and even put Troy's and my clothes in our dressers. The house was still far from clean and orderly, but it actually looked different.

"That will have to do," she said and sank into the couch.

Around eight-thirty, Mom and Dad pulled up. I looked out my bedroom window and saw them in the waning fall light. Through the windshield, Mom's face looked twisted with anger, Dad's jaw loose and ready with unhelpful responses. I knew they had fought on the way home, which was becoming routine. I watched them sit a moment and gather themselves before climbing out and coming up the steps, side by side as always.

• • •

On Saturday morning, Mom woke up and told us all, "I'm going to clean the house." Dad and I glanced at each other, knowing what was ahead. She walked into the living room in her awkward way. Because she could barely move her knees and hip joints, she swung one side of her body forward at a time, like an inelegant John Wayne, only slower and more robotic. She spotted some item she wanted to put in its proper place, stopped, bent down carefully, grabbed the object in her stiff fingers, straightened up again, turned slowly around, and walked all the way to her bedroom to put it away. Then she returned to repeat the process with another item.

"It's going to take you a thousand years to clear the floor that way," Dad said from the couch where he lay down to rest his back. "Pick up two or three things and take them with you on the same trip. See, there's an empty potato chip bag. Put that in the trash can on your way to the boys' rooms."

Mom nodded, slowly and precariously gathered several things into her arms, and shuffled to my bedroom. Once she was there, we heard all of it tumble onto the floor. She didn't have the dexterity to sort trash from treasure.

"John!" she yelled, frustrated with Dad and herself. "That was a stupid idea! Now I can't reach it."

Dad looked at me, and I went in to gather it up.

At some point, Dad must have calculated that he simply had no time or energy left to clean the house, or maybe he did not want to frustrate Mom by implying she was not creating an acceptable environment for our family. At times he did try to clean the house, but his personality was such that he became lost in small, specific tasks and forgot about the big picture. Like an artist, Dad was creative and super focused. When he started cleaning up, he would get stuck on one thing—say the countertop—and clear it; wipe it off once with water, once with bleach, then with a rinse rag; and then polish and scrub the cracks and stains to perfection over the course of hours.

"There," he would say, standing back and inviting us to admire his work. "That doesn't look half bad."

It looked great but also completely unlike the unsorted terror of the rest of the house.

Most of the time our messy house was just a backdrop—we hardly even noticed it was messy anymore. It was just a fact of life. But occasionally the mess could turn dangerous.

When Dad would get a hole in a shirt, for example, Mom would try to sew it. More often than not she would set it aside before finishing it and forget about it. And more than once Dad yanked on a shirt only to feel a sharp pain in his side or neck.

"What the heck?"

Finding the source, he would pull out a needle with the thread still hanging from it.

Mom's sewing basket was an arsenal of pins and needles that could attack at any time. She put pins in her mouth when she tried to sew, then got up to retrieve a spool of thread or get a drink and dropped pins along the way. We found those pins and needles the hard way.

"Agh!" Dad yelped one day with a worse-than-usual cry of pain, hopping on one foot and cradling the other. "That one went deep."

He leaned against the wall and pulled at the pin with his fingers. Usually he could extricate pins with one good pull. This one would not budge.

"Shawn, go get me the pliers," he said. "This thing must have gone into the bone."

I returned from the utility room with pliers. Dad carefully closed the clamps on the end of the straight pin and began pulling. His face contorted with pain. Grudgingly, the pin came loose. Dad held it up for inspection, glistening red, and shook his head. He set his injured foot gingerly on the floor, handed me the pliers, and walked toward the trash can with the pin.

"Be careful walking around here, boys," he concluded. "It's dangerous."

The kitchen, too, was a hazardous area of sorts. Drawers and cabinet doors stood open much of the time, either because they could not be closed because they were too full of things we had stuffed into them or because we were just lazy. Some cupboards had mousetraps because mice were frequent residents.

Just as dangerous was the food itself. Mom had no sense that food items expired. Troy and I learned at an early age to inspect everything Mom served us.

When I was still very young, I already had a routine when Mom offered me something that seemed suspicious. If it was a glass of milk, for example, I smelled it. I looked for chunks of cream in the glass that would indicate that the milk carton had sat on the counter for a day or two. I then felt the temperature of the milk and walked to the fridge and looked at the date on the carton. The process of validating a food's safety didn't strike me as abnormal, just smart.

The food Mom served kept all of us on our toes. Dad loved egg salad sandwiches, and Mom made them for him occasionally. One day he was eating an egg salad sandwich, and Troy and I heard a crunching sound, like he was eating popcorn.

"What's that?" Dad asked and fished the foreign items from his mouth. Eggshells.

"Aw, well. It's not all that bad," he said and ate it as it was—"crunchy style," he called it.

Dinners were adventures of their own. Mom made heroic efforts to do what "normal" moms did, including cooking most nights. But the meals she envisioned and the meals that made it to the table were two very different things.

One night we cleared our places at the table and sat down to plates of Hamburger Helper, one of our four basic food groups. But this was Mom's version: partially cooked hamburger with crunchy noodles in a watery broth. Some chunks of meat were entirely pink and raw.

Dad was inspecting his plate of food, but little fazed him.

"Dig in, boys," he said and ate his first forkful. Dad ate anything. I think he would have eaten roadkill, and he expected us to embrace the wide world of dangerous foods too. At least part of his adventurousness was an attempt to make Mom feel good and to keep peace.

"Whatever doesn't kill you makes you stronger," Dad said whenever we complained about expired milk or undercooked meals.

During my early years, I figured family meals were the same for every kid—a test of fortitude with nutritional side benefits.

Shopping at the supermarket proved daunting for Mom. One of the times we went together, Mom held tightly to Dad's arm for stability in a pose that looked like they were walking down the aisle at their wedding. Troy and I trailed behind curiously.

"Oh, look, John! Shrimp!" Mom exclaimed. "Let's get some shrimp. I'm going to make shrimp tonight."

We had never eaten shrimp in our lives, and we knew it was out of the realm of possibility for Mom to cook it. Dad looked at her sideways and shook his head. Mom always got excited in the grocery store.

"Come on, Bev. Let's keep going."

She spied a noodle product she recognized from television advertisements.

"Ooh, we need to buy those," she said. "Linda makes those for her kids."

"Ee-yeah, maybe, but they look a little complicated, and we don't really eat those," Dad said.

"Well, maybe we should," Mom snapped at him almost self-righteously. "Oh! Baking flour. I should make cookies. Would you boys like homemade cookies?"

I hoped this suggestion would fly. It didn't.

"Bev, let's just get a few things and get out of here," Dad said. We had progressed twenty feet in about three minutes.

"That's a good idea," Mom said. "We need bread for lunches."

Eventually, Dad did the shopping alone or with me and Troy on Friday afternoons when he got his paycheck.

• • •

From the start, Dad knew it would be challenging parenting with Mom.

When I was still in diapers, Dad pulled the car up to the house one afternoon after work. Mom was sitting on the front porch. I was perched in my stroller next to her. A slight incline started the stroller rolling slowly away from

Mom and toward the edge of the porch, and Mom couldn't move quickly enough to stop it. Dad's grin turned to horror, and he ran from the car to try to catch me. Even with his bounding steps, he couldn't get there fast enough. The stroller and I tumbled over the lip and onto the grass, four feet below.

"Oh, Bev," Dad said, scrambling to turn the stroller right-side up to assess how much damage had been done to their firstborn.

"I couldn't get there!" Mom cried out.

Somehow I had landed right and checked out okay.

"It's all right. He's fine," Dad said, shaking his head and walking into the house with me in his arms and Mom at his side, leaning on him for balance.

When I was just about school age, I heard a loud crash in the living room one morning.

"Mom?" I said from my bedroom.

I left my toys on the floor to see what had happened. The living room appeared empty. Then my eyes caught sight of a lump on the floor—Mom, lying on her side and shaking violently with her back to me. I went over and tentatively looked at her face. She was laughing.

"I was reaching for my coat, and I tripped over these shoes I put here," she said.

She giggled, and I squatted down and joined her in laughter. It wasn't often you saw your Mom on the floor in fits of glee, even if it was from falling down.

"I'm just going to lay here a minute and catch my breath," she said. "Then I'll get up."

She breathed deeply a few times, head resting back on the floor. Then she lifted her head and shoulders in an effort to sit upright. It didn't work. It looked like a failed sit-up. She lay back down and tried again. She got no further, her arms outstretched but not quite straight. Back she went, breathing with exertion. I sat with my legs crossed, watching her.

"Push that chair over here," she said.

I got up and pushed a dining chair, which was larger than me, next to Mom. She rolled toward it, grabbing the thin metal leg. Then, with some effort, she put a hand on the seat and hoisted herself onto her knees. Pausing a moment, she then managed to position her feet under herself and to rise to a standing position.

"There!" she said, looking proud and more or less steady on two legs. "Thank you, Shawn."

Later that week I heard another crash and came from my bedroom to inspect. Mom was on the floor in the living room, looking uncomfortably bent, as if someone had dropped her there in a heap. Her shoulders were shaking. I came closer and saw that this time she was crying.

She growled angrily. "I couldn't catch myself. Oh, my head!"

We all knew that Mom couldn't move her hands, arms, or legs quickly enough to react to sudden things, so it made sense that she couldn't arrest a fall. Now she let her head loll against her arm and continued crying, tears seeping out from her closed eyes. I looked up and noticed a hole in the wall a few feet up from the floor. White chalk dusted Mom's hair.

"If it wasn't for that stupid accident—" she said, teeth

clenched, voice descending a couple of levels into a kind of monotone hatred. "Oh, that hurt."

She rolled onto her back and straightened her body out. This made her look more normal.

"That hurt," she said again, raising a hand to feel the place of impact on her head. Fresh tears broke out for a moment. Then she seemed to come to rest inside herself and started assessing the situation. Her eyes looked around for a piece of furniture to pull herself up on. Nothing was handy. Then her eyes rested on me.

"Shawn," she said. "Pull me up."

I took her extended hand by the fingers and tried to pull her to a sitting position. She barely budged, her back remaining flat on the floor. She exhaled her remaining frustration and turned to me with a faint smile.

"Well, it'll be okay. Would you go check on Troy? Make sure he's all right?"

I ran to Troy's room and peeked in. He looked up. He was on the floor playing with toys Grandma and Grandpa Thornton had given him. I ran back to Mom.

"He's fine."

"Okay. Let's just sit here and talk, then," she said. The tears had dried on her cheeks, and suddenly it didn't seem so bad, Mom being on the floor, even if she had hurt her head. "Are you looking forward to going to school?" she asked.

"Mm, sure," I said, hoping school would be fun and involve a lot of playing on the playground.

"All your friends will be there," she said. "I know you're going to have a good time. The bus will come and pick you and Lance up. You'll ride to school and go into the classroom. Then you'll have a desk, and you can bring home things you did, and we'll hang them on the fridge."

I nodded matter-of-factly. School sounded fun, but I wouldn't be fully convinced until I got there and saw for myself.

"Tell you what," Mom said. "Why don't you bring me one of those books over there? You can sit next to me, and we'll wait for your dad to get home."

"Okay," I said.

We passed the next couple of hours talking leisurely, reading, and watching cartoons from our position on the floor. Troy came in and out peacefully. At some point we heard tires grinding on the cinders out front. Dad pulled in like a changing of the tide. He crunched up to the house with his work boots, stamped them on the porch, and opened the door. He looked at me sitting on the floor. Then he saw Mom and his face sank.

"Oh, Bev," he said. He stepped over, setting his lunch bucket down, and knelt beside her. His eyes did a quick inspection, and he put his hands behind her shoulders.

"Are you okay?" he asked.

"My head hurt for a little while. Shawn's been sitting with me."

"Here, slow," he said and gently raised her to a sitting position. He did it so easily. I watched carefully, knowing I would need to learn. Then Dad noticed the hole in the wall behind Mom. He looked on top of her head.

"You hit your head, huh?" he said.

Mom rubbed the affected spot with the back of her hand and shook it off.

"It's all right," she said. Dad glanced at the hole, sizing it up silently for future repair.

"All right, let's get you into a chair." He lifted Mom effortlessly to her feet and walked her over to her recliner. She sank into the cushions gratefully. Dad looked at her.

"You want anything?"

"Maybe some iced tea. I'm really thirsty."

She reached for a Kleenex and blew her nose. Dad went to the kitchen. Life went on.

Mom didn't fall just at home. We were at the eye doctor's office one evening for Mom to get a pair of glasses. Dad, Troy, and I waited in the car. Mom loved to shop, and picking out anything took her forever. We were content to let her enjoy herself in the nice, cool office while we sat there with the car windows down, feeling the late afternoon breeze. Suddenly an ambulance pulled up beside us. Dad eyed it suspiciously.

"I wonder if that's for your mother," he said with an unusual smile.

The medics went into the eye doctor's office with a gurney. A few minutes later they emerged with Mom on the gurney. She grinned sheepishly at us from under the big bandage on her head. Dad got out of the car as they wheeled her into the ambulance.

"I tripped," Mom said by way of explanation.

Dad got back in and we followed them to the hospital.

"What happened, Beverly?" the doctor asked.

"Well, I was walking from one side of the office to the

other, and I tripped on something on the floor—maybe a little raised part or something. I fell on the floor and think I hit my head."

That was easy to imagine because by now Mom was toppling over hard at least once every couple of weeks, going over like timber and taking out whatever was in the way—lamps, plants, shower curtains, bookcases. Sometimes I came in from playing and discovered her lying there waiting for help.

Another time Mom and Dad were out bowling with people from their Sunday school class. Our home phone rang. It was Dad.

"We're at the emergency room," he said.

"Why?" I asked.

"Your mother went to bowl the ball, and when she swung it back, she went with it," he explained.

Dad brought her home with another big bandage on her head. No stitches were required, but the doctors had given her a massive skullcap of white gauze wrapped several dozen times.

"They thought she'd had too many beers 'cause we were coming from the bowling alley and she was laughing so much when we got to the emergency room," he told us.

Indeed, we often laughed at these events as a family, as if at an inside joke only the four of us could understand.

• • •

During my early childhood years, I became skilled at pulling Mom up from whatever position she had fallen in. Sometimes she was laughing, sometimes crying, sometimes sputtering with anger. At other times, too, her emotions seemed outside the normal reaction—her laughter might be inappropriate to the situation, and even her tears often seemed to be for something greater than her latest tumble.

One afternoon when Dad got home from work, he started wrestling with Troy and me on the floor of the living room.

"It's a cocoon!" he said, pulling a blanket from the couch. He put it over the three of us and held us underneath.

I tackled him, trying to overpower him and escape the blanket. It was great fun, but it was impossible to squirm free from his big arms. I imagined all the work he did at the foundry and how I was going up against someone with massive strength. Troy was always more aggressive than I was— smaller but tough. He would eagerly take on Dad in any floor wrestling match.

"You can't escape the cocoon!" Dad taunted as we gave our best effort.

Then the hot air and my waning energy got the best of me.

"Let me go!" I hollered. "It's hot in here. Let us out!"

Troy was tiring too. We both began to whine and cry out for Mom to help us, making our cries as desperate as possible so Dad would let us go.

I vaguely heard Mom in the kitchen opening the utility drawer where we put tools and things that had no other place.

"You leave those kids alone!" Mom screamed.

"We're fine, Bev," Dad said, annoyed. I could feel his breath coming out in puffs of laughter in the darkness under the blanket. His tickling fingers stole even more of my energy.

"Dad, stop!" I said between laughs.

Troy was giggling next to me as we tried to escape the tickle torture.

"I said let them go!" Mom's voice was near now. She pulled the blanket back with one hand, and in the fresh light we saw her standing over us with a pair of scissors in the other hand. They were held high and poised to stab Dad immediately.

"Whoa, whoa, whoa, Bev!" he said, releasing his grip on us and scooting back a few feet. "I let them go! I let them go!"

Troy and I scattered. The blanket deflated on the floor. Mom looked at Dad with a feral look in her eyes.

"You may just be playing, but I can't stand hearing the kids scream!" she yelled. She slowly lowered the scissors and went back to the kitchen.

We quit wrestling on the floor that night, and when we played cocoon in the months and years that followed, we added a new dimension to the game: listening for Mom so we didn't get stabbed. You could hear the utility drawer open because it would squeak and then bump down as it dropped. Like many things in our home, the utility drawer didn't work right. But sometimes Mom would grab a knife or scissors or a jar from the counter, so the first sound we heard was her labored breathing and heavy footsteps as she clumped over to enforce justice.

"Okay, Bev! I let them go!" Dad would say, scooting us away and flinging the blanket aside. Mom would be there with a knife poised over him, eyes sizing up where she would bring it down.

Sometimes Mom simply used her hands, and her grip was

unearthly strong. She would grab Dad's arm or leg or hair through the blanket, and once she got hold, it was hard to pry her loose. Dad would suddenly let us go, and Troy and I would scamper away.

"Oh, oh, oh, Bev! Let me go, let me go! We're all done!"

"You leave those kids alone!" she would scream, holding Dad by the hair. "It's just fun to you, but I can't stand it!"

"It's okay, Monkey," he would say, employing pet names to settle her down. "Let me go, Kumquat. We're all done."

Mom was calmest when she was reading. She read more than any person I ever knew—books by popular Christian authors like Chuck Swindoll and every book in the library at Twin Branch Bible Church several times. She read romance novels and magazines of all kinds, but her core reading material was the Bible. I awoke most mornings to see her at the kitchen table with the Bible in front of her, big and blue, a highlighter in her hand moving back and forth slowly over a verse to make sure it was colored with proper intensity. It took her the better part of a minute to highlight just a few words. To underline a verse with a ballpoint pen took even longer.

Second to the Bible, her favorite book by far was *Joni*, the autobiography of Joni Eareckson Tada. It told the story of how, as a teenager, Joni suffered a diving accident that made her a quadriplegic. It told how she learned to function with that lifelong disability and to paint beautifully with her mouth and how she shared her testimony and her deepening commitment to Christ with people everywhere. *Joni* circulated from our living room to the bathroom to the kitchen in an endless loop as Mom read it time and again, highlighting it so thoroughly that the pages puckered with yellow ink.

While I was growing up, it never struck me as strange that the woman holding scissors over us, ready to bring them down hard in a fit of fury, was also my greatest example of what it means to live and love like Jesus.

CHAPTER 3

"Go for it!"

Dad and my uncles were playing a pickup game of basketball in the driveway at Nana and Papaw Gilvin's house on a late Saturday afternoon. Uncle Rick shot for the hoop from a good distance away. The ball bounced off the rim, hit the backboard, and somehow fell in.

Uncle Mark made a final buzzer noise. "The Irish win on a jumper from the key at the last second!"

He did a quick layup, then bounced the ball a couple of times and passed it to Dad, who took a leisurely shot from the lawn. My cousin Kristin and I rode a bicycle and a green pedal-driven toy tractor at furious speeds, avoiding all obstacles, including the bouncing ball and our uncles' scuffling legs.

"Papaw, can we make ice cream?" I yelled as I spun by the garage on my tractor. The garage was separate from the house and sat at the back of the driveway. Papaw Gilvin had built it as his getaway from a house full of girls.

"Next time, Shawn, next time," Papaw said. "It's not hot enough yet."

"Aw!" Kristin and I said.

Papaw sat in a chair in the shade, fixing a little metal part that belonged somewhere deep in the engine of the '39 Ford pickup truck that sat in the backyard, one of Papaw's many restoration projects. Moon-faced and still solid, Papaw wore blue khaki work pants, a T-shirt, and a golf hat—his retirement outfit. He had stopped driving the truck a few months before and had celebrated with a party at the house— including a big "Happy Retirement, Russ!" banner and a cake. Now Loretta Lynn crooned from the cabinet record player sitting against the studs of the garage wall. Tools of every size and description hung from the walls and ceiling. Loretta, Crystal Gale, Tanya Tucker, and Johnny Cash would entertain us the rest of the day.

"How much money did you make on that car you sold last month?" Uncle Rick asked Papaw while lining up his shot.

"A thousand dollars," Papaw said proudly.

"Really?" my dad said. "That's pretty good, Dad."

I was always surprised that my dad called Papaw "Dad" and Nana "Mom." It was a level of in-law intimacy and respect I didn't expect.

"Not bad for an old hillbilly, is it?" Papaw said, grinning.

He and Nana could use the word *hillbilly* safely even when others could not.

Dad came over to me, sweaty and full of life. "Shawn, go get me something to drink," he said, hands on his hips. "Water or tea or something."

I parked the green tractor, and Kristin parked her bike.

"I'll do it," she said. Kristin and I were close in age, and she was much more outgoing than I was. Whenever someone had to take the lead, she stepped up, and I gratefully ceded. I followed her inside.

Nana stood in front of a popping, hissing pan of grease on the stove top. Fried chicken was on the menu. She had saved the lard from bacon that morning in a tin can on the counter and was putting it back to use. I could smell Southern-style biscuits browning too.

Mom was sitting at the table with her sisters.

"Uncle John wants something to drink," Kristin announced.

"I'll get it," Aunt Gail insisted. "You guys keep talking." She got to her feet, grabbed a glass from the cupboard, and poured Dad some iced tea. My cousin Teri was lingering around the kitchen as well, listening to the talk. Gail looked over her shoulder as she put ice cubes in the glass.

"Teri, ask your Aunt Bev if she wants something more to drink too."

Teri turned to Mom. "Would you like something to drink, Aunt Bev?"

"Can I have some pop?" Mom asked.

Dad rarely bought carbonated drinks. He considered them an unnecessary expense. Mom looked positively gleeful.

"Of course," Gail answered for Teri.

"I really like that sweet tea, too," Mom said. Teri looked back at Aunt Gail, slightly confused.

"Okay, I'll pour you some," Gail said. "We have coffee, too."

"I'll have coffee, too," Mom said. Teri looked at Aunt Gail now with amused perplexity. Gail nodded at her as if to say, "Go ahead; it's all right." Teri looked back at Mom, and they began smiling and then giggling, for reasons neither could readily explain. Mom's giggle then turned into a deep belly laugh, and Teri responded in kind. Mom had that effect on people.

I grabbed several vanilla wafers from the box on the counter and started to take Dad his drink. Before I went out, Nana announced, "Dinner's just about ready."

Kristin and I rounded up everyone for dinner, kids and adults. It was a lot of people for one small house, but we pushed furniture out of the way and set up two tables.

Once everyone was gathered, Uncle Mark said grace. Nana passed the dishes around, and we all helped ourselves.

"This fried chicken is delicious," Uncle Rick said, and Nana nodded. We knew what she was thinking: *Kentucky style*. Nana often reminded us cousins of our Southern roots, and I got a sense that Nana believed Southern families were stronger and more God fearing than those in the cold North. Nana and Papaw still had fairly strong Southern accents.

"I'm going to have to play extra hard to work some of this off," Uncle Mark said.

"Mark and I are playing doubles tomorrow," Aunt Gail

said. "I wish you guys would play." She and Mark had been married just a few years. They swam, played tennis, and exercised together as if it were fun.

"Aw, that sounds neat," Aunt Connie said. "I wish we still played volleyball. Anyway, I can't tomorrow." She told us all about what she had going on: her in-laws visiting, a friend picking up decorations for a party, and so on. It was hard for me to keep up with her stream-of-consciousness talk. "Rick, can I get you some more corn? Butter? I think we have more rolls in the kitchen if anyone wants some."

"Connie, slow down," Nana said. "You're moving too fast for everyone." Then for good measure she added, "Shawn, stop biting your nails."

I hadn't even realized I was doing it. Anytime my hands were near my face, Nana was on top of it. Aunt April gave me a funny "What can you do?" face. We were just seven years apart in age, so she was often more like an older sibling to me than an aunt. We even went to the same Christian school for a year, and her high school cheerleading coach was my third grade teacher.

After dinner, everyone sat around groaning contentedly and praising Nana's cooking. A battery of greasy, glistening plates sat before us, proof of battle. Mom got up to go to the bathroom. When she came back, Nana watched her make her way awkwardly to her chair.

"Bevie, if you would just bend your knees, you would walk a lot better," Nana said. "Try to walk straight now. Just think about it—think about bending your knees."

At first Mom didn't resist her mother's request, but as

she began to follow Nana's instructions, I could sense Mom's emotions surging—a spark of anger and deeply felt pain. She flushed, gritted her teeth, and continued her journey across the kitchen with exaggerated, deliberate marching motions, lifting her knees high with some effort and putting them heavily on the ground as if to say, "I'm doing my best." Mom took about five steps—traversing the whole length of the small kitchen.

"Now, see?" Nana said, smiling. "You can walk just fine, if you would just think about it, Bevie. Just think about it. You won't trip. You won't fall. It'll be so much better for you if you just think about it."

"Mother, she's fine," Aunt Gail interrupted. "Bev, don't worry about it."

Dad sat quietly, perturbed. Uncle Rick cleared his throat and looked out the window. Mom made it to her chair, sat down, and drank her tea. In the silence, familiar questions ran through people's heads for the thousandth time:

Why had this happened?

Why had an extraordinary girl been transformed into a woman trapped with such limitations and struggles?

Why did John turn in front of that truck? Was he not paying attention? Was Bev's conversation distracting him? Was he just too young to be driving people around?

Why had Nana and Papaw let her go with him that night?

Had the doctors done their best? What if they had given her more physical therapy after she woke up?

Was there some way to keep her from being so stiff all the time?

And why couldn't the doctors say anything definitive about her altered mind and emotions?

On many occasions I heard snatches of conversations when visiting relatives thought I wasn't listening.

"It's such a shame about Bevie. Do you see the way she still walks?" they would whisper when Mom left the room.

"It all goes back to the accident," someone would answer sadly. "If she hadn't been in that car. If John hadn't turned in front of that truck . . ."

None of the Gilvins blamed Dad anymore. If anything, they admired him for stepping up and taking responsibility for Mom. But a sense of loss remained, and an abiding wound had formed especially in Nana's heart for the guilt she felt over Mom's condition.

Still, Nana's criticism was not limited to Mom. She had a ready correction for everyone. Every time a certain relative walked in the door of Nana and Papaw's place, Nana said the same thing: "You've got a little hanging over your belt there."

When another relative, a young woman, walked by, Nana would say in a stage whisper, "She needs to lose ten or fifteen pounds."

A distant relative went through a troubled pregnancy and a series of miscarriages. Nana's advice? "Maybe if she started eating right, she wouldn't lose those babies."

Anytime one of my cousins was putting on too much weight, Nana often shared her opinion with little filter. "You kids can have a couple cookies," she'd tell a group of us. "One's enough," she would say to the cousin in her sights.

That subtle, innocuous-sounding instruction was a

devastating indictment of that cousin's willpower, her parents' failure to instill healthy eating habits, and so on. Nana, naturally, didn't see it as criticism but as an attempt to help people improve. In her own way, she was expressing love, probably as love had been shown to her during her formative years growing up in a home for orphans during the Great Depression.

With me, it was fingernails.

"Are you still biting your nails, Shawn?" Nana would say. "Look at you, a grown boy, biting his nails like a two-year-old. You ought to be able to stop that. We're going to get some of that cayenne pepper and put it under your nails. Or maybe that bitter finger polish pharmacists used to give to people."

Nana also believed in the traditional folk culture of the Southern Appalachians known as "foxfire." These regional superstitions offered us plenty of strange "remedies" for our troubles.

One time Nana noticed a wart on my finger.

"Hmm," she said affirmatively. "Stay here."

She grabbed an onion from the counter and cut it in half.

"Give me your hand," she said. I offered it, wart and all. She rubbed the wet part of the freshly cut onion on the wart. Then she went into another room and returned with a little box. She put the onion in the box, gift wrapped it, and handed it to me.

"Throw this little box into the fork of the road," she said, phrasing it almost as an incantation.

I took the little box outside, walked to a place where the

road forked, and tossed it in the middle of the street. It felt strange and anticlimactic. I walked back to Nana's house.

"Now we wait," she said.

A few days later I walked back to the fork in the road and noticed the box was gone. I informed Nana of this.

She said soberly, "Your wart will go away soon."

The working theory behind this remedy was that my wart's poison had transferred to the onion, and whoever saw this beautiful package and was curious about what was inside would open it and get the wart. It was kind of horrible— passing the wart to someone else. But when my wart did go away soon after, Nana credited her foxfire remedy. She tried this on one of Dad's warts too. He played along, joking with Nana all the way through the process.

She offered many such cures.

"Sleep with a knife under your bed—it'll cut your labor pains," she told expecting mothers.

"If you sew on Sunday when it's not necessary, some-one will tell a lie on you for every stitch," she warned her daughters.

Connie would complain, "But I have holes in all my shirts! I've got to sew them."

"Find a shirt to wear in the meantime," Nana would say.

And, of course, Nana could wave a needle, thread, and a pencil eraser—but not a long pencil—spookily over a woman's arm and tell her exactly how many children she would have.

Still, my uncles noticed that Nana seemed to pick on Mom most, perhaps because Mom had the most things wrong with her. It lurked in the backs of their minds that maybe Nana was trying to correct the fateful decision to let Mom ride to Goldblatt's that night in 1962.

"Sue, push your glasses up on your face," Nana said, watching her oldest daughter wash dishes at the sink.

The women had stayed in the kitchen. Aunt Sue was scrubbing the green bean bowl. Aunts Connie and April were drying dripping dishes. Aunt Gail was placing items back in the cupboards and the fridge. Mom sat at the table with Nana. The men were gathered in the living room watching a game on TV. I went back and forth between the rooms depending on how interesting the conversation was.

"Hand me that bowl there," Aunt Sue told me on one of my trips into the kitchen.

"Sit up straight now, Bev," Nana instructed, noticing that Mom was slouched over the table. "You should wear something different and try to do something else with your hair to get your hair out of your eyes. Here, put your shoulders back."

Uncle Rick came in with a stray dirty dish from the table and heard Nana directing Mom.

"She's being a drill instructor," he muttered to Aunt Connie. "She's grating on Bev."

"She just wants her to be okay," Connie whispered, shaking her head and drying a drinking glass.

Mom had by now become tongue tied, as happened when she got angry in public settings.

"Mother," she responded deliberately as Nana bombarded her with suggestions. "Mother—I . . . I . . . I can do it. I'm fine."

"If you just got up after John goes to work and started cleaning the house and did that for two hours, your house would be so clean," Nana intoned.

Mom's hand stiffened and pressed tightly against her body. Her breathing quickened. I could see one of her rages coming on.

Suddenly Papaw was there. I hadn't seen him come in.

"Now, Betty," he said. He put his hand on Nana's shoulder. It was as close to chiding her as I would ever see.

"Bevie, do you want some Pepsi?" he offered.

The contrast of his kind offer was so stark against Nana's advice that it stopped the conversation.

"I'd love some," Mom said, exhaling audibly, her eyes still smoldering.

We discovered on the way home that blame was catching. Mom's emotions burst out in the passenger seat as Dad drove toward our house.

"Why does she do that? Why? I can't take it anymore! I can't!" She spoke with a guttural anger familiar to us but that would have surely frightened someone who had never heard Mom in this kind of moment.

"Why do you listen to her?" Dad yelled, matching her level of emotion. "She does that to everybody. You know your mother! She told some of her own family to lose weight. She told Troy and Shawn to stop chewing their fingernails. That's just what she does. She'll never stop. Don't let her do that!"

"Don't say that! You're talking about my mother!" Mom said bitterly, raising her volume even more.

"All right! I won't say anything!" Dad practically shouted.

"Well, I wish someone would tell her to shut up! I'm tired of hearing how bad I am. I can't take it anymore!"

"But when I say something you blame me for it!" Dad yelled. "You can't have it both ways. Stay away from her! Don't go up there anymore. You don't need her! I don't know why—"

"Because it's my mother you're talking about!" Mom screamed. With this final outburst, she began to cry and turned toward the passenger window, letting her head collapse into her hands.

I leaned over to Troy in the backseat. "Why doesn't she blow up at Nana? *She's* the one making her mad."

Troy shrugged. Like water off a slick roof, nothing touched him. He looked out the window as if the passing trees were more interesting than our family dynamics. I was pretty sure he wasn't faking it.

When we got home, Dad helped Mom up the steps, and Mom took her anger into the bathroom. The toilet seat clattered down. When she was this upset, she didn't have the patience or the dexterity to put it down softly. A few minutes later she came out, and I could see by her expression that the frustration had not gone away. Rather, it had morphed into blame. She sat heavily on the couch holding her head as if in pain. Without looking up, she yelled at Dad.

"I'm just tired of people trying to fix the way I walk and the way I am."

"Fine. We won't go over anymore," Dad said, now a little calmer than before. "I'd prefer that anyway."

"Shut up, John! If I hadn't ever met you, I wouldn't be in this situation!" Mom's anger was building a new head of steam. "I wouldn't be trapped this way. My whole family blames you. Ask my mom! Ask my dad!"

Dad was tired. He yelled back, "I'll ask them!"

I could tell he just wanted her to calm down. Both knew her accusation wasn't true.

Troy and I played in my room as if nothing were happening, but my heart seized up every time they yelled. When thirty seconds of silence went by, then a minute, I felt palpable relief. After a while Mom put her hands on the couch cushions and attempted several times to push herself into a standing position. When she finally succeeded, she walked to the kitchen with traces of the high-knee marching Nana had encouraged.

Dad noticed.

"What are you doing? Don't be so stupid! Don't do that!" he barked sharply. "There's no need for that."

It was his way of saying Mom didn't have to conform to Nana's expectations, that she shouldn't feel the pressure of needing to do something without having the motor skills to carry it out. It was also, I learned, his way of saying he loved her just the way she was.

•   •   •

"What's that smell?" Dad asked. He lifted his nose an inch or two into the air.

The one toilet in our house was having problems.

"It's that stupid field system," Dad said and stormed out

to the backyard to have a look. The screen door slammed behind him to emphasize his mood.

Because we lived just outside the city, our house had a septic tank. When it filled to a certain level, the sewage flowed into the ground under our side yard through a system of underground pipes with little holes in them. But the soil in our area was so dense that the field system was prone to stopping up. Often.

Dad burst back in.

"It *is* that stupid field system!" he said. It had already cost him a lot of money to fix when I was in kindergarten. The toilets and sinks had backed up and filled the house with wretched smells. Troy, Mom, and I had lived with Grandma and Grandpa Thornton for several weeks while it was repaired.

Now Dad leaned against the counter, his arms folded, a sour twist on his face. He shook his head as if rejecting one unspoken solution after another. No amount of calculating was going to make this cost any less. I could tell.

Finally, he pushed away from the counter with his hip.

"Don't use the toilet until I say it's okay," he said.

"But what if I have to go?" I asked.

"Go at school or pee outside," he said. I was already used to going outside when someone else stayed in our bathroom too long. "We'll let your mother use it, but until I get it fixed, just avoid the bathroom. And no water in the kitchen sink. I've got to figure this out."

The next day at work, someone gave Dad advice: reduce the stress on the field system by piping the sink and laundry water into our lawn rather than into the septic tank. That would cause the tank to fill up more slowly and would give it time to "digest" its contents.

Dad liked what he heard. When he got home, he crawled under the kitchen sink. I saw his long legs sticking out across the kitchen floor, almost touching the fridge on the other side.

"Shawn," he said, his voice oddly contained in the few square feet under the sink, "get me the wrench from the shed. The bigger one."

I got it and watched as he cut the sink pipe and joined it to a new piece, cranking the pieces together with a coupler and the wrench. Then he got up, went outside, and headed for the cellar. I followed. He flung open the wooden doors leading to the bare-earth space beneath the house. The new sink pipe was sticking down in midair. Dad stepped down there, connected a ninety-degree elbow piece to it, and ran a pipe horizontally toward the cellar doors.

"Hmm," he said when the pipe hit the doors. It would have to go through.

"Shawn," he said, "get me the little saw."

I ran and grabbed the little saw out of the shed. Back in the cellar, Dad was sizing up where the pipe would travel through the cellar door. He began sawing and whittling a hole through the wood. When it was large enough, he slipped the pipe through and connected more pipe so it extended fifteen feet into the side lawn.

"There," he said. It looked incomplete to me, the pipe lying in the grass, but I trusted him. Dad spent the next hour doing something with the plumbing in the laundry room. I grabbed my bike and found Lance.

The next day as Lance and I rode through our backyard, Lance stopped and pointed at the ground. "Ew, look at that!"

There, where the new pipe terminated in the grass, were noodles from last night's dinner. The ground was wet, covered with suds, and smelled like laundry detergent.

"Weird," I said without trying to explain it. I hoped Lance wouldn't probe into why a pipe was traveling from our house and dumping refuse where we played.

Winter came, temperatures dipped, and the pipe in the cellar broke. Dad didn't have time or money to fix it. Kitchen sink wastewater and washing machine water began flowing into the cellar, creating a large pool on the floor of the dirt-walled basement.

One day, Dad poked his head into the cellar and seemed unhappy at what he saw.

"It's gonna create mold problems," he said. The cellar stank in a strange way—like perfume dumped over rotting food. Dad closed the doors. "Stupid field system," he said ruefully.

That night at dinner he gave a new set of commands.

"I'm going to get that field system fixed when we can afford it," he said. "But right now we can't just let water go into the cellar. So nothing goes down the sink."

"Which sink?" I asked.

"The kitchen sink," he said. "You can use it to fill pots and get water but nothing else. The pipe's broken. It's all dumping into the cellar."

"What about the dishes?"

"Wash them in the bathtub and spray them clean with the showerhead."

Our house had just one bathroom and one bathtub—a strange, kidney-shaped tub where we showered and bathed. And it had just been pressed into service as the new kitchen sink.

"What about noodles?" I asked.

"What noodles?" he said.

"The ones we make on the stove."

"Get a colander and drain them in the bathroom sink," he said as if his solution were obvious. I knew that would be tricky since the sink rim was home to a forest of hairspray and aspirin bottles, cotton ball containers, a hair dryer, and a dozen other items.

"What about the laundry?" Mom asked after a moment.

"We'll see about that," Dad said circumspectly. "Until then, Grandma Thornton says she will do our laundry. After dinner let's gather it up. We're taking it over tonight."

A little while later, Troy and I dutifully picked up dirty clothes from wherever we had left them—a sock under the table, underwear behind a bedroom door, jeans stiff with dirt in the bathroom. Dresser drawers and closets were an interesting theory but not where we actually kept clothes. Rather, our clean clothes sat in piles around the house. When we thought about it, we stuffed dirty clothes into the tall, thin wooden hamper Dad had created and placed in the hallway. It had a sliding door on one side where clothes would tumble out when you opened it.

Piling the dirty clothes into plastic laundry baskets, we lugged them to our car and rode with Dad to Grandma's. She opened the front door and smiled as if seeing us with all our dirty laundry were the most normal thing in the world.

Grandma and Grandpa Thornton still had not made a serious commitment to Christ, though they carried the label "Christian" because they had been members of a mainline church for decades. Dad was raised in that church, but it seemed to function like a cruise ship, a nice place to vacation, rather than like Twin Branch, which for my family was like a raft—something we clung to desperately for life. Grandma and Grandpa were good people in so many ways, but like many Americans, they were caught up in the distractions of the modern world. Grandpa worked angles on both sides of the law to make money in politics and business, and Grandma was extremely image conscious—she wore nice jewelry, fussed over her appearance, and enjoyed life's finer things. Their way of life was in many ways so distant from ours.

In spite of this, both had a special connection to Mom. Grandpa Thornton in particular seemed to understand what Mom felt. He had been born without the muscle in the center of his right hand and the corresponding muscle in his right foot. As a result, his right hand was skinny and shriveled and always hung close to his body against his ribs. His foot dragged when he walked, and he wore a brace on it just to be able to stand. That commonality bonded him to Mom, and until I was old enough to drive, Grandpa Thornton drove me, Mom, and Troy everywhere we needed to go—daytime

Bible studies, the dentist, the mall, school events, anywhere. For years he picked Troy and me up from school every day. If I had to go somewhere, I called Grandpa Thornton to schedule it. He and Grandma wrote our appointments on their calendar, which hung prominently in their apartment.

Grandpa also defended Mom from us when needed. If we were joking around with her and she got worked up, Grandpa was the first to step in and turn the conversation in another direction. More than once he chided me for talking back to her.

"You need to be nicer to your mom," he would say, and his rare rebukes frightened me. He liked to sit in his big Victorian chair, which looked like a throne with a large side table.

Not once did I hear Grandpa or Grandma really criticize Mom—and Mom gave them plenty of reasons. She couldn't care for us the way other mothers did. She couldn't even do our laundry anymore. She didn't mask her emotions around them as much as she did around her own family. Grandma and Grandpa Thornton witnessed more of the tension and turmoil of our lives than perhaps anyone else.

For a number of years, every day about midmorning, Mom got up from her chair, lumbered over to the telephone, and dialed Grandma Thornton.

"How are you today?" Mom said.

"Fine; how are you, Bev?" Grandma's voice came across the line.

Their conversations were about daily things—minor agitations, Troy and me, little victories. Often I heard Mom complain about Dad.

"John is a terrible husband," Mom would announce evenly to Grandma Thornton. "The dresser in our bedroom is missing a handle, and he won't fix it. The washing machine is broken. He says, 'I'll get to it,' but he never does. I'm so sick of it. I'm tired of living like this."

"Is that right?" Grandma always answered. Never did she seem to take it personally or offer some argument.

"If he doesn't do something to change all of this, I am going to divorce him! I am going to call a lawyer today," Mom confirmed.

While not being argumentative, Grandma tried to provide perspective in little ways. Sometimes Mom received it; other times she just talked over it. But Grandma had a way of letting Mom vent some of the tension building up inside her.

A few days after dropping off our laundry at Grandma and Grandpa's, we returned to see our clothes in the same dirty and broken baskets. But Grandma had transformed our clothes somehow: there sat my shirts and jeans, plump and clean and smelling so good.

"Thank you, Mom," Dad said humbly as we brought the baskets of fresh clothes to the car. Grandma smiled and waved as if it had been no effort at all. The rich smell of fabric softener filled the car on the way home.

Despite our transformed clothes, in our laziness we still rarely put them away. Instead we left our clean clothes in the plastic laundry baskets or randomly placed them around the house. When I needed a shirt or pants, I knew right where to find them—by the couch or in a plastic basket in the hallway or kitchen.

We returned to Grandma's the next week, and the week after that, with dirty clothes that she magically turned into soft, symmetrical stacks of great-smelling apparel. They seemed almost invasive compared to the rest of our home.

At some point, I don't know when, Dad must have decided not to fix the washing machine plumbing problem at all. Then our dryer broke too. Mom harped on him for keeping her from her domestic duties.

"I'm not putting up with this," she declared one evening. "I'm gonna call someone and get that washing machine fixed. You make my life so hard! I can't even do the things I need to do for the boys!"

She didn't seem to recognize that Grandma had spared us much heartache—that carrying, sorting, and folding the laundry had become an overwhelming task for Mom. Some loads she made too large, some too small, some too soapy, some too wet. Often she fell in the laundry room or toppled over while trying to haul baskets to our rooms.

"John! You're a terrible husband and father!" she yelled frequently. "How can you let that washing machine sit there broken when we have so much laundry to do?"

I secretly hoped he would never fix it, even though Mom continued to complain about his failure.

•   •   •

A knock came at the front door. I looked out the window of my bedroom and saw three women carrying brooms, mops, pails, sponges, and vacuum cleaners.

"Knock-knock," said one.

I heard Mom open the door.

"Beverly!"

"Hi, Heidi! Come on in!" Mom said. I recognized the ladies from church. The Sunday before, one of them, Mrs. Kensington, had been talking to Mom and helping her gather her Sunday school materials. She noticed that Mom had trouble carrying everything. The next day she came by our house to drop off a book Mom had forgotten. Seeing the state of our home, she asked two other women to join her and bless us with a surprise cleaning.

"I hope you don't mind," Mrs. Kensington said. "We like to take a day and tackle each other's big chores. It's fun."

Mom smiled but hesitated.

"That's nice of you, but I can clean up later," she said. "Why don't you just come in and talk? Or we could sit and talk out on the bench swing in the yard?"

"Well, sure, but we already brought all these cleaning supplies, and we're ready to work," Mrs. Kensington said. "How about we do some things first?"

Mom brightened.

"Okay, that sounds good."

I lay on my bed and could hear through the wall as these women made their way through our home and evaluated each room's needs. I wondered if their homes ever got this cluttered and dirty. Strategically, I slipped out the back door as soon as I could. When I came home a couple of hours later, the inside of the house looked larger. The walls had corners. The top of our table was bare and naked, almost embarrassingly so. Features in the laminate popped out at me like never before. The counters, too, looked strangely sharp and shiny.

Where'd all our stuff go? I wondered. It was inconceivable to me that everything had a place to reside where it wasn't always visible.

"It's been great to have you visit," Mom was saying as the women reassembled. I could tell she saw it as more of a social occasion than a cleaning expedition. She was sitting in a kitchen chair watching with delight and a touch of embarrassment as the ladies gathered their cleaning supplies and rinsed their sponges.

"That should give you a good head start," Mrs. Kensington said. Then she noticed that Mom, overcome with emotion, had started crying.

"Oh, Bev," she said and put her arm around Mom's shoulders.

"It looks so good," Mom said. "I wish I could keep it this way all the time."

Another woman came over to comfort Mom.

"With a little help from John and the boys, I bet you can," she said.

"Rrrr! I get so upset—there's just some things I can't do. And John and these boys—" Mom said, winding up into an outburst. The women paused to assess Mom's escalating emotions and calculate how they should react. Then Mom cut herself short, let out a squall of pity and frustration, and held a used Kleenex up to her face as if it could shroud her from view. Our reality was coming slightly into display.

"It's all right," said Mrs. Kensington, squeezing Mom's shoulders repeatedly. "There are lots of people around you."

"God loves you, Bev. It'll be all right," said a woman by the door holding a mop and pail.

After a moment Mom dabbed her nose, then raised her fist and shook her head broadly in some type of emotion— anger? Relief? Resignation?

"You're right!" she said. "If it wasn't for him, I guess none of us would make it!"

She laughed a loud, awkward laugh that didn't seem to fit the moment. I could tell her feelings were churning inside her. If Dad were here, we would have glanced at each other as if to say, "Wonder how far this one will go?" But the women received this as the positive rebound they had been looking for.

"There you go. That's right," said Mrs. Kensington, patting and rubbing Mom's back. "Everything's going in a good direction. God has you covered."

The others quickly gathered supplies and headed out the door as rapidly as they had come in.

"Okay, Bev. We'll leave your family to the rest of your day," Mrs. Kensington said.

"Thank you for coming. It's been just wonderful. I could have gotten things cleaned up myself, but it was so nice to visit with you," Mom said, gathering herself and making her way to the front door. Dad was just arriving. He parked to the side of the driveway in the gravel.

"Thanks for coming," he said, head down a little, observing them get into their cars. Then he walked inside.

"Oh, John, it was the most special thing!" Mom reported. "We talked for such a long time, and they did so much. I could have done it, but I am glad they came. They came over to clean and talk. They love to do it for each other. I'd like to go over to one of their houses sometime and help them. I could, you know. I could do it."

"That's great," Dad said noncommittally, searching for something to eat in the newly reorganized cabinets. "Wonder if they'll come back next week."

"That would be nice," said Mom, taking this seriously and not ironically as Dad had intended.

Dad had been burned before by people's sudden interest in our family. These weren't the first well-intentioned women to come clean up or to try to help Mom with something around the house. Some even took steps toward friendship with her. They asked why she had difficulty walking and invited her to share her story, which Mom was never embarrassed to do. When she did, she always told about Dad and Papaw's commitments to Jesus. She sought in those moments to point to the Lord and his goodness to her.

But when it came to doing the things friends usually did—shopping together for the afternoon, spending time over coffee—these friendships bogged down. Mom couldn't drive anywhere and couldn't just jump in someone else's car as quickly as other people. It took her a while just to make it out the door. She inevitably forgot her purse or Kleenex, and she often needed help walking safely. Some women simply weren't physically strong enough to support her. Putting her in the passenger seat took time, and at the destination the friend had to help Mom walk so she wouldn't fall down. As bright and intelligent and fun as Mom was, her company didn't offer the freedom most people wanted in a social outing. She required time, effort, and a different set of expectations. Her high-maintenance lifestyle didn't fit normal schedules.

So despite occasional help, deeper interactions were few. No doubt some people thought they were being polite by overlooking our troubles. But overlooking reality kept relationships in shallow waters. When Mom would realize that the friend who had taken her to get her hair done or to a movie wasn't calling anymore, she became lonely and discouraged.

"They shouldn't come over once if they're not going to come over twice," Dad would say resentfully.

Worse was the unsolicited advice that arrived from random people—people who didn't take the time to get to know our family well. For some reason they seemed to think they had the key to unlock Mom from her struggles.

"Bev, if you would just put together a schedule for cleaning your house, doing a little bit every day, you could keep it clean all the time."

"The doctor should offer you physical therapy again."

"You should take up swimming. It will loosen your joints."

"John should teach you how to drive."

"You should get your GED and get a job. It would be good for you to get out of the house."

Upon hearing this last suggestion, Mom came home and made an announcement.

"I'm getting my GED so I can get a job." She stood resolutely in the living room.

Dad, Troy, and I cringed in unison—it seemed like another false start, another path to a broken dream. Suggestions like this made our lives worse because Mom had no real way of carrying them out. She could not drive. Her brain didn't function well enough to shop for food, let alone to do school-work or hold a job.

"Okay, Bev," Dad said doubtfully.

"You don't think I can do it," Mom challenged. "You don't think I'm smart enough."

"I didn't say that!" Dad said, frustrated, knowing there was no way to avoid what was ahead.

"Well, I can get my GED without you!" she said. "Then I can get a job and can buy the things I want to buy."

"You go ahead and do that," Dad said fatalistically.

"I will do it!" Mom shouted. "I'll show all of you!"

She went into their bedroom and slammed the door shut. Dad sighed.

"Wonder where she heard that?" he said under his breath.

The undercurrent of blame was obvious in people's advice. *You're not trying hard enough, Bev, John, boys. You're not thinking about this the right way. Take our advice, and your problems will be solved.*

Mom nurtured this hope for a quick fix in many ways. Among her stacks of books were some that promised heal-ing. Followers of Jesus ought never to be sick, the books said. That interpretation of the Christian faith carried a lot of weight with Mom because she was in such great need of it. She read and reread those books more times than I could count. If someone could get well by taking advice from a

Christian inspirational book, Mom would have been healed a thousand times over. But she was not healed. At times she wondered why—and whether it was her fault.

Now and then we ran across people who wanted to pray with Mom and expected God to instantly and miraculously heal her. They didn't show up at Twin Branch Bible Church. Those who believed in praying for instant healing showed up at local Bible studies or at our Christian school. Several times someone prayed for Mom's total healing and seemed disappointed when it didn't happen.

"I guess we'll keep believing until we all have the faith for it," they would say, implying that their faith level was high enough but Mom's wasn't.

Such encounters drove Mom to desperation, and she asked why God had allowed her injuries.

"I don't know why God did this to me," she said aloud one day after one of her outbursts. "I can't believe I'm this way." She put her hand over her eyes as if to shield herself from the world. I stood nearby. As angry as she got with Dad or me or Troy, she never directly blamed God. On several occasions when worked up with frustration and anger, she stopped yelling at us, looked up, and screamed with desperation to heaven, "Why, God? Why?" Her question was genuine. She never seemed to doubt that God had a purpose behind her accident. She just wanted him to more clearly answer the "why."

Today, as always after such scenes, she calmed down and reflected.

"Somehow this fits into God's plan," she concluded with

a sigh. "You kids wouldn't be here had I not met your dad or had the accident. It made us move along in our relationship. Your grandfather and your dad might not have come to Christ if things weren't the way they were. God used those three months of my being out to work in them and to get them to be more serious about spiritual things."

The last tones of *General Hospital* played on the television, which offered its constant, one-sided conversation. Mom glanced over, saw the *Joni* book on her TV tray, picked it up, and began reading from the middle, where she had last left off.

CHAPTER 4

"UNDER THE TABLE, BOYS!"

Dad's words rang through the kitchen as Mom's eyes darted here and there, looking for objects to hurl at us—a can, a glass, a spoon, a random toy. The table, piled high with junk, provided plenty of ammunition.

Troy and I knew the drill, even when we were in elementary school. We dived under the table and soon heard the crash of an object clattering across the table, taking out plates and glasses like bowling pins. We peered at each other through the matrix of chair and table legs and wondered how long this particular tempest would last.

"It's all your fault, John!" Mom shouted, her voice shrill with emotion.

"Cut it out, Bev!"

Dad was in no mood for her antics, but he also seemed increasingly feeble in the face of her unnatural rage. Like us, he could do little but stand by and try not to get hurt. On the occasions when he tried to physically calm Mom, she reacted so badly that it was hard to get her back into a normal state. I was almost thankful for Mom's physical condition at those times. If she had been fully mobile and capable, she might have taken the whole house down.

She cursed and shrieked, "I hate you, John!"

"What do I care?" he yelled back.

"I'm not going to live with this anymore!" She was screeching and cursing at the top of her lungs.

"Oh, whatever!"

"I'll tell you whatever!" I heard her grab something that scraped heavily on the tabletop. A can of corn? A Mason jar? She fired it at him. It hit a cabinet door with a sharp noise and fell to the floor unbroken. It must have been a can.

"I'm not taking this anymore!" she screamed. "My sisters don't have to live with this s—. Phyllis Cleland doesn't have to live with this s—. Neither should I!"

"Then go live with them!" Dad said. I could tell by the sound of his voice that he was standing away from the firing zone.

Moments later some nuance in Mom's movements, some almost imperceptible tone in her voice let me know her fury had peaked. I slid between the chair legs to where she was sitting, crawled up behind her, and did what Troy and I had done before—put my arms around her arms and pinned them to her waist and held her tightly. Her body still trembled with anger, her clenched hand and stiff arm pressed awkwardly and tightly against her body, and her mouth spewed curses at Dad. But I would not let go. My embrace usually pulled her back to reality—or at least to some semblance of reality. After a moment she slumped and relaxed. The frightening tension that had gripped her body disappeared with one last burst of exasperation: "I hate this!"

Now she cried—not tears of anger but tears of regret. For several minutes they flowed.

"It's just so hard," she finally said, her voice deflated and spent. "Nobody understands. I . . . I don't know why I get so angry."

Troy wriggled back into his chair and finished dinner as if nothing had happened. I kept my arms clasped around Mom but loosened my grip.

"It's all right, Mom," I said. She touched my head with her rigid fingers. Dad, standing by the inoperable kitchen sink, looked upset but ready for peace. I let go of Mom's arms and waist and went back to my seat.

Mom's fits were becoming harsher and more frequent— and her mouth was getting more vulgar. She and Dad taught Sunday school and were deeply involved in Awana, and Mom sang in the church choir, but her language during these out-of-control outbursts at home was as bad as any sailor's.

One day when I was just five or six years old, I asked her for something to drink.

"Get it yourself," she said and called me perhaps the worst obscenity in the English language. Moments later she stood in the kitchen pouring me a glass of orange juice as if nothing had happened.

When Mom cussed at us, we knew she didn't mean it. A quiet rebuke from Dad hurt a lot more than a flurry of vulgarities from Mom, which I just dismissed as one of the things she couldn't always control. I figured that she had lost her ability to shield others from her own worst words and feelings and that if other people spoke their minds unfiltered, they probably would sound like Mom.

The conflict and cursing started early each day. Mom's alarm went off at four o'clock on weekdays.

I heard the hated buzzer one morning during summer break and roused slightly. It was Monday, a typical workday for Dad. Mom turned off the alarm and made a lot of commotion as she haphazardly searched the nightstand for her glasses, knocking off items in her quest. Moments later she walked naked from her room to the bathroom, where she often left her robe. In the chaos of our home, modesty was a discarded virtue. I heard her using the toilet and brushing her teeth. When these tasks were completed fifteen minutes later, she emerged in her robe and made her way to the kitchen.

She turned on WFRN, our local Christian radio station. An early-morning host, music, and a series of popular Bible teachers formed the aural wallpaper for the rest of the morning.

Mom ran water into a pot. Moments later the coffee machine began puffing intermittently. Cabinet doors squeaked open and clattered as Mom assembled ingredients for Dad's lunch. Making his lunch took her half an hour or more.

"John!" she yelled. "It's 4:45. Get up!" Her voice echoed through the boxy house.

Dad left at 5:40 for a six o'clock shift, and the foundry was just ten minutes away. He was in no hurry to get up earlier than he needed to.

"John! It's five o'clock. Get your a— out of bed!" Mom hollered.

"I'm getting up!" Dad yelled, his face still adoring his pillow.

A butter knife clinked against a jar in the kitchen—Mom putting jelly and peanut butter on bread for Dad.

A few minutes later: "F— you, John! Get up! I'm not yelling at you again."

"Shut up, Bev! I know!" he yelled. "I can get myself up. Don't worry about me."

She set the knife down on the counter.

"Where's your bag from yesterday?" she said. "I've got to get your stuff from your bag."

"I'll get it. Don't worry about it." He still wasn't up.

A few moments later Mom was insistent, her tone getting ugly. "John! It's 5:10."

Now I heard her shuffling toward their bedroom. I opened one eye to see that she had a full pot of piping hot coffee in her hand. I lifted my head a bit from the pillow in anticipation of disaster.

"Get up!" she yelled into the room through gritted teeth. I imagined her approaching the bed where Dad lay unsuspecting.

Bedsprings squeaked as the action took place.

"Ah! Bev! Stop it!"

Dad had apparently rolled over and discovered her. From the sound of the movements and Dad's tone of voice, I knew she had begun to tip the pot so as to pour the coffee onto Dad's head, but he had caught her before any coffee spilled out and was trying to get a grip on the pot without burning his fingers.

A few weeks earlier she had roused him from bed with a lit candle.

"I'm going to burn your hair!" she threatened, bringing the flame and dripping wax down toward him.

On another occasion, after Dad bought water beds for us because he discovered they were cheaper than normal mattresses, Mom came in with a pair of scissors and plunged them down toward him as he narrowly rolled out of the way. She punctured the bed instead, and water began leaking everywhere. Dad came into my room before work that day.

"Shawn, wake up. Go get the patching stuff from the garage and patch our bed."

"What do you mean, patch it?"

"Your mom poked a hole in it when she tried to stab me this morning. Water's getting everywhere. I've got to go to work."

Today, Dad's quick reaction spared him a scalding coffee shower.

"I'm up! Now get out of here!" he yelled at Mom, who shuffled back into the kitchen without the coffeepot. I heard her open a box of cookies and put six of them in a clear sandwich bag as she always did. These went into Dad's black pail, along with the Thermos of coffee encircled by the *Our Daily Bread* devotional.

Dad's preparations lasted ten minutes or so. The voices of radio teachers J. Vernon McGee and then Chuck Swindoll resonated through the kitchen. Birds sang through the open, screened windows and doors. When the weather was fair, Dad liked to keep the doors open so the breeze blew through all night. We had no air-conditioning, which made the hot, humid Midwest nights difficult.

The bathroom door opened. Dad came out wearing his work clothes. He went into the kitchen to make himself breakfast.

"By the way," Mom informed him, "I am *not* going to sleep in this house with doors open when someone could come in and kill us and rape me." She said this with a growl of determination and pointed directly at Dad.

She was preparing a gym bag with another set of clothes for Dad so he could shower at the foundry before coming home. She must have heard a news story that prompted her resolution. She often used such news reports to attack Dad.

"No one's going to kill us, Bev," Dad said. There was no way he was closing the doors at night. He loved the cool air, and something about sleeping with everything open made him feel comfortable. He had become illogically stubborn over this, and Troy and I would get in trouble if we closed the front door or the back door at night.

"It happened to other people," Mom continued. "And you'd just like that, wouldn't you? You want someone to break in here and rape me and leave me for half-dead!"

"Good luck to him," Dad joked, putting the milk back in the fridge. He was a persevering but not a patient man. Rarely did he let things go without answering back.

"Well, f— you!" Mom yelled. Then she continued as if she had not just cursed at him, "I forgot to finish your sandwich."

"Because you tried to pour hot coffee on me," Dad said.

"You deserve it!" she said, giving him an extended, vulgar description of himself. Then, "I've about got your sandwich done."

"I've got to go," Dad said, hurrying because of the time.

"I've about got it done," she said.

"I'll have to take it as it is. Just give it to me."

"I'm going to finish it!" Voices and anger were rising again.

"No, give it to me now! I've got to get to work. I don't want to be late."

He went over and fussed with her over the sandwich, taking the knife and quickly finishing the work. She threw her hands up.

"I'm sick of this! I'm not doing this anymore. Tomorrow morning you can get yourself up. I'm not getting up before you. I'm not making your lunch anymore."

"I never asked you to make it."

"*You* can get up and make it. Today while you're gone, I'm getting a divorce lawyer. I'm ending this thing. I don't know why we are even doing this." Her body was stiffening up, and her voice dropped into its deep, glottal register.

Mom's "divorce" line was her most frequent threat. We heard it many times and in many forms, most commonly, "I'm finding a lawyer today, and I'm divorcing your a—."

Dad went along. "Fine, call a lawyer." On some occasions he would open the Yellow Pages to lawyers in our area and toss it on the table at her. He grabbed his lunch bucket and headed down our front steps. It was 5:39. Mom went to the door to yell at him.

"And don't come home!" she said.

"Fine. I'll see you later. I'm picking Shawn up after soccer practice tonight," he said.

"I don't care! I'm getting a lawyer and divorcing your a—!"

Mom shut the door. She walked back to the kitchen table, and I heard the soft thud of her Bible and the gentle clatter of pencils and a highlighter. These were welcome sounds after the yelling and fighting of the past hour.

As I lay there in the relative silence, I knew she was reading. Every so often a thin page turned, or Mom's finger got caught on a corner of her Bible as she highlighted a verse. A dozen such Bibles circulated in our home. Some she bought at Goodwill; some were given to her. A green hardback *Living Bible* with a missing front cover occupied our bathroom magazine rack. Study Bibles floated around the living room. A women's devotional Bible popped up every now and then in the sea of mess. Mom used these Bibles until they fell apart or were lost in one of our many piles of stuff.

Another page turned. I heard Mom take a drink of coffee and set the mug down with a sharp tap on the table. In the other room, Troy was snoring. I doubted he had even woken up for the earlier drama.

An hour later I woke up, not realizing I had fallen asleep again.

I heard Mom curse from her bedroom. "Shawn! Come help me find my earring."

I rolled onto the floor, stood up, and walked into her room. Mom had showered and was wearing slacks and a blouse. She sat on the edge of her bed.

"I dropped it somewhere." She cursed loudly.

Her ears were pierced, but she had a hard time putting earrings in, especially with their little metal backing pieces. Dad, Troy, and I often helped Mom get herself ready. Most Sunday mornings Dad did Mom's hair; he even gave her permanents occasionally. Often, when Dad was not home, Troy or I would be called in to help mom pull her hose up around her waist. We regularly helped her with her jewelry. She wore necklaces for weeks on end, including to bed, because it took such effort to get them on and off.

"Put this other one in my ear. I can't put it in. I got one in, and I lost the back to this one and then dropped the whole thing."

She was starting to breathe heavily, her face bunching up in frustration. I looked around. After a good while of searching among the piles of stuff that took up all but a small walking path to the door, I found the earring and its backing piece on the carpet.

"F— your father," she said. "If it wasn't for him, I wouldn't be in this situation. I'd be able to put these in myself. It's your father's fault."

I gently slid the earring through Mom's earlobe and pressed the backing piece onto the small rod.

"There. Thank you," she said, calming down a little.

She got up after me and went to sit in her chair in the living room. The TV was already on—*The Price Is Right* and its cascade of cheerful noise. Leaving it on, Mom grabbed a book that was sitting nearby, a Christian prairie romance novel. Within moments, amid stacks of household junk and aged food on crusty plates, Mom was utterly lost in 1860s America.

The sun was shining, and there was no question what my day would look like: I was going to spend it all outside, escaping the strange rhythms and environments of home.

"Mom, I'm leaving on my bike," I said a few minutes later, putting on my worn tennis shoes. I would have preferred to go barefoot, but there were bees in the clover growing in the grass and cinders on the road. A tank top and shorts completed my summer uniform.

"Okay," she said, not looking up from the book on her lap.

"I'll probably go to downtown Mishawaka or even South Bend," I said.

"Okay. Be back before dark. Get some money out of my purse. You can get a hamburger at Bonnie Doon's."

Mom meant well, but she rarely had the money in her purse for a hamburger. I didn't bother to look but went outside and mounted my blue Schwinn with its shiny silver banana seat with gray stripes. Click-click-click went the cereal box toy I had fastened to the spokes.

Lance was already doing circles on his bike, waiting for me.

"What do you wanna do?" he asked.

"I don't know," I said, happy knowing I could do anything.

"Wanna shoot BB guns?" he asked. Dad had gotten me

a gun when I was seven. He hung an old piece of carpet in the back of our old, rickety garage and fastened paper plates and cups there so we could shoot the daylights out of them.

"Nah. I wanna go somewhere," I said. I was thinking of the St. Joe River, where we could put corn kernels on the ends of our hooks and pull up carp, competing to catch the biggest one.

We sat and considered the day for a moment, resting our hands casually on the handlebars. I surveyed the neighborhood. Across a small field from Victory Road I saw the Millers' house. It wasn't much larger than ours, and Mr. Miller worked at the same factory as Dad, but their life seemed so much better than ours. They had a green, meticulously painted wire fence around the yard that Mr. Miller was always cleaning and touching up. Their lawn was a vibrant green and as thick as fur. Mr. Miller mowed it in a hatch pattern like a major league baseball field. As reckless as Lance and I sometimes were, we were always careful not to disturb the Millers' pristine fence and yard. The Millers were noticeably Catholic. Right by the front porch, Mary the mother of Jesus extended her plaster hands to receive visitors.

"Let's go to the fort," Lance eventually said, and we hopped on our pedals and headed into the woods.

Amid the trees, vines, and overgrown weeds stood our little structure, assembled with boards we pulled off an abandoned outhouse elsewhere in the woods. I well remembered tearing apart the dilapidated little shack piece by piece, then trucking boards over and hammering them together into a new shape. It was our self-designated job last summer.

"I hope the kids from Eighteenth Street don't find this place," I said, taking a seat on the weeds within the fort's limited space. Those kids were older and meaner than us. We were constantly concerned they were going to tear the fort apart. While we lived on an isolated dead-end cinder street, we often encountered kids from other neighborhoods when we traveled to the far reaches of the fields and woods around us.

"We should put a bunch of rusty nails around it," Lance suggested lazily.

After a few minutes in the peace and shade, we stirred ourselves.

"Let's go to Erma's."

Erma's was a pink house on a corner just where the city of Mishawaka really began to take shape. An elderly single woman named Erma sold Now & Laters, Bottle Caps, Pop Rocks, and wax lips, plus ice cream from a little cooler. I bought a couple of small candies while Lance bought candy and an ice cream. The trip to Erma's was quite a ride from our house but well worth it.

"Let's play Evel Knievel," I suggested. Lance nodded, his mouth full of Now & Laters. As usual, when one of us suggested something to do, the other guy pretended it was his idea.

Back at our house, Troy was awake and dressed for play. I burst in.

"Hey, Troy! Wanna play with us?"

"Yeah! Let me put on my shoes," Troy said. Usually we didn't want him around—he was three years younger than us—but lately Lance and I discovered we could have fun getting Troy to believe he was Evel Knievel, the popular 1970s daredevil, and inventing ways to test his fortitude.

Behind our house sat an old chicken coop that had been turned into a shed. The ten-foot-high roof was nearly flat with just enough pitch to let the rain roll off. The three of us climbed up via a chain-link fence and an old fence post just tall enough to give us the reach needed to make it onto the roof.

"Troy, you're gonna be Evel Knievel," I told him.

"What does that mean this time?" he said.

"It means you're gonna fly off this shed," Lance informed him.

Earlier that winter, we had played Evel Knievel with Troy by putting him on a plastic sled behind a neighbor's house and sending him down a hill toward raspberry bushes at the bottom. It took us ten minutes to disentangle him from the thorns, and his coat was snagged in a hundred places, his hands and face bloodied. Troy cried.

"I'm going in!" he yelled.

"No, no! Troy, let's keep playing. We'll do something more fun."

"I'm going to tell Mom!"

"Troy, what do you want to do? You tell us what to do, and we'll do it."

In this way we kept Troy outside and playing the terrible games we invented for him.

Now our goal was to see if we could toss him from the top of the shed over the white picket fence between our yard and the neighbor's yard. We needed to toss Troy about eight feet away from the shed to clear the unforgiving picket fence. Lance and I conferred about how to do this and decided we would swing Troy by his limbs.

"This is Howard Cosell," I said in my best announcer voice from the top of the shed. "Here we are with Evel Knievel, who is going to fly over this gorge onto the other side."

Lance and I took Troy's arms and legs and swung him once, twice, and then over the side. He landed almost directly below us with an "Unh!" sound. Lance and I looked at each other and considered our failure.

"We didn't swing him high enough."

We scampered down to retrieve Troy, who was standing up and brushing off the grass and dirt.

"I don't know if I want to do this," he said, shaking off the fall to the ground he had just experienced.

"You're Evel Knievel, Troy! You're brave," I said.

"Plus, there's thicker grass over the fence. Let's just do it until you get over the fence," Lance reasoned.

Troy seemed to conclude this was the price of playing with the big boys. We hauled him up to the top of the shed again.

"One . . . two . . . three!"

Troy went flying, and this time we put some air under him. Troy's flailing body went farther, but instead of clearing the fence, he landed partially over it with one leg caught between the pickets.

"You almost did it!" Lance said by way of congratulations. Troy's hands were patting around on the grass trying to push himself clear of the fence. He pushed up enough to get his leg free.

"Let's do it again!" I said. Troy's face fell. After a few more tries, we were able to send him soaring over the fence. How he didn't break something, I'm not sure.

That day it was Evel Knievel, but Lance and I found many other ways to involve Troy in our games. Later that summer, Lance dug out boxing gloves he had received for Christmas, inspired by the *Rocky* movie craze, and we cooked up a whole new vision of fun. In the vacant field across from our houses, we mowed the grass down and built a boxing ring. Somewhere we found poles to create a perimeter and encircled it with string.

Lance played Rocky. I played his trainer, Mickey, portrayed by Burgess Meredith in the movie. Troy, naturally, played Rocky's archnemesis, Apollo Creed.

"Get him, Rocky!" I yelled from the corner as Lance closed in on Troy with his big, new gloves. We had layered Troy's hands in mittens and winter gloves. To his credit, Troy fought back valiantly, but Lance was bigger, and inevitably Rocky emerged victorious.

"Rocky Balboa wins the biggest match of the century!" I yelled. Troy was lying on his back in the shortened grass. Lance pumped his shiny new gloves in the air as I held up one of his arms.

Brotherly love had not made it into my heart just yet.

After our Evel Knievel game, night fell. Dad would be coming home soon. Troy, still in one piece despite being thrown from the shed, headed inside, and I followed.

"See ya tomorrow, Lance," I said.

"Okay, see ya," he said, and we went into our separate realities.

The TV was still on. It rarely went off between the hours of 7 a.m. and 11 p.m. Mom was still hunched in her chair, now reading a different book. I assumed she had finished the first one and maybe another one in between. Her appetite for books was voracious. Books were spread throughout the house, and wherever Mom was, she found a book and picked up where she had left off. Often she would lose a book she was reading in the mess of our house, then find it weeks or months later and start reading again as if she had never lost it.

Dad's car crunched up the driveway. He came in moving slower than in the morning. Mom didn't say anything but didn't seem angry.

"I thought you were going to divorce me today," Dad said, testing the waters.

"A lawyer needs money," Mom said, barely looking up. "I don't have any money. I'll find some money and divorce you tomorrow."

She kept reading silently. I knew it was likely to be a calm evening.

After dinner, we did what we always did—watched potentially toxic levels of television together. Our TV set had big clunky dials and rabbit ears and picked up just five stations: the three major networks, PBS, and a Christian station run by Lester Sumrall's ministry that played a lot of old fifties and sixties classic TV shows. TV was our mutual escape— our comforter, counselor, and alternate reality. I imbibed every detail of '70s sitcoms, detective shows, and cartoons like *Laverne & Shirley, The Mary Tyler Moore Show, The Carol Burnett Show, Mork & Mindy, M*A*S*H, Happy Days, Barnaby Jones, Hawaii Five-0, Scooby Doo, Super Friends,* and dozens more. We had TV trays in the living room and often ate dinner there. Dad joked that if the neighbors saw our house without a blue glow, they would probably inform the police we had died.

Troy and I went to bed at 8:30, and Dad and Mom kept watching. Dad lay on the couch stretching his muscles from the workday. Mom chuckled at something someone on TV said. After a while she got up and got ready for bed. Dad fell asleep on the couch watching Johnny Carson. He woke up in the wee hours of the morning and moved to the bedroom.

• • •

The next morning, after cursing at Dad for an hour, Mom seemed more upbeat than usual. Then I remembered: it was her day to volunteer at the nursing home a mile or so away from the house. She was due there at noon but spent the entire morning working up to it, putting on makeup with short, imprecise motions, then picking an outfit.

"Shawn, get my bike!" she hollered around 11:30.

Dad had bought her a large three-wheeled bike with a basket on it. I retrieved it from the garage and wheeled it out front. Mom was waiting at the front door. I held her arm as she came down the front steps.

"Your father will be back in a couple of hours. You boys stay inside and watch TV," she instructed.

Gripping the handlebars tighter than necessary, she put her foot over the low frame and sat down successfully. Then she put her purse in the basket. She pressed down on the pedal and began moving forward. Pedaling was a whole leg motion for her, as if someone had glued her ankle and knee joints together so they wouldn't bend. She headed through our dead-end street to the small path that connected us to a broader world. A cornfield had bordered our street originally, with a tree line to shield crops from damaging winds. But the cornfield had recently been replaced by Blair Hills, a new housing development, and the tree line was converted to an asphalt pathway for walking and biking. This gave us easy but distant access to the rest of Mishawaka.

The nursing home Mom rode to was a simple, one-level place with fifty beds and about that many residents living out their final years in various stages of incapacity. Mom was thrilled to become a regular volunteer there. The administrators gave her a vest and a name tag, which she wore as proudly as the 4-H winners wore their ribbons at the county fair.

One time when it was raining, Grandpa Thornton drove her there, and I went along. I found it interminably boring, sitting for hours as Mom talked with and doted on the elderly residents. But I noticed they treated her like a close friend, an equal, someone who understood them and their limitations. Staff came and went, serving the people functionally and distantly. There was little common experience on which to base a connection. But the residents trusted and confided in Mom. She sat for hours giggling and laughing with them, listening to their small complaints and deeper miseries. Her encouragement, always based on some Bible verse she remembered, spoke quietly but powerfully to them. The nursing home was always brighter and lighter after Mom left.

Dad came home from work, looked over at Troy and me to see that we had survived without Mom, then jumped in the shower. Troy and I kept watching TV as if our very lives depended on it.

Dad got out of the shower, put fresh clothes on, and laid himself full length on the couch. He was perfectly still. I imagined what his day had been like: liquid steel oozing, crane arms swinging overhead, the noise, the smoke, the dust.

The phone rang. I went over and picked it up.

"Hello?"

"Shawn? It's your mother." Mom giggled for a moment.

"Hi."

"I'm at a pay phone. I'm not sure where I am. I see a Rite-Aid. And I see a gas station."

I muffled the phone against my chest.

"Dad, Mom's lost."

Then back to the phone.

"Which gas station?"

"I don't know. It's red and white."

"What's the street name?"

She fumbled around on the other end.

"I can't see from here, and I don't want to leave the phone."

"Ask her if she's hurt," Dad said without opening his eyes.

"Are you hurt?"

Mom sometimes turned too tightly and tipped the bike over or ran it off a curb.

"Oh, no," she said, giggling more. "We had such a good day at the home. People had all sorts of stories. If I can remember them, I'll tell you boys. Then I started riding around for a while, but now I don't know where I am. Can you have your father come pick me up?"

"Ask her if she sees a grocery store near the Rite-Aid," Dad said.

"Is there a grocery store?" I asked Mom.

After a moment she responded. "Yes! I see it. How did you know?"

"Tell her I'll be there in a minute," Dad said, pushing himself up from his collapse.

"He's on his way."

"What?"

"Dad's on his way."

"Okay. Tell him I have my bike."

"I will."

"Bye, Shawn."

"Bye, Mom." I turned to Dad. "She has her bike."

He was pulling on his shoes slowly as if they, too, were reluctant.

"Of course she has her bike! She didn't walk there." He groaned and huffed out to the car. Troy, lying almost on his back against a pile of clothes—clean? dirty?—hadn't moved a muscle. The show droned on.

A year after Mom began volunteering at the nursing

home, it was sold, the policies changed, and the people Mom had gotten to know had passed on. Riding the three-wheeled bike also became more dangerous as her body seemed to age more quickly than normal. She sadly stopped volunteering and looked for something else to do.

• • •

One day a package arrived for me in our mailbox.

"Hey! I got something," I said, walking into the house and holding up the box. Troy shrugged.

I tore into the box and heard a clinking. Tugging on the contents brought a cardboard sleeve into view.

"Lightbulbs?"

Mom, sitting in her chair, heard me and laughed.

"Oh, I—those are from my work," she said. "I sent them to you. We bought them! Those are for you boys, for our house."

Tucked in the sleeve were eight bulbs—two red, two blue, two green, and two clear. I left the bulbs, the sleeve, and the torn-open box on the kitchen table amid the previous clutter, expecting someone else to put it away.

The next day I came in and heard Mom on the phone. She was seated at a TV tray arrayed with some kind of paperwork and a pencil.

Someone answered, and Mom began reading from a script.

"Hello. We are the St. Joseph County Handicapped Association. We raise money to help people with special needs get ramps in their homes. We are selling lightbulbs. These lightbulbs last longer than normal bulbs—up to four years. And they come with a lifetime warranty. Would you like to buy some?"

Silence.

"Okay. Thank you."

She hung up clumsily and looked down at the sheet of paper covered with phone numbers and names. With effort she crossed out one line, then held her finger under the next number and dialed. It took her a minute or more to enter the number correctly.

A distant "Hello?"

"Hello," Mom said. "We are the St. Joseph County Handicapped Association. We raise money to help people with special needs get ramps in their homes. We are selling lightbulbs. These lightbulbs last longer than normal bulbs— up to four years. And they come with a lifetime warranty. Would you like to buy some?"

The person on the other end was talking.

"Oh, is that right?" Mom said. "So you have special needs too? Tell me about them."

She listened, chuckled, and affirmed for a long time while the person on the other end talked animatedly. Mom's posture loosened from its businesslike pose.

"Oh, I understand completely," Mom said.

Another twenty minutes went by as they talked.

"It's a good thing your grandmother came to live nearby," Mom finally concluded. "You two can take care of each other! And your daughter-in-law—she sounds so wonderful."

By now they were saying good-bye like old friends. When Mom hung up, she turned back to the paper in front of her. A look of realization crossed her face. She glanced up at the clock and her mouth registered mild panic. Nearly an hour had passed since she started. Pondering for a moment, she picked up the pencil and began filling out an order for bulbs. It took her the better part of thirty minutes to fill in the required information.

A week later another package arrived, this time addressed to Troy. I found it in the mailbox, brought it home, and dumped it in front of him where he sat having cereal at the kitchen table.

"It's probably lightbulbs," I said. He raised his eyebrows with interest, then ripped it open objectively. It was another sleeve of multicolored bulbs. He looked at me, confused. I shrugged and walked away.

Boxes of bulbs arrived regularly for several weeks, and Troy and I began to stack them against the wall. One day Dad walked in with his own box of lightbulbs, newly arrived in the mail.

"Bev! What's with all these lightbulbs?" he asked, catching on that something was amiss. Mom was in her bedroom. She began to get up and come out.

"Well, we need lightbulbs," she said defensively, as if the argument had been in her head for some time.

"I thought you were selling them to *other* people," Dad said.

"I am," Mom said, entering the room and shaking her head a bit, "but I'm supposed to sell five boxes an hour, or I don't get paid, and it takes a while to dial the numbers and take the orders."

She made a hectic waving motion with her hands.

"I thought I could earn a little extra money for me. I'm tired of waiting for you to give me any money! I want my own money to spend on what I want to spend it on!"

She yelled with increasing volume. She was getting worked into a frenzy quickly.

"And what do you care?" she continued. "This is my job. It's my money. And it's for a good cause!"

By now her rant was peppered with expletives.

"You can make and spend your own money," Dad yelled back, "but I'm seeing bulbs everywhere, and now you're just spending more money than you're making!"

He spied the stacks of sleeves Troy and I had been adding to day by day. "Are you telling me these are our lightbulbs?" he asked.

"Well," Mom said with a calmer tone and a sense of guilt.

Dad exhaled and groaned at the same time. "Bev, this is probably costing me more than when you sold Avon." Mom had sold Avon for a short time, mainly to herself. Avon sacks sat around the house like little sandbags barricading the house from a flood.

Dad looked at the sleeve of multicolored bulbs in his hand and shook his head. He walked over and added it to our stack. For quite some time, the light in my bedroom was red. Troy's was blue. Our ceiling fixtures had sockets for two bulbs, so our strategy was to get our hands on one white bulb to dilute the intensity of the red or blue. It gave our rooms a strange vibe.

One day after she quit selling bulbs, Mom fell into one of her common despairs.

"I have a headache," she announced from bed. "I'm not getting up."

"You don't have a headache," Dad said from the kitchen.

She cursed him. "Get out of here," she replied.

"It's all in your head," Dad said. "We've been to doctors. There's nothing wrong. Just get up."

Mom was always complaining about ailments and taking over-the-counter medicines for her various pains, allergies, and aches.

She cursed him again. "You live inside my body. You live inside this torment. You tell me it's not pain."

"The doctors can't find anything," he said. "It's all in your head. Here's some aspirin. Now let's get up and try to get over this."

Mom refused to budge and stayed in bed all day as promised. This happened frequently, Mom descending into a state of depression or lethargy, going to bed early all week, and leaving us to fend for ourselves.

I came home from school one day and realized that Mom was still in bed and wasn't planning to get up. Dad would be home soon, and if dinner wasn't on the way, things might get chaotic. I opened the fridge and spied raw chicken. On the counter I saw Shake 'N Bake. I picked up the phone.

"Hi, Grandma," I said. "It's Shawn. I want to cook chicken. Can you tell me how?"

Patiently, Grandma walked me through each step. "Turn the oven on to 350. Make sure nothing's in there," she said.

I set the phone down, followed her instructions, and came

back. Step by step I prepared dinner and had it ready by the time Dad got home. When he walked in the back door, he smelled chicken cooking and looked at me, puzzled. I was eight years old.

A few times Mom got so low that she intentionally took more than the recommended number of pills from her over-the-counter medicines, then became listless. Once I found her in her bed looking groggy and half-conscious.

"What's wrong, Mom?"

She groaned.

"I'm discouraged. You guys don't care. I just figured I didn't want to deal with it anymore, so I took those pills."

She pointed to an Excedrin bottle.

"How many did you take?" I asked.

"I don't know. A lot."

I had seen enough TV shows about emergency rooms and people taking pills to kill themselves that I became frightened. Dad wasn't going to be home for a couple of hours, but our neighbor, Marilyn, was a nurse.

I went next door. "Can you come look at my mom? She says she took a bunch of pills."

Marilyn nodded and quickly followed me. By now Mom was sitting up a little in bed.

"How're you doing, Bev?" Marilyn asked.

"I was feeling down, so I took a bunch of those pills," Mom said. Marilyn knelt beside her and began looking in her eyes, checking her pulse, and asking her questions.

"How do you feel? Can you stand up? How's your stomach?"

Mom enjoyed being cared for and answered readily: "My stomach hurts, but I feel okay. I'm better than I was."

After a while Marilyn patted her hand.

"Don't do that again, Bev," she said. "Shawn, if this happens again, come get me."

A few days later Mom pulled out of her funk and bounced back in her own way. She came into my room at 3 a.m. and hit the switch. Pink light filled the room.

"Shawn, I'm vacuuming the house today, and then I'm going to make breakfast," she said. "It'll just be a few minutes. Would you like some eggs?"

I squinted at her, shielding my eyes from the pink light with my sheet.

"Um, eggs sound real good, but maybe later," I said, glancing at the clock and trying to convince myself it wasn't really the middle of the night. She beamed.

"Okay! We'll have eggs later."

She turned the light off and shuffled away. Moments later a blue light went on across the hall. I heard Mom having the same conversation with Troy.

Later that morning before school, Troy and I sat eating cereal. Without talking about it, we both knew the situation: what goes up must come down. Mom's burst of energy was surely going to crash and burn, probably that afternoon, resulting in some bad times in the Thornton residence.

The storm arrived right on schedule.

"Hey."

Dad walked in from work, sooty and metallic-smelling.

The TV was on. Troy and I were watching a kids' show. Dad dropped his lunch bucket on the counter.

"What's for dinner?" he asked optimistically.

Mom had been sitting quietly for hours without any outward sign of agitation. Now she flung words at him like boiling water.

"Do you think I've just been sitting around all day, waiting for you to come home and make you dinner!" She shot a few choice obscenities at Dad.

Dad glanced at me and Troy—a quiet assessment, even a solidarity. He wisely waited a few minutes, getting himself some water from the sink. There he noticed a pink hunk of meat sitting in a bowl of water.

"What's this?" he asked.

Mom looked over, then dropped her hands in her lap regretfully.

"We were going to have cow tongue, but I just got it out of the freezer." Cow tongue was a fairly frequent part of our diet.

"You just got it out?"

"Yes. I forgot to get it out!" She pressed the words through her teeth and then started crying.

"It's all right, Bev," Dad said. "Next time if you just got it out in the morning and put it in the refrigerator—"

"I know!" She cut him off and loudly began cussing him out, using every bad word I knew in just four sentences. She seemed frustrated there weren't more available. Troy didn't budge. My heart twisted with pain.

Dad stood by the counter, pondering his options.

"Well, we've got to find something to eat," he stated as if reading a status report. He rifled around in the cupboards and pulled out a couple of cans of Campbell's soup, crackers, and some lunch meat and bread.

The next day Mom still seemed off kilter from the high she had hit the day before. She banged around in the kitchen for an hour before Dad got home, putting pans on the stove, cursing everything. The result was supposed to be Shake 'N Bake chicken with a side of instant mashed potatoes.

We sat down to eat. None of us seemed interested in talking. It was getting toward the end of the week, and we were all tired. A few bites in, Dad held his piece of chicken up for inspection.

"This chicken's pink in the middle," he observed with a hint of agitation.

"I followed the recipe exactly as it says," Mom said.

"Well, you might have followed the recipe, but this chicken isn't done on the inside," Dad said, displaying the raw pink from the part he had bitten.

Mom banged the table and began to curse. "You just go off to work, and you work all day, and you expect me to have dinner ready. I tried to make the chicken, but I dropped the bowl with the water, so I'm not sure how long it really thawed before I put it in. But I followed the recipe to a T!"

I decided not to mention that the instant mashed potatoes were crunchy. Troy had no such tact.

"The potatoes are dry and crunchy, too," he said.

"Well, s——!" Mom said to Troy. "I work in this house, slaving all day, and you don't show me any appreciation. You're just like your father."

She got up and huffed over to the trash can. There she pulled the instant mashed potatoes box out.

"Here! I did exactly what it said," she said, tossing the box toward the table. It landed on the floor.

She sat down and broadened her complaint, using more obscenities as she became more agitated. "It's hard to work around here. I'm tired of this hell! And I'll tell you what! I'm not putting up with it anymore. If you don't fix that washing machine by next Tuesday, I'm leaving you. It's been years! Connie's washing machine works. Do you think Rick would ever let Connie have a washing machine that didn't work for this many years? Rick and Jack and Mark would have fixed my washing machine! Any other husband would fix the washing machine for his wife!"

"Calm down, Bev!" Dad said, his annoyance piqued.

"No, *you* calm down, John! I am not kidding. I am tired of this!"

Her whole body stiffened as she talked. Expletives colored every phrase. She called Dad every name in the book at the top of her lungs with an almost demonic tone.

"I had to learn to walk all over again! Do you know what it's like to crawl on the ground and have to learn to walk all over again? Or when I couldn't put my thoughts together because I knew what I wanted to say but couldn't get it to come out my mouth? Do you know what it's like to have to work to get one sentence out sometimes? Do you? Well, *do you?*"

She was going higher in her rage now, and we knew what was coming. Troy and I ducked down, making a shield of the table. Mom's facial expression and body posture had telegraphed what she was about to do. Her eyes flamed with emotion, and she scanned the area for something to throw. I made note of the possibilities: a drinking glass, a kitchen utensil, and a pair of scissors, all within her reach. Then her eyes flicked to the right—a handheld can opener. She reached for it. I scrunched down farther.

The can opener, fairly weighty, glanced against Dad's glass and splashed milk on him before clattering to the kitchen floor behind him.

"D— it, Bev!" he yelled and held up his arms, wet.

"If you wouldn't complain, I wouldn't get so angry!" she said. "It's all your fault, John!"

The kitchen was so cramped and obstructed that Dad couldn't move around the table quickly enough to stop her from throwing. A few times he had come across the table and tried to reach her arm before she could let loose. On those occasions she grabbed his wrist with superhuman strength, dug her nails in, and growled, "I hate you!" Mom's nails caused real pain and only made the argument worse.

I leaned my head sideways against the chair back and waited, knowing I was safely shielded for now. Troy had caught a pizza cutter on the forehead recently, and his wound had bled like a sieve. I took a Mason jar in the back. We never blamed Mom when one of us got hit—rather, we blamed ourselves for not getting under the table quickly enough. "You should've moved," Dad informed us, or "You'll learn to duck." And it was true. We had both delayed for some reason that time, counting on Mom's slow reaction time, and had caught the brunt of her anger.

One time Mom got upset while holding a pot of boiling water. She began to spiral into fury while standing in the middle of the kitchen with a steaming pot. All three of us knew it was a situation that required teamwork.

"Get her, boys!" Dad said. We approached Mom the way you would a wild animal, hands at the ready, eyes looking for an opportunity to safely snatch the pot from her before she threw it at one of us. While Mom's attention was on me, Dad's hand darted in, and he grabbed the handle, safely wrestled it from her, and dumped the boiling water down the kitchen sink, not caring that it went straight into the cellar.

Another time, Mom became incensed with Dad while holding a heavy skillet in which she was cooking slices of Spam, one of our common entrées because it was so cheap. Troy and I stood nearby but didn't move quickly enough to stop her. She hurled the skillet, and it hit Dad painfully in the arm. The pan clanged to the floor, flinging Spam slices and grease everywhere. Mom put her hands over her eyes, horrified by what she had done. Dad grabbed his arm and looked at me and Troy dolefully, rubbing the sore spot.

"Why didn't you get her?" he asked.

It always took Mom some time to wind down from an outburst. Sometimes she retreated into the living room, or her bedroom, or the bathroom.

At some point, someone gave Mom a small, eight-by-eight-inch metal loom that she used to make pot holders or squares for a quilt of sorts. The loom had metal posts that Mom threaded yarn around, using a little crochet needle to work the yarn back and forth. When she was finished, she lifted out a thick, square pot holder made of yarn.

"Look at that, Shawn!" she said, holding up a pink and yellow one.

"Good," I said, not really excited by kitchen items.

"That'll be very useful," she said, setting it aside and threading her needle for the next one.

She began producing pot holders by the dozens. The loom became one of Mom's central activities, particularly after her outbursts. Having cussed us all out and targeted us over dinner, she often retreated to her chair, put the loom on her lap, and spent the next several hours creating multi-colored pot holders while watching TV. When she built up a surplus, she learned to sew them together to make heavy blankets. We slept under those blankets for years. Some were so heavy, I despaired of getting out from under them in the morning, let alone rolling over in the middle of the night.

The loom, as simple as it was, was a godsend for Mom and for all of us. But we would need more than a loom to calm her in the years to come.

CHAPTER 5

"I'LL KILL YOU!" Mom screamed, drawing out each letter and giving the words a horrifying depth. Ironically, we were on our way to church, one of the safest places I knew.

"Shut up, Bev!" Dad yelled back.

The windows vibrated with their shouting. Troy and I didn't even know why they were fighting this time, but some of the worst fights happened on the way to church. It was woven into the fabric of things.

"I'm going to dance on your grave when you die, John!" Mom yelled.

She was heaving with anger, and her words were becoming unrestrained. Troy and I sat silently in the back waiting to see what would happen next. I shoved Troy's leg to get it off my side of the seat, then studied my thumbnails, which I had chewed down to the flesh. Troy sat as if thinking with real interest about something entirely outside our world.

We pulled into the church parking lot with Dad yelling and Mom not backing down. For me, the sight of Twin Branch's glass double doors could not have been more welcome. Dad pulled up near the front so Mom wouldn't have so far to walk. She flung open her door, and I imagined all the vulgarities piled up inside her spilling onto the asphalt. Troy and I got out too. Mom was still in a high state of agitation, and when the greeter at the door offered a "Good morning, Bev," Mom's "Hi!" sounded a little harsh. The greeter came down three or four steps to help her up. The gesture softened Mom's mood. Inside the front door was Pastor Jones, who reached out and shook Mom's hand, then bent down to shake mine and Troy's.

"Good morning, Bev. Good morning, boys."

"Good morning, Pastor Jones," Mom said. Whatever rage had been there a minute earlier had evaporated. It always seemed that as soon as we passed through those doors, our family weirdness disappeared. Love and acceptance enveloped us and changed us, at least for a few hours.

"All right, I'm heading upstairs," Dad announced, coming in the door from parking the car. He served as the junior high boys' Sunday school teacher. The teenage guys liked Dad, who served in a wide variety of children's and student ministries. Dad disappeared up the steps.

Mom headed for her classroom, then stopped suddenly as if remembering something. She abruptly yelled my name across the small church lobby.

"Shawn, I have some flannelgraph figures that still need to be cut out before I teach the kids," she said. "Can you come? Do you mind being late to your class or even missing it today?"

"No, Mom, I don't mind," I said.

I almost didn't care where I was within the church. My soul felt comforted just being there.

In the very small fourth- and fifth-grade classroom downstairs, Mom dumped her Sunday school materials on the table with satisfaction.

"Okay. Grab some scissors. I don't even know where to find them," she said.

"Okay, Mom."

I knew exactly where the scissors were, as I knew where everything in the church was, down to the stapler refills. I came back with the scissors, searched through her disorganized and crumpled Sunday school materials, and began to cut figures out of paper to accompany the lesson.

Soon Mom's first student arrived—Cheryl, the daughter of the church song leader and the church pianist. Cheryl was in her thirties and had Down syndrome. She could not speak or read, so she grunted, squealed, and used gestures to communicate. She attended Sunday school with the elementary-age kids. She looked grumpy until she caught sight of Mom. Then she brightened like an instant sunrise.

"Hi, Cheryl!" Mom said. Cheryl sheepishly approached Mom and then hugged her with a long, slow, firm bear hug. "Oh, it's good to see you, too," Mom said. "Now go ahead and take a seat in one of the chairs, and Shawn will give you this week's take-home paper to look at until the others get here."

Cheryl plopped down cross-legged in one of the chairs and settled in, pleased with her obedience. I gave her the lesson sheet, which she immediately rolled up tightly like a newspaper. She began bobbing back and forth, tapping the rolled-up lesson sheet on her knee rhythmically, as if she heard a specific song in her head. Soon she would begin her regular routine of tearing it into small pieces, methodically creating a pile of shavings on the floor throughout the course of the morning. She did this every Sunday.

Even though everyone loved Cheryl, plenty of people struggled to work with her because she was willful and easily upset. "That girl's a handful," church workers commonly said after a morning with her and the rest of the kids.

But Cheryl behaved well around Mom. It seemed to me that Cheryl became normal in Mom's presence. She even sought Mom out at other church activities and every now and then would sit next to Mom during church services.

Kids trickled in faster and faster.

"Hi! Hello! Come on in," Mom said, greeting each one. After a bit she walked to the end of the classroom table, extended her right hand, and planted her left hand on the short table for balance. She attempted to lower herself into the child-sized chair, but her planted hand caused the opposite end of the table to pop up five or six inches off the ground. The table slammed back down hard, and Mom landed fast and awkwardly in her chair with a stunned look on her face. The look turned into a self-deprecating grin, and the startled kids giggled behind their hands. They knew Mom was more or less immobile from that point on and enjoyed helping her get things she needed.

"Oh, I forgot my pen," Mom said. "There's one on that shelf over there."

Before I could move, several girls jumped into action, bringing back several pens for her to choose from. Mom took them all.

"Thank you! You are all so helpful," she said. One little girl remained standing in front of her.

"My puppies were born Thursday in the middle of the night," she said.

"Oh! Are they cute?" Mom asked.

The little girl nodded smugly. "They are the cutest puppies in the world. And the mommy licked them until they were clean."

"I bet those puppies loved it. But I don't want to lick a puppy," Mom said.

The girl cracked a reluctant smile and nodded her head in agreement. Another girl popped up.

"A boy likes me at school," she said.

"He must be a very special boy," Mom said.

"He's kind of weird."

Cheryl interrupted with an insistent grunt. She could say no intelligible words, but we knew what her request was.

"Orr . . . eee . . . ovvve," she said while making an arch with her hands over her head. She wanted to sing her favorite song, "His Banner Over Me Is Love."

"Okay, kids, let's start the singing time," Mom said, using Cheryl's request as a transition. She began singing. "The Lord is mine and I am his; his banner over me is love . . ."

Everyone did the motions and sang. Cheryl sporadically

did the motions with us and attempted to grunt out key words in her deep, abrasive voice. For the rest of the songs, she went back to pinching off pieces of paper. After singing time, Mom led the kids gently through a lesson, welcoming interruptions from those who wanted to share stories and off-topic observations. Mom laughed with them. The lesson was secondary to these impromptu conversations.

As the kids left the class at the end of Sunday school, Cheryl hugged Mom tightly and moved to a larger gathering room for children's church. As the lights to the church basement were turned out, Cheryl's pile of shavings remained at the base of the chair where she sat. Often I would be at church later in the week for one reason or another and would clean up Cheryl's weekly mess.

Mom leaned on my arm as we made our way upstairs to attend the main worship service. People were coming and going happily, greeting each other and shaking hands. Mom's eyes sparkled. She loved gatherings. Coming back from the drinking fountain, I found her engaged in several conversations.

"How is your new grandbaby?" she asked one friend in passing. "Is he cute? You should bring pictures."

Another friend passed by and leaned in to share some news with Mom.

"A car accident?" Mom said. "Let's pray right now."

In the din, they clasped hands and prayed. When they were finished, the woman hugged Mom, and Mom hugged her back with real feeling.

"Okay, we'll keep praying," Mom said. "Tell them to get better."

Shirley, a regular attendee, came through the doors. Some people turned away instinctively. Shirley wore a fur coat and long white gloves, though it was hot outside, and her mouth was smeared with red lipstick. She had an old scarf around her head and seemed to be wearing an ill-fitting wig. She smelled like she hadn't bathed in some time. Her son was twelve and still wet his pants in Sunday school.

"Hi, Shirley!" Mom chirped. Shirley turned and recognized Mom. Her face relaxed, and she went over.

"How's Kevin?" Mom asked, putting her arm around Shirley and rubbing her back by way of greeting.

"He's good," Shirley said in her strange, slow voice. "We've all got problems, but he's doing better."

Shirley's husband had left her some years before, and Shirley was never right after that.

"I'm so glad to hear that," Mom said.

Mom's tone of voice and enthusiasm were the same for Shirley as for Pastor Jones. I couldn't help but notice that certain types of people gravitated toward Mom: widows, accident victims, people in wheelchairs or on crutches, misfits, awkward people, the uneducated, the elderly, and anyone going through a life-altering challenge, including in their marriage or family. Somehow they concluded that Mom was safe, that she understood something deeper about them. Whenever a child with special needs came to church, Mom always went directly over and made conversation. People who moved too slowly for the rest of the world were just her speed. She dwelled in the margins with the overlooked, the ignored.

Mom and I arrived at the top of the steps and reunited with Dad and Troy in the busy lobby.

"How was your class?" Mom asked Dad brightly.

"Good," Dad said. He played things down, but I could tell he got a lot of energy out of teaching. "Let's head on in."

"Oh shoot! I've got choir," Mom said. "I've got to go back downstairs and get my robe on. Here."

She handed me her lesson materials, and Dad helped her back downstairs. Once he rejoined us, Troy, Dad, and I walked into the sanctuary. There was no question where we would sit for the main service. Dad insisted on the second row. He didn't like to see other people whisper or rattle their bulletins or hear them rustle the wrapper of a mint or lozenge. Plus, when Dad committed to something, he did it all the way. Going to church and sitting anywhere but in the front didn't count to him.

My friend Jeff came up to me.

"Wanna come sit with us?" he offered.

"I can't," I said, thinking that if Jesus himself sat in the third row and invited me to sit with him, I would have to decline.

"Why?" Jeff asked.

"My dad won't let us."

He gave me an apologetic look and went to where our friends were gathering. Nana and Papaw sat toward the back of the sanctuary with other family members, but we may as well have been in separate buildings.

Cheryl's mom started playing the organ. The choir filed onto the platform from a side door, each person equidistant from the other. Then there was a long, unexpected gap in the line. Seconds later Mom emerged from the door, smiling at a private joke or at the fact that she couldn't quite keep up. She tried to hustle to make up the space. I hoped there was nothing for her to trip on. She made it safely to her spot and stood in ranks with the other choir members in their matching robes. Cheryl's dad, Louie Grant, was our church song leader. Mr. Grant introduced the opening hymn.

"Let's sing together, number 44," Mr. Grant said, holding his hand up like a baton to lead the congregation.

We opened our songbooks and sang with enthusiasm, but not too much. Nobody wanted our congregation to be confused with the overly emotional church across town. Still, it seemed that Mom sang with greater gusto than anyone. Her face was full of expression when she sang with the choir.

I spotted Mr. Franklin, a guy in the church for whom Dad expressed the highest respect. His daughter had Down syndrome, and his wife had muscular dystrophy. They both needed a great deal of care and couldn't do many things for themselves. Mr. Franklin was relatively successful as a manager in a local factory and was a faithful member of our church. He was also an innovative thinker. To get his wife from one room to another in their house, he had bought a ceiling track with a sling hanging from it. He used it to transport her from the bedroom to the bathroom and back. Mr. Franklin was on a church leadership committee with Dad, and during meetings he would occasionally pull out a walkie-talkie and check in with his wife to see if she needed help.

"That guy's a real example," Dad told me more than once,

marveling at the cheer with which Mr. Franklin served his wife and daughter.

There were many such people at Twin Branch whose examples we drew strength from. I was proud that my dad was respected among the leaders there as a man truly committed to Christ and to the church.

Pastor Jones took the pulpit and began preaching a Bible-based sermon infused, as usual, with a sense of rightness, embattlement, and urgency. I had heard people call Twin Branch a "fighting fundamentalist" church. I didn't know what that meant, but I got the impression that many other churches were straying into unbiblical teachings, and only churches like ours were standing for truth in a generation prone to error. At times it seemed we were against more things than we were for. But that was unimportant to me. The structure, love, and sense of family the church provided was like pure oxygen compared to the atmosphere of our increasingly chaotic home.

●　●　●

"Let's get in the car, guys," Dad said one Saturday morning.

"Where are we going?" Troy asked with irritation.

"We are going to go out on visitation," Dad said cryptically.

I didn't know what that meant but knew it had to be some church thing. Mom and Dad served our church the way some people do branches of the military: with fierce loyalty and faithfulness. Whatever the church was doing, the Thorntons did it without question. When Twin Branch introduced Evangelism Explosion classes on Thursday nights, Dad signed up, learned all the relevant Bible verses, and was ready to tell perfect strangers about Jesus. When our church started a formal evening Bible institute, Dad and Mom were in the first classes. Dad's high sense of commitment dictated a lot of what we did as a family.

He drove Troy, Mom, and me across town to a neighborhood I recognized as the place where he picked up children in the church bus every week—kids whose parents wouldn't take them to church. I could hardly imagine such a household.

"Where are we?" Troy asked.

"Just get out and follow along," Dad said without explanation.

He went around the car, took Mom's arm, stood her up, and began walking toward the first house. Troy and I trailed behind. Mom caught her toe on a cracked portion of pavement and stumbled. Dad stopped until she regained her footing, then continued on. The gate and front porch steps presented another obstacle. Finally they made it to the front door and knocked. It opened. A woman's face peered out from the interior gloom.

"Hi," Dad said. "I'm John Thornton. Your son has been riding our bus to church. I'm the bus driver who picks him up, and I'd like to tell you a little more about what we do at Twin Branch Bible Church."

"Okay," the woman said, neither opening the door wider nor shutting it.

Dad shared about the various programs our church offered—Sunday school, Awana, and Vacation Bible School.

"Can I give you a flyer inviting you to come see what Twin Branch Bible Church is about?"

"Sure," the woman said. She stuck her hand out the screen door and took it. *Appreciative but not enthusiastic*, I thought. Troy and I stood to the side, stealing glances at the inside of her house, which, while very modest, looked unnaturally tidy and smelled like baking bread.

Where's all their stuff? I wondered.

"We hope to see you soon," Dad said.

"We'd love for you to come by," Mom chimed in. The woman looked at her and smiled for the first time.

"That sounds nice," she said.

"Oh, it's a lot of fun!" Mom said. "There are such good people there. I bet you'd really learn something, too. It's a lot of fun."

The woman smiled more.

"Okay," she said. "Thank you. I'll—I'll think about it."

She shut the door and Dad, with Mom attached, navigated the steps, gate, and uneven pavement on their way to the next house. I quietly calculated how long this boring venture would take.

About three houses in, it struck me as strange that Dad, usually so reluctant to talk first in social settings, was knocking on doors and initiating conversations with people. Put Dad in a room with a stranger all day and he might not share ten words. Yet here we were spending a precious weekend morning speaking to total strangers about their eternal destiny and deepest beliefs.

We were already at church almost every day—Sunday

morning, Sunday evening, and Wednesday evening for services, and Tuesday evening for Awana. Dad also served as Twin
Branch's part-time janitor in addition to his job at Dodge's, so
on various evenings and many Saturday mornings, Dad, Troy,
and I headed over to clean the building. I could count on not
being at church only one or two nights a week. By the time
I was in grade school, I knew every crack in the floor at the
church, every loose toilet seat, every dripping sink, and every
lopsided shelf because I was often the one scrubbing, tighten-
ing, or repairing them. I sometimes spent more waking hours
in a week at church than I did at home.

Dad was also the commander of Awana, meaning he
ran the entire club of a hundred kids, which was a lot for a
church our size. Awana offered unique games and a sense of
belonging that wasn't available in many places in town. Kids
flocked to it for the fun and found themselves learning the
Bible as well.

Our Awana nights began with Dad leaving to drive the
church bus to pick up kids in our area. Then the church sold
its bus, and our car had to do the job. Dad drove us on a
circuit around town to pick up kids.

"Open that door, Shawn," Dad said at our first stop.

He was pushing ten-year-old Tracy down the path in her
wheelchair. Tracy had cerebral palsy. I pushed the door open
and held it there. Dad lifted her from her wheelchair and
gently lowered her into the seat next to me.

"Watch her head," Dad told me. I put my arm around
her, as one of us always did, to keep her head from slumping
over. She was unable to hold it upright on her own.

Dad closed the door, folded up her wheelchair, and placed it in the trunk.

"Woo-hoo," Tracy vocalized. She couldn't say words.

"That's right. We're going to church," Mom said in response.

"Woo-hoo," Tracy said again, her chin pressed against her chest. Tracy looked like just skin and bones and wore diapers. Her head slumped and her eyes were out of sync with her head movements. I held her upright as Dad pulled away from the curb.

The next stop was for brothers Tim and Scotty. Tim was not disabled. Scotty had a milder case of cerebral palsy. He wore braces on both legs and dragged them when he walked. His hands were still nimble and his mind quick. He talked a mile a minute but slurred his speech so you had to listen carefully to understand what he was saying. Like Tracy, Scotty was ten years old. They went to the same special-needs school.

In the backseat with us, Scotty leaned over and kissed Tracy on the forehead.

"You're my girlfriend," he said. He told her this every week.

Tracy smiled and made appreciative cooing noises.

A few stops later my location had changed to under the dashboard. I, Troy, and six other kids had crammed into the car, along with Mom and Dad. Troy was balled up in the footwell of the backseat with Scotty's feet in his face. There were two kids on the bench seat between Mom and Dad.

"You okay down there, Shawn?" Mom asked me, her voice seeming to come from a distant, muffled place.

"Fine, but your feet all smell," I said.

"That's what I'm saying!" I heard Troy shout from what seemed like far away. Mom laughed in her loud, over-the-top way.

"In ten minutes we'll be at church," Dad said.

The heat from the engine and other people's bodies warmed the air unnaturally, stiflingly. Asphalt raced by just below the floor of the car. When we arrived and Dad turned the engine off, I was the last one to extract myself from the car and escape into the cool evening air. Dad was getting Tracy's chair out of the trunk, setting it up, and placing her in it. Scotty waited eagerly, legs held straight with braces. The cramped ride didn't bother any of us because we knew the fun was about to begin. We made our way inside and took our places.

"Right-hand salute!" Dad called us to attention and led us in the Awana salute. "I pledge allegiance to the Awana flag, which stands for the Awana clubs, whose goal is to reach boys and girls with the gospel of Christ and to train them to serve him."

We stood saluting the Awana flag, having already pledged allegiance to the American flag, and from that point on I was like a fish put back into water. The highly structured, rewards-based activities fit me just right. I loved the Awana games we played with Olympic fervency in the church basement with its low ceiling, gray tile, and pea-green walls.

But what I did best was memorize Bible verses.

"Okay, Shawn, let's start with you," our handbook leader said during handbook time, one of three main activities at

Awana. Five other boys and I were sitting in a stairwell with a young college-age adult named Jack, who later married my aunt April. Other groups had found their real estate in the sanctuary, hallways, even the boiler room. The church was full of little knots of young boys and girls reciting Scriptures to their handbook leaders and earning points for their teams.

Jack opened the handbook to the correct page.

"Tell me, Shawn, how much does God love us?" he said.

My reply was instantaneous. I had memorized it that afternoon.

"God loves us so much that John 3:16 says, 'For God so loved the world, that he gave his only begotten Son, that whosoever believeth in him should not perish, but have everlasting life.'"

Jack nodded. Scripture memorization was conducted as question-and-answer exchanges to simulate dialogue with kids who did not understand or had not heard the message of the Bible.

"How else do we know he loves us?" Jack asked.

"We know he loves us because Romans 5:8 tells us, 'God commendeth his love toward us, in that, while we were yet sinners, Christ died for us.'"

I said it so fast that he had to digest it for a moment to see if I had done it right. The other kids watched with hope and despair—hope that I was racking up points for our team, despair that they had memorized comparatively little and would be put on the spot soon.

Ten verses later, Jack looked ready to be done with me.

"Shawn, you're doing great, but you could probably go

all night. I've got to give these other boys a chance," he said. Some of my friends had stopped cheering me on and were becoming antsy and bored. Jack turned to them. "All right, let's see what you know. You heard Shawn say these already, so it shouldn't be too hard for you."

After handbook time everyone assembled in the sanctuary. Tonight Dad was giving the lesson. He walked forward wearing his gray, short-sleeved uniform with a red tie and a big "Commander" patch above his pocket.

"All right, it's lesson time," he said, knowing full well that kids liked games a lot more than listening to an adult give a Bible lesson. We were all wearing our gray scouting-style uniforms too. The boys' red scarves were held in place by little gray plastic Indian heads or covered wagons. The girls had bolo ties with emblems significant to their Awana group.

Dad held up a needle.

"Anybody know what this is?" he asked.

"A pen!"

"A hair!"

"Nothing!"

"A needle!" someone shouted.

"Who said needle?" Dad asked, and a girl raised her hand. "That's what this is—a needle. This needle is temptation. It's sharp. It's bad. Now watch this."

From behind a table he pulled out a balloon. The kids cheered.

"This balloon represents you trying to live your life for Jesus."

"Is it a water balloon?" a boy yelled.

"No, it's not a water balloon, but it represents your life. Now watch here."

Dad brought the needle toward the balloon ever so slowly. Kids yelled with excitement.

"Don't do it!"

"Do it! Pop it!"

Dad brought it closer and closer. As he did, he spoke.

"Now this needle is temptation, and it's coming closer to you. It's going to pop the balloon, which is the good way we're supposed to live. Let's say this needle is tempting you to lie to your parents. Have you ever lied to your parents?"

A chorus of "Yes!" and "No!"

"Well, you shouldn't lie to your parents, but let's say this needle is tempting you to lie so you won't get in trouble for dropping the cookie jar or something."

Kids laughed.

"And here it comes. Now what's stopping it?"

"Nothing!" some boy yelled.

"That's right. There is nothing stopping it now, 'cause we can't do it on our own," Dad said. "But there is something that can stop it. What is it?"

"God's Word!" another boy yelled.

"Who said that?" Dad said. A boy raised his hand.

"Give that team extra points. That is the right answer. Come up here and help me."

The boy bounded up to the platform.

"Take that Bible there and hold it between the balloon and the needle," Dad said, and the boy obeyed. "So right when the needle is about to pop that balloon, the Bible comes between them and stops it. When you memorize God's Word, it says, 'Thy word have I hid in mine heart, that I might not sin against thee.' That's how it stops it."

Kids seemed disappointed that the needle hadn't popped the balloon.

Dad got his ideas from a book he bought, *52 Object Lessons to Teach Children the Bible*. It resided for several years in the bathroom magazine rack at our house.

A few weeks earlier, Dad had demonstrated anger and jealousy by pouring vinegar over baking soda, creating a bubbling, overflowing mess in a glass on a table. The kids loved it, and the emotions came vividly to life.

"Anger boils up inside us," Dad said, "but the Bible says, 'In your anger do not sin.'"

Of course, if anyone knew how anger worked, it was Dad. Nobody at Awana knew that anger was vividly demonstrated almost every day in our home.

"Who wants me to pop the balloon?" Dad asked after the boy helping him had sat back down.

"Pop it!" kids screamed almost in unison.

"Okay, count it down. Three . . . two . . . one!"

Dad brought the needle into the balloon, and it exploded in his hand. He couldn't help laughing while the kids cheered.

By fifth grade I had earned the highly prized Timothy Award, marking a significant level of achievement in Awana. You received it by memorizing hundreds of Scriptures, earning badges for writing letters to missionaries, and doing things like giving a gospel tract to someone. Lance had all kinds of sports trophies in his room, to the point where they bored him, but the Timothy Award was one of my few awards and by far the largest. I was proud of it like I had never been proud of anything else.

• • •

Though church was an oasis, sometimes Mom's outbursts threatened to break out even there.

One Sunday evening, Pastor Jones said, "While we're turning to the next hymn, would anyone like to share a testimony or word of encouragement?"

Services were looser in the evening, almost like family gatherings. Mom immediately began to get to her feet.

Uh-oh.

Troy, Dad, and I glanced at one another. Mom had melted down pretty badly that afternoon. She was more fragile than usual. While people at church knew our lives were not quite normal at home, they did not know the extent of it. It occurred to me that this might be the moment our private and public lives collided.

Thankfully, Pastor Jones called on someone else. Each time he asked for another testimony, Mom gripped the pew in front of her to pull herself up and opened her mouth to say something, but other people were faster. Each time she missed the opportunity, Dad, Troy, and I felt a wave of relief. Finally, Mom used the pew to steady herself, shot up, and said, "Well, I have something to say."

"Bev, go ahead," Pastor Jones said.

Clenching the pew to hold herself steady, Mom began speaking.

"John and I have been married thirteen years, and I still don't know why I married him."

She meant this, but people chuckled, thinking she was joking. At home her next sentence would have naturally been, "That's why I'm calling a lawyer tomorrow and divorcing his a——!" I grimaced.

"It's not always fun, and we all have struggles," she continued. "They say that's just how life is. I was thinking the other day how . . ."

She paused. Her jaw tensed, and her muscles became rock-hard. Usually this signaled she was about to break out into a string of accusations, complaints, and expletives. She seemed on the verge of doing just that.

". . . how God lets us go through things, and we wonder why, and it hurts sometimes! It doesn't always seem fair."

She was working herself up emotionally, her mood evident in her hands and face—taut muscles, tight fingers, flared nostrils, widened eyes, a higher pitch to her voice. All of this was all too familiar. At home it meant she was about to take flight into a dangerous, vulgar rant. I scooted to the edge of my seat as if preparing to bolt from the sanctuary. Mom caught sight of me and changed topics.

"Let me tell you about my son. He can be a real . . ." she said, starting to say a foul word to describe me, but before it could come out she turned away from it.

Whoa! I could not believe she had veered away from the word. Was it the Holy Spirit? Or some extraordinary display of willpower? Troy, Dad, and I looked at each other as if to say, "How did she *do* that?"

"He's a good boy most of the time, and I'm proud of what he does in school, Sunday school, and Awana," she said. "But sometimes he does things that make me so mad!"

Her voice suddenly sounded deep and angry.

Oh, boy.

"But then I think, well, he's so helpful in other ways," she continued.

For no apparent reason she let out a high-pitched, almost crazy laugh. The congregation laughed with her because they thought they had missed something or that Bev was just being funny.

These people have no idea she's on the edge of an outburst, I thought. *Thirty more seconds, and they'll be treated to a torrent of cuss words like they've never heard in this place before.*

"These kids!" Mom went on, gesturing at Troy and me. "Sometimes having two boys . . . it's so hard, and you just want to . . . But praise the Lord—God is good all the time!"

She cut herself short and clumsily lowered herself back down to the pew. People said "Amen," and someone else stood up. Attention went elsewhere. A lady near us whispered, "What a wonderful testimony," and patted me on the back.

Dad's eyes displayed a sort of astonished happiness that we had avoided the worst-case scenario. If I needed any evidence of the power of God at work in our day, we had just witnessed it. Mom had stayed within a decent boundary against every expectation.

If only we could have bottled that restraint and brought it back home.

CHAPTER 6

MOM HAD ALWAYS entertained dreams of getting her own driver's license. Every mother she knew drove children to little league games, school, and the park.

"I ought to be able to drive!" Mom told Dad one day, working herself up about it as she had numerous times, punctuating her speech with expletives. "I ought to be able to take the kids to their games or to school on my own. My sisters can do it. There is no reason I shouldn't. You won't stop me. We need a second car. I need to go get a driver's license."

"Whatever, Bev," Dad said with a dismissive edge.

I suspected Mom knew she didn't have the skills to drive, but I wasn't sure. Dad just bore it and tried not to get trapped.

"Oh yeah?" she said. "If it wasn't for you, I could have gone to college! I could have graduated from high school! If I hadn't ridden with you in that car that night we—"

"Yeah, yeah, I've heard it before," Dad said. "Tired of hearing it again. Just shut up!"

Mom stood up and leaned into her fierce words.

"You're going to hear it until you rot in hell! And I hope you die and go there soon! I won't shed a single tear. As a matter of fact, I'm going to roller-skate on your grave! There! How do you like that?"

Dad took a different tack now and went all sappy sweet to quell her fury.

"Now, Monkey, calm down. Just settle down, Kumquat." He slowly moved closer to her, smiling and trying to gently hug her.

His goofy romantic names injected a conciliatory note into her symphony of anger. These were his favorite pet names for Mom, maybe drawing on memories of their best times together. She calmed down a bit. This tactic worked often for Dad. What it told me was that deep down they both loved each other.

"Well, I should get one," she said in a gentler tone. "It's not fair to you or the boys."

"It's all right, Kumquat," Dad said. "We'll think about it some other time."

One day he was unable to shake her loose from the idea of a driver's license and finally got so irritated that he changed course altogether.

"You want to drive?" he said. "Okay, you get to drive. I'll teach you."

He grabbed the keys to our car, got Mom into the passenger seat, and drove to the top of Victory Road. Once there he turned the car toward the opposite end of our dead-end road and put it in park. He threw Mom the keys across the bench seat. She wasn't quick enough to catch them, so they landed between her legs. Mom looked stunned and pleased all at the same time. They both got out of the car, and Dad helped Mom into the driver's seat. He got into the passenger seat, where I had never seen him before. Mom looked so strange behind the wheel.

I sat on my bike so I could watch from the safety of our lawn.

Dad helped Mom put the car in gear, and Mom steered the car toward the end of the street at a crawl.

Maybe she can actually do it, I thought. *This could change everything.* Troy watched from the porch. I spun the pedal on my bike with my toe, fascinated.

Mom turned the car around with Dad's help and proceeded back toward our house. She was doing pretty well. Closer and closer she came, her hands white-knuckling the steering wheel. I watched the car come closer, closer, the grill now facing me as she turned imprecisely before our driveway and proceeded to drive on the lawn. She was picking up speed.

When is she going to slow down? I wondered.

The hair on my neck stood up, and I realized she might not slow down at all. Our car was coming straight at me and the house. If I didn't move, it was going to run me over. I stepped on my pedals and rode laterally about twenty feet.

A second later the car barreled through the yard right where I had been. It continued straight toward the house. Just in time, Dad got his long leg over and stomped on the brakes. The car came to a sudden, ungainly stop, rocking on its chassis. I could hear Mom screaming at him from inside the car. A moment later she fumbled with the door, got out angrily, slammed it shut, and walked toward the house in silence. Before climbing the porch, just a few feet from the car's bumper, she turned to Dad and pointed through the windshield at him with her body stiff and tight.

"The reason I can't drive today is because you never let me learn when I was younger!" she yelled.

She spent the rest of the day in her bedroom, out of sorts. That wasn't the last time Mom bugged Dad about getting her license, but it was the last time either of them even suggested Dad let her get behind the wheel.

•   •   •

"What's the story behind the pink truck?" Dad asked the salesman at the used car lot.

He motioned to the bread truck that looked like someone had converted it into a camper. The salesman, in his short-sleeved shirt and tie, scratched the top of his head.

"Hmm. Not sure what the story is," he said. "But let me look at the paperwork and let you take a look inside it."

He walked into the trailer that served as his office. A moment later he came back to where Dad, Troy, and I waited in the hot August sun.

"Here's the key and all the information we have about it," he said, a hint of doubt in his voice. "Not sure what you're going to think about it. It's an old delivery truck that some hippies apparently converted into a camper a couple of years ago. It's large and kind of . . . unusual."

He motioned for us to follow him across the small lot. There, amid bland four-doors and nondescript pickup trucks, sat a large, twelve-foot-tall delivery truck. Except for its color, it looked like a modern UPS truck. It was tall, boxy, and painted the color of Pepto-Bismol. Undoubtedly, whoever the hippies were who converted it would have called it flower-power pink. The roof was white. On each side someone had painted the words "The Magic Bus" in an iconic 1960s script. The words and script matched the cover of The Who's 1968 album of the same name.

"It's a '66 Chevy—converted by somebody, obviously," the salesman said. "We bought it just recently."

He seemed to hold his breath, anticipating a bad reaction.

Dad stood and stared at the behemoth as if seeing a strange vision. He didn't immediately respond. Quietly he walked around to the side, with Troy and me trailing behind. The eminent pinkness of the vehicle seemed to cast a rosy aura over the surrounding cars and us.

"Hmm," Dad said. His nonrefusal seemed to give the salesman hope.

"Go ahead and take a look inside," the man said.

Dad opened the big sliding door on the driver's side. I'd never been so close to such a vehicle. I poked my head in below his. The floor and walls were covered with wall-to-wall green shag carpeting. A two-and-a-half-foot-long gearshift handle protruded from the floor next to the driver's seat. The windshield seemed as big as a movie screen. There was no passenger seat. Dad turned his gaze upward, and my eyes followed his. Bolted to the ceiling above the windshield was an eight-track cassette player.

"Can we climb in?" Dad asked.

"Sure, sure," said the salesman. "Go right ahead. I think you'll see it has everything any camper or RV would have."

Dad pulled himself up by the steering wheel and disappeared into the back. Troy and I scampered up behind him.

Our eyes adjusted and were greeted by an unexpected sight. Vanity lights and wood paneling had been installed in a couple of places. To the right was a table with booth-like benches on either side. The salesman stood by the driver's door and yelled, "The kitchen table collapses and converts into a bed for two." Across from the kitchen table there was a stove, sink, and small propane refrigerator, all built in. Once we passed through the "kitchen," we saw a full-size bed against the back wall. It stretched across the whole back of the truck. Large windows in the back wall, which had originally been two delivery doors, allowed a great view out the back.

"This is pretty cool," Dad said under his breath so the salesman couldn't hear. I could tell the funky design both inside and out appealed to his bohemian side. Dad had always been more creative than his job as a foundry worker implied. He would often wear socks of two different colors because he liked the contrast. Every tie we gave him he embellished with puffy paints, and for many years Dad grew a handlebar mustache that he twisted and curled up with wax on either side, giving him a modern hipster vibe. The salesman might not have been able to tell, but Troy and I knew this bus seemed like Dad.

Dad wiggled the different elements to see how well they were installed.

Satisfied, Dad climbed out the passenger side, which also had a sliding door that seemed to crash open.

"It drives all right?" Dad said.

"Oh, sure," the salesman said. "You're welcome to take it for a spin."

"How much are you asking?" Dad said.

"Four thousand is what we have it marked as," the salesman said.

That was cheaper than the other cars and campers Dad had scouted and concluded we couldn't afford. Dad thought for a moment.

"If it drives all right, I'll take it for twenty-eight, plus the sedan trade-in," he said.

"Well, I guess that's all right," the salesman said. "That was easy."

Just like that, the Magic Bus became our sole means of transportation. Troy and I climbed in the back and perched on the seats. Dad slid behind the large, black steering wheel like a man at the helm of a supertanker. With a press of his foot on the oversized accelerator and a fearsome rumble from the engine, he guided the truck onto the city streets.

I can't believe we're going home in this, I thought, caught between a sense of complete awesomeness and total lunacy.

One of the first things Dad did as he tinkered with our new car/camper was to install a plastic, stackable, classroom-style chair as a passenger seat for Mom. It looked strange, this bright green piece of school furniture in the empty space at the front of a delivery truck. He positioned it just so and bolted it to the floor using a metal plumbing pipe, a flange, and plywood.

"That oughtta do it," he said, jiggling it. It resembled an odd but sturdy pedestal. He then procured a seat belt and bolted it solidly to the bottom of the seat on either side.

We began traveling everywhere in the Magic Bus—school events, church, grocery shopping, and vacation. There was no hiding us. That didn't bother me. I was enamored of our new vehicle.

The Sunday after Dad purchased it, we pulled up to an apartment building in Mishawaka as we had done each Sunday for several months. The building was seven stories high, probably the tallest building in town. It was a senior citizens retirement facility and had very small apartments. We idled loudly for a moment and waited. Then a sweet older lady named Olga came out of the building's doors, smiling. She was in her eighties and stood all of four feet and one inch tall. Dad helped her into the Magic Bus.

"Good morning," Olga said to Troy and me, her voice weakened by age but still resolute and cheerful.

"Hi, Olga," we said. She always insisted kids call her Olga or Miss Olga.

We rumbled off. Olga held her Bible on her lap and smiled as if she always took carpet-lined delivery trucks to church.

Olga was an institution at Twin Branch Bible Church. A 1930s graduate of Moody Bible Institute, she had never married. She was Mom's third-grade Sunday school teacher and Troy's and my third-grade Sunday school teacher too. She served for years as our church secretary. She was the gentlest woman I ever met. Mom told us she used her money to support missionaries. Olga often left little books for Mom to read and wrote notes of appreciation and encouragement.

"First stop, Twin Branch Bible Church," Dad said from up near the windshield as we bumped into the church parking lot. "That's our only stop too."

For once my family's weirdness made me feel cooler than my friends. The Magic Bus was a point of pride, and I wanted them to see us pull up in this new family vehicle, which really stood apart from the boring cars everyone else was driving.

We picked Olga up for church every Sunday morning, Sunday evening, and Wednesday evening. She usually waited in the same place, on a balcony several floors up, visiting with friends. When she saw the Magic Bus pull in below, she took the elevator down, got in the passenger door, and sat at the kitchen table with Troy and me, smiling.

About a year after Dad bought the pink truck, Lance's dad, Larry, walked over. It was a Saturday night in early June, the kind of night when the sun stayed up forever, the cinder road was warm even after dusk, and we could play in the yard right up to bedtime. Dad was tinkering with something near the house. Larry put on a look of disappointment and sadness.

"John, I know you go to church. You proclaim to be a Christian. But I'm really ashamed of you."

"What the heck are you talking about?" Dad said. I turned circles at the end of our dead-end road and listened.

"Well, you don't act like a Christian."

"What?" Dad said.

"I mean, I hear you talking about it, but when it comes to doing it, you're setting a different example," Larry said.

"You are not making any sense, Larry. I have no idea what you're talking about," Dad said, letting his hands fall to the sides of his body, holding his tools.

"Take, for example, the fact that you're driving everywhere in that 'Magic Bus.'"

"Yeah?"

"Have you seen what's on top?"

"Why would I? It's too high," Dad said.

"And yet you've been driving it all around town, showing everyone," Larry said, shaking his head.

"Yeah. We take it everywhere. Why?" Dad was growing impatient.

Larry couldn't suppress a laugh anymore.

"You might want to climb up there and see the message you've been spreading around," he said.

Moments later Dad had our ladder against the side of the truck. He climbed up while Larry steadied the ladder, grinning ear to ear the whole time. When Dad got on top, shock passed over his face as he looked at the roof. Then he laughed, groaned, and shook his head in disbelief.

"When did that get there?" he asked. Larry could hardly speak, he was laughing so hard.

"My friend knows the people who owned it," he managed to say after a while. "When he saw it parked in your driveway today, he told me the full history."

"What is the full history, Larry?" Dad asked.

"The owners were hippies, two couples. They turned it into a camper and traveled the country."

"But why'd they put *that* there?" Dad asked.

Larry saw me and Lance hanging around below.

"I'll tell you later," he said to Dad.

They both climbed down the ladder, and before I knew it, they were pulling away in the Magic Bus. Half an hour later they returned with half a dozen cans of white spray paint. They climbed on the truck and began spraying the roof white. The smell filled the driveway.

Years later, I asked Dad what was so urgent that they had to go to the hardware store on that Saturday night to spray-paint the top of the Magic Bus. That's when I learned that the previous owners had not just painted the truck pink but had added an "artistic" touch on top. In a dark color and in strong contrast to the white of the truck's roof, they had painted a huge, bold hand giving the middle finger. Because the couples lived right next to the South Bend airport's main runway, they thought it was hilarious that every incoming and outgoing aircraft would see the universal symbol of ill will painted on the roof of their Magic Bus.

We then realized that though the obscene gesture was not visible from street level and most people probably hadn't seen it, for a whole year Olga had looked down from her seventh-story balcony on the unsanctified pink truck with the white roof. The image of a large hand flipping the bird had greeted her every Sunday—twice—and on Wednesdays.

"That poor saint was looking down on that thing from her balcony three times a week and never said a word," Dad marveled. "Wonder what she and her friends must think of us?"

We picked Olga up the next day in our newly sanitized van and nothing was said. Olga smiled as usual, the picture of acceptance. When she died at age 104, we were pretty sure she had seen everything.

• • •

We were driving in our car one evening before Dad bought the Magic Bus. Something in my parents' conversation lit Mom's fuse.

"I hate you!" she screamed. "I'm not taking this anymore!" Suddenly she threw open the passenger door and leaned toward it as if to jump from the car. We were traveling at forty-five miles an hour.

Dad flung his right arm over her chest to hold her inside. Mom then leaned left and grabbed the steering wheel, pulling down hard. The car swerved, but Dad held it from running off the road. Mom then snatched the keys out of the ignition. Instantly the steering wheel almost locked up. Our car engine was off, and we were traveling at near highway speeds. Dad muscled the car to the side of the road and came to a stop.

"Why'd you do that, Bev?" he yelled.

"Leave me alone!" Mom shrieked. "I hate you!"

Dad felt around on the floorboard for the keys. In the meantime Mom pulled herself out and began walking down the side of the road, fuming, cursing, and throwing her hands around. Dad got out and went after her as cars swished by. He tried to turn her around, but she swung at him violently. He dodged her blows and for a moment didn't seem to know what to do, his car stopped on the side of the road and his wife in a full-blown altercation with him. Troy and I sat inside the car, watching. Dad managed to herd Mom back with his words and his hands. It took several minutes.

Back in the car everyone was silent at first. Mom tried to stir things up a few times, but Dad just ignored her, and she had gained a bit more control of her emotions by now. We went straight home. Nobody said anything about the episode. Mom didn't seem to treat it any differently than their usual fights at home.

Mom tried jumping from the car again a week or two later, and this time we were ready.

"I can't stand any of you!" she shrieked and cursed as we drove to the mall.

She grabbed the door handle and pushed it open.

"Hold her back, boys!" Dad said, throwing his hand over her chest.

Troy and I leaned up from the backseat and put our arms

around Mom's shoulders and neck. She heaved forward, trying to dive onto the asphalt and gravel speeding by. We had the advantage of leverage to keep her in place. She then tried to lift her foot and put it outside. While still holding her against the seat with my left hand, I leaned over farther, grabbed the door handle, and pulled it closed. Troy minded Mom's left hand so she didn't grab the steering wheel.

With a scream, she rammed herself back against the seat, giving up. Instead of slowing the car down, Dad sped up. Within minutes we were back home. I understood Dad's logic. If he pulled over and she got out of the car again, she would endanger herself—walking into traffic, refusing to get back in the car, or falling down hard on the pavement. Mom was frighteningly strong during her outbursts. Better to speed up and get home.

Mom's attempts to leave a moving car at high speeds were an obvious sign to Troy and me that at times she lost her handle on reality. In the moment, she framed her actions as part escape, part suicide attempt, and part homicide.

"I'm ending our misery right now!" she yelled on more than one occasion.

While these irrational outbursts frightened us a great deal, we knew that deep down she didn't mean any of it. She was not in control mentally or emotionally in these moments.

Mom had similarly begun walking away from our house when she flared up.

"John, I'm leaving you for good," she said one night after an argument, cursing Dad and us kids. Mom's declarations of the marriage being over and calling Dad, Troy, and me foul names had become ordinary, mundane background noise to our everyday life together.

"Yeah, yeah!" Dad yelled back. "Quit talking about it and do something about it."

Out the door she went, pulling it shut hard behind her. Twenty minutes later she shuffled back in. She hadn't even reached the end of Victory Road, less than 100 yards from our house, before turning around.

The next time she went farther. Dad put us in the car, and we found Mom walking down Dragoon Trail, the dark, wooded, and windy main road off which our dead-end street branched. He pulled alongside her and slowed the car to a crawl.

"Bev, get in," he said through the open window.

"No," she said. "I'm not doing this anymore."

"Just get in," he implored, opening her door for her. "We can talk about it at home."

"No."

She kept crunching along the gravel on the side of the road in the dark, the lower half of her body lit by our dome light.

"Bev, get in now!" Dad said, seeing headlights in the distance. Mom finally stopped.

"Fine, but I'm calling a lawyer and divorcing you tomorrow," she said.

"Fine, you can divorce me tomorrow—just get in," Dad said. Mom began the awkward motion of getting into the passenger seat. Troy and I helped her. Then Dad turned the car around, and we headed back home.

Sometimes Dad couldn't convince her to get in, and he would eventually turn around and drive home. Mom would walk until she reached a pay phone and call Dad or one of her sisters for a ride. To force her into the car when she refused or to keep her home against her will was to invite physical rage and screaming such as most people never experience. It didn't feel good to have Mom walk into the dark alone at night, but it usually turned out better than if we held her back.

One evening Dad was driving us home from church via our normal route. Suddenly Mom was enraged by something one of us had said.

"F— you, John!" she said and pushed the door open with a mighty heave. We were going fifty miles per hour.

Dad didn't have to tell us anymore. I shot forward and in one motion grabbed Mom's shoulder and the door. This time she had locked her arm straight, and her stiffness now worked to her advantage. The door was at a forty-five-degree angle, the cool air rushing in like great waves. She kept her arm extended and tried to get her leg out. With her left hand Mom grabbed the steering wheel, sending our car across the road.

"Bev!" Dad said, wrenching her fingers off one at a time and punching her arm in anger and to keep her from doing it again. Our car swerved back onto our side of the road. Dad accelerated to sixty miles per hour, striving to get home as quickly as possible.

I was trying to pull the door closed when we came to a section of road with three houses in a row on the passenger side of the car. Before we knew it, loud, shuddering bangs rattled the car and my hand. I looked behind us. The open passenger door had taken out two of the mailboxes as if they were made of matchsticks. The impacts freed Mom's iron grip. I pulled the door closed. Dad sped up even more.

We got home safely and acted as if nothing had happened, but Dad didn't drive that route again for several months. I asked him why.

"I don't want anyone to recognize us as the people that took out their mailboxes," he said.

The Magic Bus complicated this aspect of Mom's outbursts. Mom's new seat was higher. Often in warmer weather we kept the sliding side doors wide open as our air-conditioning while we were driving, and she had an easier time lunging toward the open door. In the car we could pretty much hold her in by pulling on her arms and shoulders. But her upright position in the pink truck and our distance from her seat made things more difficult.

After exchanging heated words with Dad one day, Mom released her seat-belt latch, groping for some place on the dash to push off to get through the open door. We were traveling down Lincoln Highway at around forty miles per hour. She had managed to get her hand on the dashboard to launch herself when Troy and I rushed from the back and grabbed her. We held her shoulders and arms to keep her from diving out of the truck.

"Let go!" Mom yelled through gritted teeth. "I hate all of you! Just let me out!"

Dad ran a stop sign. A block later he ran a red light. We were getting nearer to home.

I had positioned myself between her seat and the door,

the only place where I had enough leverage to counter her. Turning my head I looked down to see the road rushing by just a few feet from me.

If she doesn't calm down, I thought, *I'm out that door and onto the asphalt.*

Within minutes we were home. Mom went inside, threw some things around, stormed into the bedroom, and then lay on her bed for a couple of hours. Dad retreated to the bathroom. It didn't matter to me that we didn't end up going where we were going. Mom and the rest of us were safe. Mom was calm again, even if for only a brief time.

Once, after nearly succeeding at jumping from the Magic Bus, Mom called Troy and me to her when we got home. We sat next to her at the kitchen table. She pulled us close—uncomfortably so since we were not a family that hugged often.

"I want to apologize to you boys for what I did," she said, crying. "I know it scared you, and I'm sorry. I shouldn't act that way when I get angry."

"It's okay," I insisted, and Troy nodded his agreement. Something told me she didn't have to apologize, and I wanted to interrupt her apology and nullify it somehow. I felt embarrassed for Mom but not angry at her. I was pretty sure she still didn't realize the consequences of jumping. Rather, she regretted how it made us feel.

• • •

The Magic Bus accomplished one of Dad's goals by opening the outdoors to us like never before. Mom was always calmer in nature, where the hectic pace of life couldn't touch her. She liked taking walks on tree-lined paths and watching the passing countryside out of the truck's gargantuan windshield.

In late July, during the annual two-week shutdown at the factory, every employee took a forced vacation. Dad used the first week to paint the exterior of our house green. At some point he announced, "We're going camping in Michigan." Michigan was just half an hour away, but to Troy and me it was another world of campgrounds, fishing ponds, swimming pools, and miniature golf courses. In the days leading up to our departure, Mom, Troy, and I tried to stock the converted camper with food and supplies we would need.

We made it to a KOA campground the first night without a single outburst or yelling match. The campground had a small lake for fishing. It was quiet except for the sound of other campers and a distant generator. We knew from experience that Mom rarely had outbursts in public. She enjoyed meeting new people and seeing new scenery, so we were virtually guaranteed a peaceful time away.

"Let's go for a walk," Mom suggested to Dad soon after we parked.

Dad grunted as if to hide his delight.

"You want the boys to come, or should they stay here?" he asked.

"Let's just go, you and me," Mom said. "It'll be quiet for a little while."

Dad turned to Troy and me. "You hang around here. Don't go anywhere."

He took Mom's arm, and they walked slowly toward the lake, which was encircled by trees and an inviting pathway.

I was reaching the age where I noticed that between their frequent arguments, Mom and Dad were actually affectionate sometimes. "You kids keep playing," Dad would often say before closing the door to their bedroom on Saturday or Sunday afternoon. Usually their bedroom door was open, even at night. I realized as I got older that a closed door meant they were being physically intimate. Other times they sat on the swing on the side of the house, drinking iced tea and talking for hours.

Seeing them walk out of our sight around the lake felt like the promise of a sane life in some intangible future. It was the way things could be if only we could subtract the chaos and craziness that pervaded our household. The feeling reminded me of other peaceful times, when Troy was a baby. Dad had bought a red Schwinn tandem bicycle. It was built for two, but Dad piled all four of us on it—Dad on the front seat, Mom on the back, me (a toddler at the time) in a child's seat behind Mom, and baby Troy on Dad's back in a baby-carrier backpack. To get us started, Dad held the bike steady so Mom could get onto her seat, and then he pedaled like mad to get enough momentum to carry us forward without tipping over. Once we were up and riding, Mom could actually help Dad power the bike by adding her force to the pedals. We rode around town many times, four people on a red bicycle built for two—not exactly inconspicuous, I would imagine.

Less than an hour later, Mom and Dad came back. Dusk was falling.

"Oh, boys, we saw so many birds and turtles!" she said. "You should have seen them."

"You didn't let us go," I said.

"Maybe tomorrow you can see them," she said. "I've got to go to the bathroom, John."

"Shawn, take your mother to the bathroom, you and Troy," Dad said. He handed Mom to me and went into the Magic Bus, presumably to put together dinner from whatever we had packed.

We walked to the campground restrooms, and Troy and I were done quickly. We stood against the outside wall and waited for Mom to come out of the women's bathroom.

"I want to go swimming in the pool," I said.

"I want to play mini golf," Troy said.

"I wish I brought my bike," I added.

Mom's voice came through the windows near the ceiling. She was laughing and talking with somebody in the restroom. After what seemed like forever, I shouted up at the window.

"Mom! Can we go back?"

She and the stranger kept talking. Troy and I felt almost dead with boredom.

"Mom!" he yelled, emboldened by my effort. "We're done!"

Mom laughed at something the stranger said. Finally, the door swung open, and Mom came out holding the arm of an elderly woman.

"Boys, this is Frances. She's from Ohio."

Frances nodded to us. She seemed to be unsteady on her feet from some injury or simply from age.

"This is Shawn and Troy."

"Nice to meet you boys. It's been good talking to you, Beverly. I'd better go back and make dinner for Sam."

"If you're leaving tomorrow, I'll say good-bye now," Mom said. "Say hi to your kids and grandkids for me."

"I will. Nice to see you," Frances said to all of us and began walking slowly over to her camper.

"Who was that?" I asked Mom as we walked back to our pink camper. I expected that Frances was some old friend Mom had bumped into.

"Oh, that was Frances," she said. "I just met her. She's from Ohio. She has the most wonderful family, which they're going to see in Washington state. I told her that's quite a ways to drive, but Sam is up to it, and he loves to drive anyway. He's retired and really likes to see different places. Doesn't that sound like so much fun?"

We were back at the truck, and Dad had made sandwiches for us all.

"What took you so long?" he asked.

"Mom," I said by way of explanation.

"I met the nicest lady in the bathroom," Mom said. "She's from Ohio, and she's passing through here on her way west. She has seven grandchildren, and three of them live near Seattle, so she's going out there to stay for a few weeks."

Dad munched on his sandwich and listened. He always seemed befuddled and admiring of her innocence all at once.

"You don't want to make friends in a campground john," he said halfheartedly.

"I wish you could have met her, but it's dark now," Mom said. "Anyway, sit down, boys, and eat your sandwiches."

After four days of relative calm, we piled in the Magic Bus and headed home. Dad treated us to breakfast at a pancake house. While we drove, he left his door open so the air blew through.

"Look there. Amish people," Mom observed, pointing to a horse and buggy clomping down the side of the road.

A little while later: "Look there. Kids riding their bikes. Just like you guys."

We stopped at a McDonald's for a bathroom break.

"You guys be quick," Dad said and waited in his seat.

Troy and I were in and out in two minutes. Mom took longer. After ten minutes we saw her come out of the bathroom and head toward the opposite side of the restaurant, away from us.

"Look, there's your mother," Dad said, waiting to see if she realized where she was headed. "There she is, going the opposite way again."

He fired up the truck and pulled around to the other side of the building in time to meet Mom coming out the other door.

"Where were you?" she asked almost scoldingly.

"Right where we parked," Dad said.

"Oh, I must have gotten lost," Mom said, laughing a loud, cheerful cackle. She buckled herself in.

A few miles later she lit up. "Oh! A garage sale."

There was a sign tacked to a telephone pole. Dad didn't have to be told twice. Mom loved garage sales so much that to drive by would have been criminal. Normally we didn't have time to stop just because we saw a sign. But we were on vacation.

Dad parked in front of the lawn, shedding pink light against the house, and pulled out his well-worn wallet. It was part wallet, part planner, part filing cabinet. In it he kept little notes to himself, reminders of projects to do, and always a hidden twenty-dollar bill for unexpected costs. He found a five-dollar bill and gave it to Mom.

"Here," Dad said, putting the bill in her hand. "Buy whatever you want."

He helped her down the Magic Bus's step, and she walked up the driveway to the garage. She rummaged around for a while, then returned holding a paper grocery sack labeled "Mystery bag: $1. No peeking." With the playful curiosity of a little child, Mom had no resistance for such surprises.

"What's this?" Dad said, helping her up.

"I don't know!" she said. "Let's open it."

Inside the bag were a pair of socks, a paperback dictionary, and a set of coasters.

"That's a waste," Dad concluded. "You should have gotten something else."

"I'll look at the next one," she said.

"If there is a next one," he muttered.

Twenty minutes later Dad saw another garage sale sign and pulled into a neighborhood. Odds and ends were laid out on someone's lawn. People milled about.

"Now use that money to get yourself something," he commanded. "Some books, a hat, a dress, or something."

Mom fumbled happily with the door, and I helped her down. She browsed at leisure for a while, then pointed at things, which the proprietor put into a plastic grocery bag for her. She came grinning to the Magic Bus. Troy took the bag for her, and Dad hoisted her up.

"What'd you get?" he asked.

"Oh, lots of things."

Dad peered into the bag. "A rubber ball, a set of marbles, dominoes, jacks, pencil erasers," he said. "What's all this?"

"It's for the kids at Sunday school," she said matter-of-factly. Other Sunday school teachers bought "treasure boxes" of toys as rewards for kids who performed well. Mom couldn't easily afford the official treasure box sold at the Christian bookstore, so she supplemented hers with trinkets from garage sales.

"What'd you get for yourself?" Dad said.

"Well, I got some shirts," she said. Clutched in her other hand were several articles of clothing. She held them up.

"That's a man's shirt," Dad observed.

"I thought it would look good on you," Mom said. "And these are for the boys."

More shirts.

"But none of this is for you!" Dad exclaimed.

"Well, it was mostly boys' stuff," Mom said. "And I got a stuffed chipmunk for Shawn and a stuffed cat for Troy."

She handed me the brown striped plush toy, which looked like it was designed for a three-year-old.

"Thanks, Mom," I said, trying not to sound disappointed.

She buckled in. I went back with Troy, who was already

playing with his stuffed cat and some of the other little toys Mom had bought. We pulled onto the highway. Mom hummed songs from church. Dad drummed the steering wheel with his thumbs. We crossed the Indiana state line, and Mom turned around to me.

"That chipmunk—I forgot to tell you, Shawn. I bought it because when you were two years old, you saw a chipmunk outside the window, and you wouldn't stop looking at it and pointing at it," she said. "I thought that was so sweet."

She laughed at the memory and then turned back around.

I clutched my chipmunk a little tighter. Suddenly, I wouldn't have traded it for the world.

CHAPTER 7

SHABOO, OUR CAT, sat contentedly on Mom's lap one Saturday morning.

"How is your day going?" Mom asked her. "Oh, good," she continued. "I bet you have all sorts of things planned. You are a busy kitty. Yes, you are. I'm busy too. I have so many things to do today."

She stroked the cat with all tenderness. Shaboo provided Mom with hours of comfort and companionship. She related to the cat as if it were human, often having full one-sided conversations with it. Troy and I were lying on the living room floor, plowing through hour after hour of Saturday morning cartoons. We didn't plan to stop until the boring programming came on. Then we'd head outside.

Mom went into her room to get dressed. A few minutes later something clattered behind me. It was Shaboo on the counter, a common sight. She had learned that the quickest way to get fed was to jump onto the avalanche-prone counters and start knocking things off. This was the most reliable way to get Mom's attention.

Crash!

Shaboo knocked a bowl and spoon onto the linoleum. She meowed.

"Mom, the cat!" I yelled. Usually, Mom began cursing Shaboo the way she did the rest of us. This time there was nothing. It sounded like Mom was fussing around in her room with jewelry.

During a commercial I got up and poured a bowl of cereal. Shaboo was slinking between cups and stacks of plates. With her paw she knocked a margarine tub loudly into the sink.

"Can't you wait?" Mom hollered, as if Shaboo understood her. "I'm not going to feed you right now. I have to get ready to go to Nana's later."

Shaboo meowed, sat for a moment, then batted an empty bottle off the counter. It thudded to the ground. I waited for Mom's curses, but none came. Instead, Mom herself emerged from the room half-dressed. I was sitting at the table, eating my cereal. Without a word, Mom picked a tube sock from a basket of dirty clothes. She shuffled over to Shaboo, who watched her with hopeful expectation and stepped to the edge of the counter. Mom took the sock, carefully wrapped it around Shaboo's neck, and tightened it. I watched for a moment, wondering if this was actually happening.

"Mom, you can't kill the cat," I said.

Mom didn't acknowledge me. Her face betrayed no emotion. Shaboo seemed to realize she was not going to be fed but rather was suddenly in danger. Her eyes went wide, and she shook her head a few times to get loose. Mom pulled the sock tighter around her neck. Shaboo bared her teeth in agony and batted the air with her paws. Mom's hands were too far away for Shaboo to reach them. Shaboo strained to pull her head back, but it was no use. Mom was strong.

"Mom, let go of the cat," I said with a little more urgency.

She paid no attention to me. Shaboo's head slumped to the side as if she were going unconscious. I got up to intervene, and as I approached, Mom seemed to notice me for the first time. She looked over and smiled sweetly.

"Did you get any sugar on your cereal?" she asked.

She dropped the tube sock and Shaboo, who hit the floor and scampered away. Mom brought the sugar bowl over and set it next to me as if nothing had happened. Then she went back to her room to finish getting dressed.

A few days later, Mom got angry with Dad and came after him with scissors in their bedroom. He scooted out quickly and pulled the door shut behind him.

"Your Mom's in there," he informed us. "She's trying to stab me." He was holding the door handle.

Mom banged on the door with the scissors, making a metallic sound.

"Let me out!" she said.

"You can't come out of the room until you put the scissors down," Dad said.

"You can't lock me in here!"

"I'm not locking you in. I'm waiting for you to put the scissors down."

She tugged on the door handle. Dad held it shut. Mom was silent for a few moments.

"Let me out of here now! I'm going to wet my pants! I'm going to pee on the floor, and you guys'll have to clean it up!"

"Just put down the scissors, Mom," I said.

A pause.

"Okay. I put them down."

"Slide them under the door."

With a scraping sound the scissors appeared under the door. Troy grabbed them and took them to the utility drawer. Dad let go of the door handle and walked away. I slowly opened it. Mom came out cursing and went straight into the bathroom.

We had learned by now how to manage many of her outbursts. A hand placed firmly on her shoulder was enough to keep her seated in a chair. In just a few minutes, the storm would pass, and she would calm down, cry, and apologize. As Troy and I got older and she started to throw something, we simply leaned over the table and knocked the object from her hand before she could launch it.

Mom seemed most at peace when nobody was home. She worked on her loom, sat in the bathroom and read for forty-five minutes, and took slow, methodical showers. Left alone at her own pace, she was content. Outbursts happened when we disturbed her world or placed any expectation on her.

Mom and Dad continued to work on their marriage,

attending activites with other young couples and listening to special speakers. As time went on, though, the marriage advice seemed less and less fitting to their circumstances. One retreat speaker said that married couples should spend six minutes of "couch time" together when the husband comes home from work before dealing with the kids. Mom came home excited about this new solution. But for a dozen reasons, "couch time" never materialized. Mom blamed Dad.

"You still won't do six minutes of couch time with me!" she yelled at him in the midst of an argument.

"How can I?" he said. "When I get home, you tell me, 'John, I want you to kill the kids right now.' You won't even sit down."

Dad concluded that standard Christian marriage advice was not going to cure our household. We were so far from normal that mainstream advice seemed to come from outer space.

Television remained our portal to a more stable world— a world with goofy housekeepers, friendly neighbors who dropped in unannounced, and spotless kitchens. A place where nobody flew into fits of rage. A place with predictable relationships and interactions that always resolved. A place where you didn't have to make excuses or explain the way your house looked to your friends. I leaned on these fictional environments for support. They held out hope that the world beyond my sight was different and better.

I especially related to characters like Bob Newhart's Vermont innkeeper on the show *Newhart*. He was a normal guy surrounded by crazy people. There were always moments when Bob would stop and give a look that said, "Tell me, why are we all acting like this is normal?" Mr. Douglas from

Green Acres was the same way, a normal person surrounded by people living in a form of insanity. He would stop mid-conversation and say something like "Do you realize we are talking to a pig?"

That's how I felt: a normal kid living in a crazy situation. And my situation, it seemed, always got crazier.

We had finally installed a new field system just a few years earlier, but this one failed too. Our septic tank filled up again, and again Dad didn't have money to fix it. So he bought a portable camper toilet and wedged it between the real toilet and the bathtub. It was two feet high, two feet wide, and two feet deep. It had a small toilet seat and lid.

"Dad, what's wrong with our real toilet?" I asked.

"Doesn't work right now," he said.

"What do I do?"

"Use the other one."

I soon learned the particular ways of the camper toilet. It worked on weak pressure we pumped up for each flush. We had to push the flush button correctly to make the toilet carry all the way through to a successful flush. When it was full of our waste, we unlatched the bottom tank, which was about the size of a briefcase, put it in the car, and took it over to Grandma and Grandpa Thorntons'. There we held it over *their* toilet and slid open a release hatch, letting all the refuse go into the toilet. Back home we put two blue tabs in the refuse tank, added a couple of gallons of water to the clean water tank, and reattached it to the bottom of the camper toilet for another week of service. The real toilet became the place we stacked books.

The camper toilet was our only commode for the next

year. I made a habit of using the bathrooms at school or church and relieving myself outside. Mom, of course, was stuck with the camper toilet most of the time, and she yelled at Dad about it a lot.

"This is just like the washing machine," she said. "Rick would fix their toilet. Jack would fix their toilet. They wouldn't leave us using that portable toilet. If you don't fix our toilet *and* our washing machine, I'm divorcing your a—."

But when I complained about it, she told me reasonably, "We can't afford to fix the field system just yet, but when we do, we'll have our toilet back. Won't that be nice?"

The difference between my life and my friends' lives became glaring. Not only did most kids have one or even two functioning toilets in their house, they had the money and talent to pursue life's finer things. So when Dad came home one day and announced, "We're getting a pool," I was ecstatic. *Finally, we'll have something better than everyone else*, I thought, imagining neighborhood kids coming over to swim in our backyard.

"Where are we getting it?" I asked.

"From Claude Kinder."

Mr. Kinder and his family lived across the street from Nana and Papaw and attended Twin Branch Bible Church. They had a nice above-ground pool, and I had tried it out on several occasions. The shallow end was four feet deep, and the deep end was eight feet deep. A metal frame and white braces held it together, and wood decking went all the way around. It even had a diving platform. I was beside myself with anticipation. With one stroke, our house would become the coolest on our little street—the only one with a pool. All-day pool parties filled my imagination.

Dad made a deal with Mr. Kinder. He had to tear down the pool at the Kinders' and move all the parts to our house. He did this and laid everything in our front yard for examination. He walked around the pile of metal, wood, and plastic parts, studying and measuring.

"Gonna have to replace that liner," he mused to himself and to us. The original liner was torn beyond repair in several places.

Then he walked to the backyard and looked at the space where he intended to put it. It was all covered with grass, like a regular lawn, but I saw the vision coming together in Dad's head.

An hour later we were at the pool supply store in South Bend.

"That specialty liner shape isn't available anymore unless you order it custom," the man at the store told us, looking in his catalog.

"That'll cost way too much," Dad muttered. "How about a standard liner?"

The man punched up the price.

"That'll be fine," Dad said.

"Standard liner?"

"Yep." Dad had a plan to scale back the depth of the pool a bit so that a standard liner might fit.

We took the liner home and got to work setting up the frame. Dad laid the new liner out to see how it would fit. It was too short on one side, but Dad didn't seem bothered.

The next day we were back at the pool supply store.

"How'd that liner work out?" the man asked.

"Good, but I'll need another one to go with it," Dad said.

The man cocked his head, trying to understand. "You want another liner?"

"Yeah, a smaller one," Dad said.

"Just so I can try to help you, why do you need another liner?" the man asked.

"The other one's not the right size," Dad said. "But if I cut the liner I bought yesterday in two and glue this smaller liner to the middle, I think it'll cover the ground I need it to cover."

"Don't cut that liner, sir," the man said. "Don't cut the liner."

Dad had cut the liner before we left home.

"Hmm," Dad said.

They looked at each other for a moment.

"I'll still take the smaller one. And a hundred tubes of liquid pool-patching cement," Dad said.

Back home Dad looked at the standard liner he had cut in half. It was laid out on our lawn. He laid the smaller liner between the halves. He now had a would-be liner in three pieces. He took the same razor he had used to cut the big liner and cut a strip ten feet wide from the smaller one. He had determined that was all he needed to make the new liner he was creating to fit the custom-size, larger frame.

He's going for broke, I thought.

Dad placed the smaller strip between the bigger liner halves, essentially creating a large patch in the middle.

"Guys," he said. "Get the tubes of pool-patching cement from the car."

Troy and I did as he asked. Dad was on his hands and knees now. He overlapped the pieces by eight inches or so and glued them together. The sutures zagged unevenly.

"Won't the water run out the bottom?" I asked.

Dad grunted and stood up.

"Not if I did the glue right and the water weight holds the overlapping flaps down," he said.

The next task was to dig out the ground to establish the pool's depth. Dad got a shovel, and for two weeks he labored in the yard after work and on weekends, digging down six inches, one foot, two feet. Troy and I helped as well. Troy loved working on this kind of project with Dad—me, not so much. It was hard going, and our efforts produced a shallow, uneven landscape of pits and drop-offs.

"That's it," Dad said one afternoon, leaning on his shovel, arms glistening with sweat, shirt soaked. "I'm done. I'm not doing this anymore. This is as deep as it's going to be."

The next thing I knew, a bunch of sand was delivered and put in the area we had just dug. Dad attached the liner to the frame and began filling our new secondhand pool with the hose. It took hours. As it filled, the liner molded to the ground beneath it, revealing the lumpy topography of our yard. I watched for water flowing out of the patched area but couldn't see any.

After what seemed like a whole day, the pool was mostly full. Everything seemed to be holding, to Dad's great satisfaction. He then assembled the wood decking, discovering in the process that some of the wood was rotted out, leaving gaps. He went to the lumber yard and bought two-by-fours, stained them, and created makeshift bridges over those areas.

The pool had looked pristine at the Kinders' house, like a picture from a magazine. At our house it was shallow, gap-toothed, and sitting awkwardly on top of the ground. It had more of a lake bottom than a pool bottom, with unexpected drops and contours. Dad's premature halting of our digging efforts impacted our pool depth. The shallow end was just over two feet deep. Our "deep" end was three or four feet deep, depending on which side of it you were on. Diving was strictly prohibited.

Somehow the pool never leaked. But with your toes you could feel the flaps where the liners were glued together. Dirt gathered there, and one of my jobs was to clean them out when I vacuumed the pool.

My vision of pool parties drawing friends from school and church dimmed. I would have to be content to splash around with Troy and Lance. Dad procured tractor-tire inner tubes, and we floated in them. Even Lance thought it was cool. We got masks and snorkels and swam underwater, pretending we were seasoned scuba divers. Even with its imperfections, we had a pool. It kept us cool in the summers, and it gave us hours of fun.

But our new pool did bring some unexpected dangers to our household. One day the school bus dropped me off as usual at the top of Victory Road. As I approached our house, I heard a voice.

"Shawn! Shawn!"

It was Mom, and she seemed to be calling me from outside somewhere. I walked around back. There, in one of the tractor inner tubes, Mom was floating in the pool. In her hand was an empty plastic cup, the tea that was in it long since consumed.

"Shawn, help me. I can't get out. Your Dad didn't know what he was doing when he built this pool!" she yelled, cursing and paddling futilely toward the side of the pool. I set my backpack down and climbed up on the decking.

"How long have you been in here?" I asked. The entire front side of her body was cranberry red.

"All day!" she said, groaning and laughing her distinct, gregarious laugh. "I couldn't get out once I got in. Here."

She was close enough to hand me her cup. I set it aside, took her hand, and pulled her out of the inner tube and onto the decking.

"Thanks," she said. "I wasn't sure I would ever get out of there."

In the early fall, Dad and I returned to the pool supply store.

"This is pool shock," the man at the store said, patting a gallon bottle. "You'll need about ten of these for a pool your size. It'll help it get through the hard, cold winter without allowing the water to freeze and damage your liner."

Dad eyed the bottles. They were a whopping eight dollars apiece.

"Shock, huh?" he said.

"Yes, pretty standard stuff for pool owners," the man said.

I could see Dad's gears working.

"What's in it?"

"It's a chlorine-based compound of some type," the man

said, turning a bottle around to see the ingredients. "Carefully blended for pool use."

Dad nodded.

"All right. Well, I'm not going to buy it now, but if I need some, I know where to get it," he said.

Our next stop was the grocery store. Dad went down the household goods aisle and peered at the bottles.

"There we are," he said. He pulled a white bottle from the shelf that read simply "Bleach" in black letters. It was thirty-nine cents a bottle. Dad bought twenty of them.

Back home, Dad began uncapping and dumping bottles of pure bleach into the pool. He had purchased pool chemical strips to test the levels. After a while he tested the level and then added more bleach. Eventually, he just poured in all of the bottles. I was beginning to learn that Dad lived by an unspoken motto: anything good in moderation is even better in excess. All that late fall and winter the pool sat unused and covered with a pool cover the Kinders had sold us with the rest of the equipment. It smelled like a chemical truck had overturned on the highway.

It wasn't the glamorous pool I had hoped for, but it was better than nothing.

• • •

"Dad, who are we playing tonight?" I asked on the way to a softball game one Thursday night. Dad glanced at his schedule.

"The blue hats," he said.

It was my first softball season without Lance. For years, he and I were a dynamic duo, with Lance pitching and me catching. We were usually selected as a pair. We played in the fast-pitch underhand league that met at the field behind Elm Road Elementary School, where I had gone to kindergarten. There were no uniforms, no sponsorships, no field stripes, and no permanent bases. Fathers organized the whole thing, and we wore baseball caps with different colors to distinguish teams. There were the yellow hats, red hats, purple hats, blue hats, and green hats.

Now Lance had moved over to the city league, which wasn't a surprise. Lance was the consummate competitor. His parents paid for him to have all kinds of lessons: golf and tennis at the YMCA, baseball, basketball—even bowling. When Lance practiced these sports, he needed someone to practice with, so I was usually invited along. Many of my big experiences in childhood came from hanging around with Lance and his family. His older sister, Lisa, even taught me how to ride a bike.

So the city league fit him well. The teams had real names—the Dodgers, Tigers, Cubs, and so on. Their baseball field complex had four very nice fields with dugouts, bleachers, and concession stands. Each team had a sponsor: Weaver Electric, Jim's Tire Shop. Those names adorned the back of their crisp, white uniforms. I began seeing Lance get into his car wearing cleats, baseball pants, stirrups, a jersey, and a hat with a real team name on it. His league played several times a week and even had announcers. As far as I was concerned, he was in the major leagues already.

Our country softball league had no dugouts and no bleachers, just a couple of benches some dads built. Our backstops looked homemade. Many of us didn't know what it felt like to wear cleats. We wore whatever shoes we wore to school.

Dad pulled the Magic Bus up to the field where the other boys and dads were assembling. We got out.

"Who brought the bases?" one of the dads asked generally.

"I've got some," another dad offered. "Gimme a minute. I'll put 'em out."

One of the fathers lugged a big yellow water jug with a red spout toward the field. Moms and dads carried lawn chairs and positioned them along the first and third base paths. Our infield was indistinguishable from our outfield, the base paths visible only by the wear on the grass. Looking at our setup, I was envious of Lance's league, which had dugouts that were sunken into the ground and a big chain-link backstop. The players could lean on the dugout railing, chew sunflower seeds, and harass the batter, just like in real baseball.

I put on my hat and glove and began warming up with the other boys. Dad and another father walked around, hooking bases onto stakes in the ground. The grass hadn't been mowed and was eight inches tall. A ball hit to the outfield would just sit there, making it easy for those playing outfield to retrieve it and throw home. I prepared myself for plays at the plate.

The pitcher on my team was a kid I barely knew. He didn't know any of Lance's and my hand signals. Even if we got into a groove and won our tournament, it would feel anticlimactic to me in a way. Our team would receive generic trophies, the kind that say "First Place" with a golden plastic man swinging a bat on top. Lance's trophies were large, heavy, and personalized.

"Play ball!" shouted the umpire, one of the dads from a team not playing at our diamond, and I sank into my catcher's crouch. But it was hard to think about anything other than what had happened at home before the game.

Mom had served cow heart, the kind of inexpensive, tough meat that even though it was slow cooked like a roast required a steak knife and a lot of patience.

I don't remember what was said, but Mom had become suddenly angry. She screamed obscenities at Dad.

"Oh, get over it!" he shouted back.

It seemed like just another night of tension at the dinner table. Then Mom's eyes flitted around for something to throw. Perhaps we had grown complacent, counting the milliseconds and knowing we had time to reach over and knock an object from her hand. But this time she was faster than expected. Before we could react, she had grabbed her steak knife and whipped it through the air at Dad.

I watched the knife, as if in slow motion, flying over the table, crossing between Troy and me, and plunging straight into Dad's ear, penetrating the hollow area just above his earlobe. It went through all the way to the wooden handle and stuck there horizontally. Blood began to flow down his neck. Troy and I glanced across the table at each other, stunned that our mother had just stabbed our father. Our eyes said it to each other: we should have stopped her before this happened.

"D— it, Bev!" Dad screamed angrily.

He reached up, grabbed the knife handle, pulled the blade out of his ear, and slammed it onto the table. Mom realized what she had done and wailed hysterically. Dad took his red handkerchief from his pocket and pressed it against the wound. Deeper red spread through the fabric.

"Why'd you do that, Bev?" he shouted.

Freeing one hand, he immediately threw his glass at her. It hit Mom's arm, bounced off, and shattered on the floor. He got up from the table and stormed around his end of the kitchen area, then wove in and out of the nearby bedroom doors. It seemed he was trying to deal with the physical pain and gain control of his emotions.

Mom pounded the table in confused exasperation. Troy sat with his fork above his plate, watching what unfolded. Dad checked the handkerchief for blood and felt his ear. Still bleeding. He pressed the hankie against his head again and turned away from Mom, who was bawling like a child and sputtering, "If you wouldn't . . . you just get me so . . . if you guys would leave me alone, I wouldn't . . ." Her voice trailed off.

Dad went into the bathroom to wash the wound and look at it in the mirror. Mom kept crying and muttering the same incomplete phrases, each time with a deeper sense of guilt. Dad replaced the blood-soaked hankie with a small bathroom hand towel from one of the baskets of clothes just outside the bathroom door. Still applying pressure to his bleeding ear and having calmed down substantially, he began to sense the need to help Mom, Troy, and me through what had just happened.

"Bev, you have to stop this!" he said, referring to Mom's crying. "Don't worry about it. It'll be fine."

He went and stood next to her. She grabbed his free arm and sobbed into it. A stunned silence remained over us. Troy and I looked at each other across the table again as if to acknowledge that this was a whole new level of crazy for our family.

"Guys, go to your rooms," Dad said. "Dinner's over."

We hadn't finished eating, but I wasn't thinking about food anymore. Alone in my room, I lay down on my bed.

What if the knife had hit Dad's eye? His face? His forehead? His temple? His chest? A handkerchief wouldn't have solved that one.

Dad never went to the doctor about it. His ear healed with no noticeable scar, and nobody mentioned it again. But a sense of foreboding and danger seemed to have crept into our home. If nothing else, my heart felt wounded. Whatever sense of stability and normalcy I hoped to retain in our household was quickly evaporating. Uncertainty consumed my feelings.

As I crouched behind home plate that night, on a makeshift field with a kid I barely knew pitching at me, my mind kept circling the same question: *Why? Why do we have a home with violence and yelling? Why does everything in our lives seem so broken?*

"Strike two!" the ump yelled. I tossed the ball back to the pitcher. The outcome almost didn't matter to me.

Just a few months before the knife incident, a black and white mutt showed up in our yard. We had never seen her before.

"Go on home," I said after petting her awhile. She didn't seem to understand me. "Go home, girl," I repeated, pointing to the road. She took two steps away, then turned back as if to ask if I was coming too.

I left her in the yard and went inside.

"Dad, I can't make that dog go home," I said.

"Don't worry about it," he said. "Just wait awhile. Someone'll come looking for her."

We waited a week. Nobody came looking for her, and she continued to hang around our house like it was her own. We fed her and gave her water from the hose. It didn't make sense that out of all the houses in Mishawaka, she seemed to have chosen ours. Dad surmised that maybe someone had abandoned her in the fields or woods nearby.

We named her Lady. Dad, who had worked with dogs as a sentry in Korea, spent some time playing with her in the yard one day and concluded that she had been abused. When you said her name or even gestured toward her, she cowered and put her tail between her legs. At times she got so low that she seemed to be trying to bury herself in the ground. Lady's pain resonated with me.

When I got home that night after my game, I lay on my bed with Lady. Now I had someone who would listen as I poured out my heart. I considered Lady a gift from God to me.

I didn't know how badly I would need her.

CHAPTER 8

"DAD, I NEED NEW JEANS. Mine are too short," I said, pointing to my pants legs, which terminated north of my ankles.

"Time for you to pay for your own blue jeans," he said. It was a half-serious remark, but I knew what he meant: "Don't ask me for what you don't absolutely need." He was also communicating to me that, as a thirteen-year-old, I needed to take some responsibility for my life.

An advertisement in the back of a *Boys' Life* magazine I read at school said kids like me could make money selling *Grit* newspaper, so I signed up. Like the boy in the ad, I pictured myself raking in money selling *Grit* to friends and family as well as to people outside of Dorbin's, a neighborhood grocery store. *Grit* was a small weekly that was folksy, patriotic, and "down home" in its style. It contained little if any current news but had interesting, warm stories from America's heartland.

The newspapers arrived, and I stationed myself at the entrance of Dorbin's with my cheesy-looking *Grit* newspaper bag (for which I had to pay). I held up a sample newspaper, just like the kid in the ad.

"*Grit* magazine! One quarter! Buy yours now!"

I stood there several times a week for three or four months, even in the pouring rain. I earned fifteen cents per magazine, and the publisher earned a dime. At the end of that time, I had made less than four dollars. Blue jeans cost eight dollars.

I gave Dad an update on my financial status, and he seemed to soften.

"Tell you what," he said. "You put in what you have, and I'll put in the rest." He knew what it was to be a working man.

But expenses kept piling up. I joined the junior high basketball team and needed a certain type of Converse high-top shoes.

"High-top shoes?" Dad said. "Why don't you play in your regular shoes? Who is going to pay for these high-top tennis shoes?"

But the coach required high-tops, so I started looking for any kind of extra money. I even asked God to help me. Aunt Gail had me babysit her three boys several times. Then one day I got a call from Uncle Buddy.

Uncle Buddy was Grandma Thornton's younger brother, so he was actually my great-uncle. Something about him was a little off. He functioned well enough to hold a job and to take care of himself, but he had no idea how to handle money and lived a simple, meager life. Grandma Thornton went to Elkhart every week to spend an afternoon with him. She helped him reconcile his checkbook and made sure his bills were paid.

At age seventy, Uncle Buddy met and fell in love with a woman named Ruth, who was sixty-eight and also had never married. Ruth was tall, impossibly thin, and wore "cat" glasses that looked like they had been with her from the early 1960s. She was not "off" in the same way as Uncle Buddy, but she was odd in her own way. She worked at Miles Laboratories in Elkhart for fifty years. Miles was where they made Alka-Seltzer tablets and Bactine antiseptic spray, the stuff we put on cuts and scrapes when we fell off our bikes. Ruth had lived in the same house her whole life, a structure ordered from a Sears catalog decades earlier when Sears, Roebuck and Company sold prefabricated homes. A man in Elkhart had purchased eight identical Sears homes and erected them all in a row, making one of the largest collections of Sears homes in one place.

Buddy and Ruth dated for six months and were as giddy as teenagers. Then they got married, and for their honeymoon they drove through the Upper Peninsula of Michigan into Canada. Eight days later Ruth's factory called Grandma Thornton.

"We're worried about Ruth," they said. "She has never missed work before, but she was supposed to come in yesterday and today, and we haven't seen her."

Grandma called around. Uncle Buddy and Aunt Ruth had disappeared. Later that day Uncle Buddy called Grandma from a diner three hours away.

"We were having such a good time that we traveled farther, and on our way home we ran out of money," he said. "Can you wire us some for gas so we can drive home?"

The happy couple arrived safely and moved into Ruth's Sears home.

Mom connected well with Buddy and Ruth and embraced them at face value. Like so many other people who crossed her path with unique problems, challenges, or quirks, Uncle Buddy and Aunt Ruth accepted Mom as she was too. Mom and Ruth would laugh together like junior high schoolgirls when we gathered as a family at Grandma and Grandpa's. Buddy always listened to Mom's thoughts on discussion topics, even if the rest of us casually dismissed her input. Mom seemed to understand the couple's quirkiness better than the rest of us and had keen insight into how they thought and behaved.

Uncle Buddy was pleased to offer me work around his house and suggested I come over for the weekend to spend time with him and Aunt Ruth. I loved the idea of making money and hanging around with them.

Grandpa Thornton dropped me off in front of the line of Sears homes. Uncle Buddy was outside one of them smoking a cigar. He was never without a cigar, and his shirts and pants had little holes in them from the ashes. So did the driver's seat in his car.

"Hi, Shawn!" he said, as happy as could be. He appeared

to be enjoying retirement and married life. He invited me inside.

I set my backpack down next to the couch and noticed a dog there that stood stock still. It was Clarence. Clarence had been their pet, and Uncle Buddy and Aunt Ruth had had him stuffed when he died. They did this with some of their former pets, placing them around the house like furnishings. A deceased pet parakeet adorned a shelf in the living room, perched lifelike on a twig. A few dogs stood at attention in various corners and beside end tables.

I noticed Rusty standing in a far corner. He had been alive the last time I visited.

"What happened to Rusty?" I asked.

"There he is," Uncle Buddy said as if Rusty were still alive and well. Rusty's glassy eyes stared permanently toward the living room window.

Aunt Ruth was in the kitchen wearing a simple cotton dress. Her legs were as thin as chair legs.

"Shawn's here," Buddy said.

"Shawn!" she said, coming in and hugging me with her tree-branch arms.

We sat in the living room and chatted for a while. They asked me about school. Then Ruth got up, sat on Uncle Buddy's lap, and put her arms around his neck.

"What are we going to have for lunch, Daddy-o?" she asked, stroking his balding head.

"I don't know. What do you think?" I was fascinated that they were in their seventies but acted like high school kids.

Their cupboard was always stocked with good food, but

they loved the adventure of the simple journey to the local grocery or butcher shop. Ruth had a good deal of money relative to what Uncle Buddy had, having lived with her parents in that home from her early childhood.

"I want something different," she said.

"Me, too," he said.

"Come on, Daddy-o! We're going to the grocery store!" Ruth jumped up excitedly, and Uncle Buddy grinned around his cigar.

We got in the car and drove to the corner market, two blocks away. Everybody knew them there because they came as often as twice a day. When we got home with the groceries, Aunt Ruth started making lunch, and Uncle Buddy waved me outside.

"So you want to make a little money?" he said.

"I do," I confirmed.

"I'll give you twenty-five dollars if you take the trash to the curb," he said.

I couldn't believe my ears. Without looking too excited, I said, "Okay." I carried the can to the curb and came back. Uncle Buddy looked around.

"I'll give you fifty for trimming those bushes," he said. I nodded, thinking I had fallen into a wonderful dream. I found shears in his garage, came back, and started cutting the bushes. The whole task would take me two hours. Uncle Buddy smoked his cigar and watched pleasantly.

Aunt Ruth poked her head out the door in the middle of my new assignment.

"Let's have lunch," she said.

"Let me pay Shawn first," Uncle Buddy said. He often paid me long before a job was done. We walked inside, and he headed toward the television. Ruth joined us.

"Here, kitty, kitty, kitty," he said.

"Here, kitty, kitty," she said too.

On top of the television was a jar full of cash and change they called the kitty. When Uncle Buddy or Aunt Ruth put money into the jar, they said, "We're going to feed the kitty! Come watch us feed the kitty."

Now he said, "Oh, the kitty's going to have to cough up some money for you, Shawn."

He stuck his hand in and pulled out seventy-five dollars' worth of various bills and change.

"Ooh, the kitty doesn't like that," he joked. "There, there, kitty."

He handed the bills to me and I pocketed them, half believing he would ask for them back at some point. But he didn't. By the time I left, I had enough money for high-top shoes plus a bunch of other things I had been needing. It didn't occur to me that Uncle Buddy didn't know how to manage money. I just thought he and Aunt Ruth really wanted the work done.

Six years into their marriage, Uncle Buddy died. At his funeral Grandma Thornton walked forward in her dignified way, draped herself over the casket, and sobbed with sorrow. I had never seen her cry before.

Soon after Uncle Buddy's death, Aunt Ruth began to show signs of dementia. Mom and I visited her one Saturday afternoon with Grandma Thornton. Mom got along famously with Ruth. Neither one had a driver's license, and both loved to laugh and did so at socially awkward times.

"Would you all like some Tang?" Ruth offered once we were seated.

"Sure," Mom and I replied. Aunt Ruth went to prepare it.

When she was gone, Grandma Thornton said in a low voice, "We need to check what she gives us because recently she tried to give us milk that was a week old."

Ruth came in with glasses for each of us. She was always proud of what she served and liked to explain what it was. She handed me a little empty packet.

"We have had this Tang since mother lived here," she said. That was twenty years earlier. "Let's have some ice cream, too," she said and went back into the kitchen.

I looked at the packet. The "Tang" was actually heart medicine in orange powder form, and the prescription made out for Ruth's mother had expired almost twenty years earlier. I showed it to Mom and Grandma.

"What are we going to do?" I asked.

Mom said, "I'll tell you what we're going to do. Everybody pour it in that plant."

We dumped the orange drink in the dirt, in sight of the stuffed pets but not Aunt Ruth, who came in moments later. She saw our empty glasses and said, "Oh! Would you like more?" We politely declined.

Back home, Mom became my advocate for money. While Dad was in the bathroom one morning, Mom grabbed his wallet off the dresser and pulled out a few dollars for me.

"That's for the new belt you need," she said. She was

so slow handling the wallet that Dad came out and caught her.

"What are you doing in there? Get out of there," he said, holding a towel around his waist.

Mom's tone of authority was unusual.

"John, he needs the money. We're his parents. We need to provide for him."

Dad relented.

"I was always going to help him. I just wanted him to learn that money doesn't grow on trees."

I took that lesson to heart and became an entrepreneur. I discovered I could buy candy at our local grocery store—Twizzlers, Blow Pops, Tootsie Rolls, Bottlecaps, bubble gum—pack it in sandwich bags, and sell it from my locker at school. It cost me thirty cents, and I sold candy bags for a dollar. I was selling convenience. Soon, although I was in seventh grade, I was selling candy to high school students who had jobs already and money to spend.

By eighth grade, I got an opportunity for my first real job, working in a local plant nursery. The wife of our part-time youth pastor at Twin Branch Bible Church introduced me to the nursery owner, Mr. Coffman. He hired me to do manual labor around the greenhouses. I moved clay pots, mixed and moved soil, and carried flats of seedlings from one greenhouse to another. The greenhouses were hot and humid, and the work was dirty. The minimum wage was $3.10 an hour, but Mr. Coffman paid me a dollar an hour under the table. Still, to me it was a big deal when in the summer and on breaks, at the end of a full week of work,

Mr. Coffman reached into the old cash register and handed me forty dollars. I had made more working for Uncle Buddy and Aunt Ruth, but those golden opportunities were short lived. This was real pay for a good week of work.

But no matter how much money I made selling candy, "working" for Uncle Buddy and Aunt Ruth, or working at the plant nursery, it didn't change my home environment. And I couldn't keep up with friends whose parents made more money than we did. Plus, their homes had clean counters and visible carpeting. They washed their sheets weekly, and their parents didn't yell, as best I could tell.

I became acutely embarrassed that our house was never clean and that Mom and Dad barked and cursed at each other throughout the day. On the rare occasions when friends came over, I prepped them about what to expect.

"My mother was in an accident in 1962," I would say, sitting on the back porch before we entered the house. "She has a hard time doing some things, so our house is always a mess."

I'm not sure they wanted or needed to hear it, but it made me feel better to mention it before they went inside and encountered our chaotic piles of clutter.

Personal insecurity enveloped me, as did the fear of losing friends or looking bad in front of them. I felt I couldn't speak with anyone about my day-to-day life because my family's circumstances were so unusual and even off-putting.

I envied Lance. His family defined the normal life I wanted. His dad was an electrician who worked hard and earned enough money to invest in a few rental properties, then in an entire apartment complex. Lance's family had a satellite dish and could pick up channels from around the world. For Christmas, Lance always got the hot toy that year. While my family did have a few Christmases with some incredible toys, more often than not Troy and I received a bizarre collection of stuffed animals and random items from thrift stores and garage sales, all mummified in tape, wrapped in newspaper, or stuffed into shopping bags because Mom couldn't wrap well. On Christmas Day I was always eager to go over to Lance's house and see what he had gotten.

Lance's house was brand new and had a sliding glass door that led out to a patio. Our house was all original and barely holding together. Lance's house had a finished basement, which served as a recreation area. Our cellar basement had a cement slab floor and dirt walls and was really a glorified crawl space with a broken kitchen drain pipe hanging down into it. Half a dozen bottles of Dad's homemade apple cider, made from our backyard apple trees, sat on a makeshift shelf in various states of foaming, explosion, and unintentional fermentation on their way to becoming vinegar.

And even when they argued, I never heard Lance's parents fight like mine did. I was sure the few and distant neighbors we had could hear everything we said because our windows were open for much of the year.

"John, you're worthless!" Mom told Dad one evening, yelling obscenities at him. I lay on my bed with Lady, who seemed content to stay beside me forever.

"Just shut up, Bev," Dad said, his patience worn thin by a day at work.

I hugged Lady close and began to cry.

"Why?" I asked Lady aloud. "Why am I in this situation? Why did God put me in this family? Why is our household so crazy?"

Lady looked in my eyes without judgment, listening. I stroked the fur on her head over and over. I wished I could disappear into the television set and become part of the world there. When crazy things happened to the people there, it was always funny and always ended up okay.

Mom picked up the phone. I knew she was calling one of her sisters.

"Sue?" she said. "I'm going to kill him, I'm so mad at him."

Silence.

"Well, I want a divorce. I can't stand it. I have to do something."

Silence.

"Okay. Okay. Okay, bye."

She hung up, and that was the end of it. Sometimes just hearing someone else's voice put Mom in a different frame of mind. Sometimes one of her sisters would come and get her, and she would cool down before coming home. This time just a call was enough.

I looked back at Lady. She had not moved. She was still looking at me as if I were the most important thing in her entire universe. I hugged her and fell asleep.

• • •

Strife at home affected my behavior at school. I attended a Christian school, and despite my earlier good performance in Awana, I was becoming trouble for my teachers. One day I was clowning around in class, and the teacher sat me in a chair facing the wall.

"Let's see if you talk to Mr. Wall the way you talk to Roger," she said.

"Hello, Mr. Wall" was my immediate rejoinder.

Her face reddened with frustration and disapproval.

"Get up," she said and marched me to the hallway. She sat me in a chair. When she went back inside the classroom, I began talking to the hallway. She came out, totally exasperated.

"Shawn, what has gotten into you?" I'd had a good relationship with this teacher and had had her the year before as well. I was usually respectful, but with boundaries falling apart at home, I guess I felt like testing the ones at school.

I served as a crossing guard at school, just like Mom had. One day in sixth grade I was holding the stop sign for the little kids to cross the alleyway safely when I spotted my classmate Ricky. He was at the wheel of his brother's car.

"Hey, Shawn!" one of my friends yelled, sticking his head out the window. A bunch of guys were crammed inside with Ricky, who drove out of the school parking lot into the surrounding neighborhood.

Ten minutes later they pulled back up. I had just finished my start-of-recess crossing-guard duties. Ricky stopped the car in front of me. All of the guys in my small class were crammed inside the car, and many were hanging out the windows.

"Hey! We're driving around. Get in." They opened the door, and without much thought, I joined them.

Ricky took us slowly around the quiet neighborhood near our school. It seemed thrilling but also natural. Houses crept by. Ricky pressed gently on the gas and the brake. After a few minutes he cruised back and parked the car where it had been before. I got out and did my end-of-recess shift of crossing-guard duty. Then we all went to class.

Our teacher, Miss Timothy, was a large woman and wore dresses that seemed to be made of a single piece of cloth. She had a big mole on her nose. I liked Miss Timothy, and we got along well, but she was beside herself when she found out that a bunch of young junior high boys had gone for a joyride during lunch. One by one she called us out of class and took us upstairs as if to an execution chamber. Ricky was first.

Minutes later, Ricky came back, crying. It was quite a contrast, seeing the boy who had just been piloting his brother's car around the streets of that little neighborhood now sniffling at his desk.

"They paddled him!" someone whispered.

The next boy went up the stairs. He, too, came back crying. He winced when he sat down and then sat in such a way that his bottom didn't touch the seat but his weight was on his upper thighs on the edge of the chair.

The class sat quietly. I could see the pattern. Miss Timothy was starting with the leaders and moving down to the followers. Soon even Darin, the best student and the most well behaved of the eight boys in our class, had been paddled.

Uh-oh! I thought when Darin returned to his seat, crying uncontrollably.

I had never been in this kind of trouble. Troy was the

one who got paddled in our family. He had been paddled at school many times in kindergarten alone. Once he looked at the teacher after she had whacked him with the paddle and said, "Just so you know, that didn't hurt." Many times we would come home, and Dad would be furious because Troy had been paddled again at school.

Troy actually caused his third-grade teacher to quit the profession. One day he winged his Bible textbook at her in anger and hit the mark. The moment she got hit, she sat down on the floor, cried, and had some kind of breakdown, right in front of everybody. One of the girls in the class went and got another teacher, who came into the room and took over.

Mom and Dad were called in, Troy was paddled, and Troy's teacher quit and became a missionary in a small village in Brazil. Apparently working with South American natives was easier than dealing with my little brother.

Now it was my turn. Miss Timothy beckoned me to follow her upstairs. She was quiet and resolved as we headed to the principal's office.

Dr. Bowling was a tall man with a sturdy, strong frame. I came in and sat in front of him. The paddle, which was probably still warm from being used on my buddies, sat crossways on his lap. It was long, wooden, three-quarters of an inch thick, and carved from a single piece of wood. Three drilled holes helped Dr. Bowling get it up to speed.

"Were you in the car?" he asked me.

"I was," I said, trying to sound confident in my ultimate innocence.

"Why did you get in?" he asked. One of his hands rested on the paddle now.

"I wasn't even thinking," I said. "I had just finished my crossing duty when the car pulled up. They kind of forced me in, and before I knew it, we were going down the road."

Dr. Bowling looked at Miss Timothy as if to ask, "Is this credible to you?" She gave him a conflicted look. I knew that my having cultivated her favor might yet pay dividends.

"I was only in the car for ten minutes, not the whole half hour," I continued. "Then I was back for my crossing-guard duty. Then I came in. I'm really sorry I did it. It happened so fast, and I didn't really want to. I must have been tired from my crossing-guard duty."

It was terribly slick, but they seemed to be buying it. Dr. Bowling studied my face as if studying my character.

"What punishment do you think you deserve?" he asked.

My response was ready. "I'd take away my recesses for the next week."

Dr. Bowling slowly nodded. "All right," he said, tapping the paddle with his thumb. "That's what we'll do." He looked at Miss Timothy. She seemed in agreement with him.

They both bought it. *I think I just talked myself out of this,* I thought with a sense of cunning pride.

Dr. Bowling stood up. "You can go back to class."

With that, Miss Timothy and I walked back to class. Neither of us spoke a word. When I entered the classroom, my friends scrutinized my face for signs of pain—tears, red eyes, a grimace. Nothing. I went back to my seat and sat down normally.

"You didn't get paddled?" one of the boys asked. His nose was still red from crying.

"No," I said. The truth spread quickly to the other boys and so did their shared fury.

"How come you didn't get paddled?" they asked after school. I explained my logic. They just about disowned my friendship.

That was the first time I realized I had a gift to speak persuasively. I had taken Dr. Bowling logically through what had happened and explained my point of view convincingly. Of course, I had used this talent for wrong, and I became convinced I could talk myself out of anything.

Learning that I could persuade others made me realize that words are powerful. Because of the turmoil I was feeling at home, I began using my words in another powerful way—to tear people down. Harshness entered my vocabulary. I denigrated teachers and students alike. In a way that sickened even me, I maintained them as friends while treating them terribly. I wanted the best of both worlds—their friendship and loyalty and the freedom to put them down in order to push myself up.

One day I walked into my bedroom and noticed that my Timothy Award from Awana was gone. I immediately knew what had happened: Dad had recycled it for another kid out of thrift. But it didn't bother me much. I had already drifted from my interest in Awana. In truth, I had grown cold toward the church and toward the Christian life, bending every rule I could while keeping up the appearance of a good Christian teen.

One day when Lance's parents were gone, we broke into his dad's liquor cabinet and drank some vodka. A few days later we rode our bikes around and banged up people's mailboxes with baseball bats. I began using bad language, every word in the book.

If Mom can use them, why not me? I thought.

In the back of a pickup truck on the way to a soccer game for our Christian school one day, Ricky reached into his gym bag and pulled something out.

"Check this out," he said. He tossed several pornographic magazines to us. Before the truck stopped, he gathered them up again, but not before we had filled our eyes and heads with the images.

One day while Lance's parents weren't home, we stumbled upon a stack of *Playboy* magazines his dad had stashed somewhere. The "education" we received went way beyond what I had learned from reading the Harlequin romance novels Mom left lying around the house. Then Lance found some pornographic stations on their big satellite dish and invited me to come watch with him. I knew it was wrong, but it became difficult for us to resist.

Up the hill on the other side of Victory Road, my friend Steve's parents owned the gravel pit. In that pit, Steve and I found pornographic magazines that truck drivers had thrown out. Steve hid them in an abandoned house there, and we hung around and cussed like junior sailors. We really thought we were something.

As much as I had drifted from the church individually, the situation with the other youth at Twin Branch Bible Church was hardly better. We had a new pastor whose son, Jeremy, was two years older than I was. Jeremy and I started hanging out and going to his house, the church parsonage, which was a couple of doors down from Nana's house. We talked about two subjects: girls and sex. Jeremy knew a lot more than I did, and I became his young sidekick.

Once while Dad was cleaning the church, he picked up the extension to call Mom. The church had one phone system with lines in different parts of the church, so when you picked up one phone, you could hear if someone was already on the line. Dad heard Jeremy and the church secretary's daughter saying vulgar things and using bad language. Another time he caught them kissing somewhere in the church.

A few days later, when we were in the car, Dad confronted me. "I don't want you going over to the pastor's house anymore," he said. "And I don't want you hanging around with Jeremy."

I was shocked. Jeremy had become one of my closest friends that summer. And after all, he was our pastor's son. Was Dad actually telling me I could not go to the church parsonage anymore?

"Why?" I asked.

"I overheard Jeremy and Jenny on the phone, and I heard the language those two are using," Dad said. "You're probably using it too. Plus the stuff they were talking about with each other should not be talked about that way by kids your age."

Embarrassment crept over my face. I had no defense. Unlike my time in the principal's office, I saw no way to persuade Dad to change his mind. And I knew he was right. I responded with a sheepish "Okay."

A few moments passed. Then he added, "You've got to be able to choose better friends. I'm going to help you choose them until you're old enough to choose them on your own."

I was not happy to hear Dad's assessment, but I also admired him for taking a bold, direct stand with me. I had been caught, and his strong response impressed me. That ended my friendship with Jeremy.

In the middle of my seventh-grade school year, a ministry group from Michigan called Life Action came to do a week's worth of presentations at my school. The group was made up of young people and couples who traveled in RVs, performed skits and music about what it means to be a Christian, and took students through a thick, impressive notebook that tackled life's biggest issues in an inviting way with lots of illustrations and diagrams. It was called the Master Control seminar, and it was like nothing I had ever seen.

Every session and each page seemed to be speaking just to me. The seminar addressed what it looked like to live as a Christian, how to wrestle with temptation, how to address sins and failures, and even our purpose for living. The entire week I felt as if the leaders knew all about my current struggles.

The notebook covered so many topics in such practical, real-life ways. I filled the margins with notes from the presentations and engaged with the various interactive illustrations and diagrams. At some point in my listening and jotting, I realized just how far from God I was—but I also knew there was the possibility of rescue.

In the gymnasium of the school where we met for the week, transformation began in my heart at a deeper level than in my early days of Awana or with my decision to follow Christ at the birthday party for Jesus. I had been told and preached at all of my life, "Start living your life for Jesus Christ now." I felt I had made the commitment to do that but didn't understand the next steps. I had been left asking, "How do I do that?" Life Action answered that question for me and gave clear, Bible-based guidance on how to live my life as a young Christian.

I was especially surprised when the leaders addressed "Dating, Marriage, and Sex"—and pornography specifically. I had not heard that topic addressed in my church, and here was this group of young people talking openly about battling it. With my life in a state of turmoil and duplicity, I deeply wanted the "master control" the seminar offered.

While I didn't talk to Mom or Dad much about what was going on, they both were consistent examples to me of the struggle of the Christian life. Within all the chaos of our home and their relationship with each other, I observed their desire to follow Christ. Their attempts to read the Bible and pray, their commitment to our church, their desire to live out what they were hearing from the pulpit at Twin Branch and on the Christian radio station—all of this was obvious to me. Yes, it was occasionally drowned out by the brokenness Mom exhibited in her outbursts and by Dad's misguided attempts to respond to her effectively. But their commitment was still apparent. The transformation they showed as they walked with Christ was real, even with all of the abnormalities of their lives.

With my own internal struggle between the way I was living and the way I knew I *should* be living, I began to see my parents' struggle differently. I could see how they had grown in spite of Mom's challenges and Dad's poor responses. This new perspective added greater fuel to my resolve to live the Christian life.

As convicted as I felt, my behavior and words were still in the process of changing, and I still had a reputation among my friends for being as rebellious as they were. Most of my teachers and the adults at church thought I was the picture-perfect Christian kid, but my friends knew the real Shawn.

At the end of the school year, we all gathered in the gym for the final assembly. Dr. Bowling droned on, handing out awards to various students. One award caught my attention.

"Each year we ask the faculty and staff to pick one young woman and one young man from the entire junior and senior high student body who have demonstrated the highest levels of Christian maturity and character," he said. He named the female award winner, who made her way up amid applause. She received a nice plaque with her name on it. I was happy for her and knew she deserved it.

"The male student chosen this year—" he said.

I sat in my seat feeling smug. Whoever was chosen was bound to be someone my friends and I had harassed.

"...to receive the 1980 Christian Character Award is . . . Shawn Thornton."

I was shocked. While the other kids clapped, I stood up, face red with embarrassment. My friends whispered under their breath mockingly, using words they knew I used—words that did not match the award I was receiving.

"Christian Character Award, huh?" Ricky whispered. "You? What a joke."

I walked forward. Dr. Bowling shook my hand and then interrupted the applause to say something.

"I have to apologize to Shawn," he said. "Your plaque came from the trophy company with a few errors. We will have to get a new one made, and you can come by the school and pick it up later this summer."

That only made the moment more awkward. I returned to my seat empty-handed and sensed God telling me, *You don't deserve that award. Adults in your life see one thing, and your friends see something else. You are living a double life.*

I recalled a specific teaching from the Master Control seminar that had struck me. The book of James talks about a double-minded person being unstable in all of his ways. I realized that was me. As much as I wanted to follow Christ fully, I remained double minded. God used the award to make me realize this. I knew things needed to change.

The school never called me that summer about a replacement plaque.

Dad, who drove a bus part-time for the school I attended, must have caught wind of the bad influences there. He pulled Troy and me out and put us in another, smaller Christian school in town. Troy was in fifth grade, and I was in eighth. The move infuriated and discouraged me since I was forced to leave the familiar environment and all my friends. But God also seemed to be whispering that this would give me a greater chance to break some bad habits and do what Dad had challenged me to do—pick better friends.

To my amazement, my new school brought in Life Action for a weeklong seminar during the second week of the new school year. I sat through the same presentations and went through the same book without a moment of boredom. I knew God was purposefully seeking me out. I filled the margins with even more notes.

Soon after my second trip through the Master Control seminar, I was walking down Victory Road heading back from our mailbox. As I walked, I felt the close presence of God in a way I had never felt it before. His love, peace, and purpose for me were so plain, so real. His words, though not audible, pressed upon me: *You need to stop what you're doing with Steve, Lance, and the others. You now have an opportunity to make new friends. You can start fresh. I'm going to do things with your life. It's time to make some choices.*

God felt so close and so attentive to me that I was sure this was a defining moment.

"You're right," I said aloud, staring down at the black, shiny cinders crunching under my feet. "I'm deciding now: I will never look at those things again."

The next day I had a chance to test that decision with my closest friend, Lance.

"Hey, let's go look at my dad's magazines," he said. Lance and I were alone in his house.

I looked directly at him. "I'm not going to do that

anymore," I said. He looked back at me blankly. "I can't do that anymore," I repeated.

"Don't be an idiot. Of course you want to."

"Yeah, I want to, but I'm not going to do that anymore—or at least that's my plan," I said. I felt a new power behind the decision, but I also understood my own weaknesses enough to know that my strength would have to come from God.

Lance shrugged, and we did something else.

Throughout this time, Mom often mentioned to me that she was praying for me. She said this genuinely, not applying motherly guilt. I doubt she knew all that I was doing with friends. At first I resisted her mention of prayers for me. *You might want to pray for yourself*, I would think. *Your language and behavior isn't all that pleasing to God.*

As time passed and God continued to work in my heart, Mom's reminders that she was praying for me became little milestones of how God was at work in my life—even though Mom was completely in the dark about my struggles with insecurity, vulgarity, and pornography.

A week after taking a stand with Lance, I was walking up the forested, sloping highway alongside the gravel pit on the way to Steve's place. We were going to meet at the abandoned house.

But I felt God speaking to me again as I walked. *You know when you get there, you're going to have to tell him the same thing you told Lance. You're going to have a moment where you make a decision: Are you going to live for me or not?*

I know, I thought, feeling the weight of the decision again—and the potential loss of friendship.

I looked down at the gravel and my worn-out shoes as I

walked. A knot of determination formed in me: *I'm going to tell Steve I can't do this anymore.*

God wasn't done. *You're going to have to decide what kind of language you're going to use too.*

Whenever Steve and I got together, we cussed a lot, making ourselves feel grown up and powerful.

I responded, *I will from this point forward never, ever, ever use foul language again.* While this commitment seemed like a big one, a key principle I had learned from the Master Control seminar was that when we submit ourselves to God, he gives us the self-control needed to deal with our personal vices. Removing pornography and cussing from my life would be my first steps of trusting God to demonstrate his power in my life.

The abandoned house was small. The doors and windows were all gone, the fixtures and copper stripped away. Gray paint peeled off the exterior boards. Graffiti scarred the inside walls. Trees grew through some of the floorboards. It was dark, shadowy, and empty and sat near the pond we swam in at the gravel pit.

"I don't have the magazines anymore," Steve said as I walked up. "Someone took them."

I wondered who. Maybe his parents. Maybe other kids. But I was relieved. We sat there and talked for a while, but the energy seemed to have gone out of our meetings. No foul language came from my lips. I walked home feeling light, free, and certain that God had a vision for my life that was just beginning to unfold.

I didn't know the worst times for our family were just ahead.

CHAPTER 9

THE FRONT DOOR SLAMMED. Mom's words hung in the air: "I'm divorcing you tomorrow!" She walked off into the night, fuming and cursing. The conflicts in our home were growing angrier, more frequent, and more personal and were escalating. Mom often threw things at Dad, called her sisters for help, and pledged to kill Dad and Troy and me. Sometimes Dad called one of Mom's relatives and simply said, "Come get her." We knew it was bad when Dad reached out for help. Mom's lows afterward got even lower. Our dismal routine was compressed into one long blur of tension and irresolution.

Twenty minutes after Mom left, Dad walked out the back door. I heard the car (which had replaced the Magic Bus) start and pull away. Lady and I lay on my bed waiting for them to return. I scratched her head and smoothed her fur as tears ran down my cheeks. Troy played in his bedroom.

"Why do things have to be this way?" I asked God directly. "Why couldn't they be more normal?" I didn't even know what *normal* meant.

I never got a direct answer.

We celebrated my fourteenth birthday just before Christmas. A week later, on December 28, 1980, a petty argument broke out between Mom and Dad and turned into a real battle in the kitchen.

"Go to your rooms," Dad said sternly to Troy and me after a while. We closed our doors behind us gently, as if this act would help calm things down.

Outside our doors, Mom was screaming, things were breaking, and Dad was yelling back.

Crash-crash-crash!

"You're the reason I'm this way! If it wasn't for you and your stupid driving!"

"Oh yeah?"

"Yeah!"

"Well, who needs you anyway?"

It seemed like whole counters were being emptied of piled-up junk with the sweep of an arm.

This is not a normal fight, I told myself. *This is a freak storm.*

"Ow! Beverly!" Dad shouted. I imagined her scratching him with her nails as she was prone to do.

"I'm getting a lawyer!" she shrieked.

"Get one! I've heard it all before. Nothing ever changes!"

The paper thud of the phone book let me know he'd thrown it in her direction, daring her to call.

It seemed the craziness would never end. Usually Dad backed down, or Mom grabbed her loom or a book or walked out the door or called one of her sisters. Tonight both were all in. It was a fight to the finish. Neither would give up.

Peering through the gap between my warped bedroom door and the door frame, I saw some of the action. Dad was holding Mom, and she was grappling with him in a sort of boxer's clench. They were standing in the kitchen.

"Ow, John! You're hurting me!" she yelled. She had been switching back and forth between crying and screaming.

He equaled her volume as he shouted back, "You let go of me, and I'll let go of you!"

Mom relented, but as soon as Dad let her go, she caught him off guard and shoved him into the fridge. He shoved her back, knocking her off balance and against the stove. She almost fell to the floor, barely catching herself as she stumbled. She had scratched her arm, and this produced an angry rage that was beyond anything I had ever seen from her. She began to hurl anything and everything at Dad and around the room. Dishes, glasses—anything she could reach soared and shattered everywhere.

Dad backed off and retreated to the bathroom, peering into the mirror to check his wounds. He left the bathroom door open to keep track of Mom's movements and actions. She headed to their bedroom and moved past a mirror that hung in her route.

"F— you, John!" she screamed, among many other

obscenities. She pulled the mirror from the wall and flung it to the floor, where it shattered into hundreds of pieces. She slammed the bedroom door behind herself, uttering one more loud obscenity at Dad.

At that point, Dad seemed to believe the fit had passed. He came into the kitchen to assess the damage. It was the normal pattern of calm following a horrendous storm.

Just then their bedroom door swung open. Mom spewed vulgarities at Dad and threw his toiletries and personal items out the door. Everything exploded again with renewed screaming, throwing, cussing, shoving, and name-calling. It seemed it would never end. I knew instinctively that something was different tonight—that Mom was having some type of emotional or nervous breakdown.

With my arm wrapped tightly around Lady, I stared at a certain spot in the ceiling tile in the corner of my room. I often fixed my eyes on this spot for long stretches while Mom and Dad fought. I could sense Lady looking at me with her gentle eyes as if she wanted to give me the answers I needed to hear. Clutching her and with tears streaming down my face, I looked at the corner of the ceiling and prayed, "God, why am I here? Why this family? Why couldn't I have been born into one of my friends' families? One of the normal ones? Lord, just do something. Get me out of this mess!"

I wanted out any way possible, and I meant it.

Just when I thought the house might collapse from the violence, Mom and Dad stopped yelling. An eerie silence pressed against my ears. I settled back into bed wondering what was happening outside my room. I didn't want to get up and look. Lady lay still beside me. I listened intently to the silence. I had longed for it. Now it seemed frightening and as unwelcome as the disturbing sounds of the night-long fight.

The silence was interrupted by the sound of car wheels on the cinders of Victory Road.

Blue and red lights flashed across our lawn and against our house. I looked out my window to see a squad car. Then there was a knock at our front door. Dad opened it, and a police officer came in. I heard them talking but could not make out their words. Mom flared up again several times, with each episode followed by Dad's scolding, irritated voice. After a while the front door opened again. I looked out my window and saw the officer escorting Mom to the car, holding her tightly as they walked across the bumpy lawn. I felt like someone had hit me in the stomach, and I was glad that Troy's window did not face the front of the house. I did not want him to see what I was seeing. The officer closed the door for Mom, and the car pulled away, leaving us in vacant silence.

For the first time I wondered, *Is Mom ever coming back? Is this really how our journey as a family ends?*

She and Dad had used the word *divorce* so many times over the years. Maybe this time they would act on it. How would they ever reconcile after a fight of this magnitude? Who was wrong? Who was right?

After a while another car arrived. I waited for what seemed to be the appropriate amount of time, then opened my bedroom door. Grandma Thornton was there, quietly sweeping up piles of the glass and mirror fragments that littered the kitchen and hallway floor. Troy slowly opened his bedroom door and noticed Grandma too.

"Hi, Grandma," I said, as if everything were normal.

"Hi, boys," she said to both of us, as if it weren't nearly midnight.

Troy and I glanced at each other with a sense of relief. Someone else was here now, and not just anyone—Grandma. Mom and Dad weren't going to fight anymore tonight. Mom was gone—where, we didn't know. Dad was piddling around the house, helping Grandma a little but mostly trying to keep his mind occupied, it seemed. He flitted around the house like a bird that was not allowed to land, as though he were concentrating but could not settle his thoughts. I knew he was conducting a mental evaluation of what had just happened.

I was too. Perhaps the months of heightened conflict would stop and normal patterns would be reestablished somehow. Or maybe this night had truly changed everything, and my family was done for.

Throughout the entire next day, I felt sick to my stomach, wondering where Mom was and what would happen when she returned. *She must be at Aunt Sue's house,* I thought. *But why so long? Will Mom finally call the lawyer and go through with a divorce?* In that numb waiting period, Troy and I watched TV and tried to disappear into its alternate reality. Grandma set out plates of snacks and sandwiches for us.

Dad came home from work late in the afternoon. He

and Grandma talked quietly in the kitchen. I listened as best I could.

"She's at Memorial Hospital in South Bend," Dad said.

"Okay. Where?" Grandma asked.

"Seventh floor. Mental ward."

"Really?"

"That's where they put her."

"When will they release her?"

"I have no idea."

"Are you going to go visit her?"

"That's the thing. I can't!" Dad said, shutting a cabinet door hard and filling a glass with something from the fridge. "Sue's the only one who can visit. Because there was a 'domestic dispute' involved, they won't let me near the place. Domestic dispute! I wish they'd been here and seen who was disputing who."

Grandma took it in quietly. When she left a little while later, Troy and I went home with her to stay with her and Grandpa indefinitely. Grandpa took us home most mornings before school to get clothes or other things we needed for the day. It wasn't easy living between two homes. But it was best for now.

One morning while we were at our house getting stuff together for school, Mom called.

"Hello?" I said, picking up the phone.

"Hi, Shawn. It's your mother."

"Hi, Mom," I said, my heart beating faster. "Where are you?"

"At the hospital."

I felt some relief and sadness in that.

"How is it?" I asked.

She sighed. "Oh, fine, I guess, except that the Virgin Mary and Santa Claus are fighting."

She laughed.

Maybe Mom has *gone crazy*, I thought. "What are you talking about, Mom?"

"The Virgin Mary and Santa Claus both live here, and they're not getting along," she said. As she talked, it made sense: the Christmas season had just passed, and two of the new residents had taken on the identities of key figures of the season. Everyone else in the ward called them by their imagined names because it was easier.

"How are you doing there, Mom?" I asked.

"I like the food," she said. She seemed relaxed and funny, in such contrast to the last time I had seen her.

"Yeah?"

"And the puzzles and games," she said. "And most people are calm because they're on medicine."

"It sounds like you're having a vacation," I said.

"Well, maybe not a vacation, but it is peaceful in some ways. I just wanted to call and see how you boys were. Tell Troy I love him, and I love you, too. I'll see you soon."

"Okay, Mom. Bye."

We hung up.

Where did she get access to a phone? I wondered afterward.

The next day about the same time, Mom called again.

"Good morning, Shawn."

"Hi, Mom. How are you doing?"

"Better. Santa Claus quit yelling at everyone."

"That's good."

"I don't think your dad can come visit me. They won't let him."

"I think you're right."

"But I need a couple of things," she said.

"What?"

"Could you have him send them up to me?"

"Okay. What are they?" I asked, grabbing a pencil to write it down.

"Just have him bring me two things," she repeated.

"Okay. I'm ready."

She paused, then said, "My Bible and the *Joni* book."

I wrote them down, and we said good-bye. When Dad got home, he studied my note, put the two books in a small box, and set them aside to give to Aunt Sue for delivery.

Aunt Connie went to see Mom before Aunt Sue's next visit, so she delivered the books and a vase of flowers, which the doctors wouldn't allow on the seventh floor. Orderlies escorted Mom to a visitor's room, where Aunt Connie was waiting. Mom looked refreshed.

"Are you feeling better?" Aunt Connie asked.

"I'm working on it," Mom said. "There's a lot of crazy people in here, but I like the activities."

"Maybe they'll get you some help—some counseling or therapy or something," Aunt Connie said.

"Oh! My books," Mom said, noticing the Bible and *Joni*. She eagerly grabbed them.

A few weeks into her stay, Mom called the house again.

"Shawn?"

"Yeah, Mom?"

"Come get me out of here."

She didn't sound as peaceful this time. I heard funny noises and voices in the background, obviously coming from fellow patients. Mom sounded tired and done with her experience there. Unlike most of her fellow seventh-floor patients, Mom did not have ongoing mental problems, at least not the way they did. She did not need to be on heavy medications. Once her outbursts passed, she was completely sane. Now she was surrounded by people who were unable to function in normal society at any level.

"I don't think I can get you out," I said. "I'm fourteen. I don't even have my driver's license."

"I've thought it through," she said. "If you come at night to visit me, we can go through a door in the visitors' room that leads to the elevator. Once we get to the ground floor, we can walk to the pay phone at the drug store nearby, so they won't be looking for us. Then we can call a taxi to take us home."

"Uh, Mom, we'd better just wait and see what the doctors say."

She sighed. "I don't know what I'm doing here."

"I know, Mom. I know it's hard."

"This woman came into my room last night," she said.

"Who was it?"

"I don't know, but she was naked and hysterical and wanted to get into my closet."

I had no ready response for that. "Did they take her out?"

"Well, yeah, but it was weird, and it woke me up," Mom said.

I didn't know what else to say. "What are you doing today?"

"There's a group therapy meeting," she said. "Oh, Shawn! They have lots of coloring books here, and they like us to paint and create artwork. I like that a lot."

In some ways, being in the mental ward sounded like day camp. And Mom didn't have to deal with Dad, Troy, or me.

"But I miss you boys," she said. "I'll call whenever I can. Next time I'll talk to Troy."

"Okay. Bye, Mom."

Mom's sisters continued to visit her. While Aunt Sue was the main contact, Connie and Gail were there frequently. Aunt April lived out of state and checked on Mom via Nana and my aunts. Soon Aunt Sue began telling Dad of an almost miraculous recovery reported by the psychiatric staff at the hospital.

"Bev's starting to walk normally," she said several weeks after Mom was admitted. "She's regaining her fine motor skills. She's more mobile and flexible. She can bend her knees."

"Really?" Dad said. It didn't seem possible.

The doctors confirmed Aunt Sue's report.

"She is improving rapidly," they told Dad by phone. "When she comes home, she will be able to do normal housework, and there will be no more angry mood swings."

"Okay," Dad said, daring to believe. "That's great."

He pictured Mom riding a two-wheel bike, perhaps

driving a car, cooking and cleaning, jogging, shopping, taking Troy and me places, and living as a typical mother and wife. The spark of a dream they both shared came alive again. Perhaps normal life was within reach.

Dad arrived on the seventh floor with Aunt Sue for his reunion with Mom. Dr. DeLasalle sat him down with gravity and occasion.

"John, I want to prepare you for what you are about to see, because Beverly has had some real breakthroughs in these few weeks," he said. "We are amazed at her progress. You need to be ready, because your wife is not the same person who came in here that night. She has been released from the emotions that were locking her up. I don't know if I've ever seen this kind of improvement from someone who came in like she did. She is a different woman."

Dad took it in soberly. Hope soared in his heart. The curse of the accident was about to be lifted. Mom's torment, and ours, seemed to be at an end.

Aunt Sue looked at Dad with a reassuring look.

Dr. DeLasalle turned to the nurse. "Bring Beverly in."

The nurse went through a side door. Moments later the door opened and Mom stood there. She spied Dad, and her eyes lit up. She couldn't suppress a smile.

"Beverly, walk across the room," the doctor said.

Mom began. In her normal, stiff fashion, she made her way across the room. Dad wordlessly tried to discern some difference.

"Now show John the mobility you have in your arms," Dr. DeLasalle said.

Mom stopped in the middle of the room and made circular motions with her arms and hands. Her range of motion and fluidity were no better than before. Fingers stiff, arms slightly bent.

Dr. DeLasalle looked at Dad with evident pride. Mom beamed at him as well. Dad sat there not knowing how to react.

It's the same woman I've seen every day of our fifteen years of marriage, he thought. Then, *Maybe* I'm *the crazy one. Maybe I'm jaded or can't see the improvements they see. If this medical doctor and psychiatrist and Bev and her sister all see her as cured, maybe I'm nuts.*

It occurred to him that he might be in a *Twilight Zone* episode where the twist at the end is that Dad was the one who had been disabled by the accident and there had never been anything wrong with Mom.

"In three weeks she won't even be walking with those minor difficulties," Dr. DeLasalle said. "She will continue to improve until she's completely whole."

Dad began to say, "She's been walking like that since she was fourteen, buddy. I don't see any difference at all." But he held his tongue.

"Thanks for your work" was all he could manage. Dr. DeLasalle took this as deeply felt gratitude. He let Mom say good-bye to Dad. The nurse escorted her out, and Aunt Sue followed. Dad was still not able to visit Mom alone yet. Dr. DeLasalle smiled, took his chart, and walked to the door.

"Congratulations," he said turning back, then he was gone.

Dad's disappointment crescendoed as he left the hospital. That night, lying in bed alone, he pieced together what must have happened. When Mom left the house the night of their fight, she had been almost completely locked up with stiffness and anger. She could barely walk, talk, or move her arms. Normally this stiffness would subside after these kinds of outbursts. But since this one pushed Mom further than before, she must have stayed physically locked up for days, even after the emotions dissipated. When she arrived at Memorial Hospital, they must have thought this was Mom's usual state. When she finally relaxed, as she always did after an argument, it must have seemed to them like a miraculous recovery.

They didn't even ask about the accident, he thought. *They don't know anything about her medical history. They thought it was all in her head.*

Dad smoldered in the dark, feeling anew the devastation of Mom's condition and ruing his gullibility.

"I was a fool," he said. "I believed them."

•   •   •

"We're going to see your mother at Aunt Sue's," Dad said. Troy and I hadn't seen Mom for weeks. Dad had been able to visit her at the hospital, but she was not allowed home yet, and as minors we were not allowed to visit the psychiatric ward. We put on our cleanest clothes and went to the car.

Mom was sitting on a sofa in Aunt Sue's living room when we walked in. Aunts Connie and Gail were there too, keeping Mom company.

"Hello, boys. You can spend some time with your mom now," Aunt Connie said with a smile and walked into the other room.

Mom's eyes were glowing with excitement to see us. Troy and I looked at her awkwardly, not knowing how to "spend time" with her outside of our normal context at home. She was more relaxed than we had seen her in a while. She looked good and well cared for. Dad stood behind us. There seemed to be a different dynamic between the two of them, a kind of peace agreement.

"Don't just stand there. Come over and give me a hug," Mom said. Troy and I walked over to her outstretched arms, and she pulled us close for the first time in so long. She was real, flesh and blood, not just a voice on the phone. After squeezing us, she reached behind her and pulled out a canvas.

"I want you to have this," she said. "It's a watercolor painting I made at the hospital."

I took the painting in my hands and looked at it. It wasn't half bad. I could kind of tell it was a barn in a field with a sunrise behind it.

"Thanks, Mom," I said. "That's real nice."

"Yeah," agreed Troy.

We were both on our best behavior. Dad had demanded it.

Mom gripped our hands and pulled us in closer. I thought she might hug us again. Instead she spoke in a low voice so no one else could hear.

"You've got to get me out of there," she said.

Troy and I looked at each other helplessly.

"You'll be home soon," I reassured her.

"Yes, but you've got to get me out," she said. "Think of something."

After visiting a little while longer, we said good-bye and went home with Dad. Aunt Sue took Mom back to the hospital.

"That was good," Dad said on the way to Grandma and Grandpa's, going out of his way to praise the visit. "It's good you boys got to see your mother."

We had three other visits with Mom. Every time she showed us more of her art, gripped our hands, pulled us in, and made the same request: "Get me out of that place."

I took it as a good sign: she knew she had emotional and mental challenges but was more lucid than many of the folks on the seventh floor. And she wanted to come home.

Though Mom was doing better, I was in turmoil. Nothing about the previous year and that terrible night seemed resolved. I desperately needed to talk about it, but Dad was a man of few words, and Troy was young and didn't seem to care as much as I did. My friends had no idea what was happening, and no one who knew our situation suggested we see a counselor or even talk to someone at church.

But one evening at church, not long after Mom went into the mental ward, I was just leaving the men's room when Mark DeMateo, our youth pastor, approached the door. Mark worked part-time at our church and part-time as an orderly at Memorial Hospital.

Mark saw me and paused. No one else was in that area of the building.

"Shawn, I wanted to tell you that I was there at the hospital the night your mom arrived," he said. "I was assigned to help transport her from the emergency room up to the seventh floor."

The simple fact that someone outside my family acknowledged what had happened brought two parts of my life together. I felt like healing began instantly.

"I just want you to know that she's doing well," he said. "Your mom loves you. She'll be okay. God's going to take you through this. Trust God."

In that moment I was so comforted that I felt I could get through months of uncertainty, if necessary. I had never been so thankful for the church in my life. Mark became a key voice for God in my life during the months that followed. After Troy and I got to see Mom at Aunt Sue's, Mark was the only person outside our family I felt I could talk to about our visit.

But I decided to widen the circle. One day at school my Bible class teacher asked, "Before we begin, are there any prayer requests?"

For the first time in the weeks since Mom was hospitalized, I got up the gumption to request prayer for her. Fearing my classmates would find out she was in the mental ward, I slipped my hand up and simply said, "Pray for my mom. She's been in the hospital."

A concerned girl in my class blurted out, "Why is she in the hospital, Shawn?"

"Because she's sick," I replied with no further explanation.

My answer seemed to satisfy the class, and the teacher prayed for Mom. Something told me others were praying too. I was comforted that we were bringing Mom and her problems before God.

When class was dismissed, my teacher pulled me aside as my classmates filed out of the room.

"Shawn, I know the situation with your mom, and I want you to know I'm praying for your whole family," he said.

By this time many other people had told me the same thing, but for some reason my teacher's words carried significance. I knew God had given them to me as a special gift.

"Thank you," I said awkwardly. "It means a lot."

I continued to lie on my bed for long stretches, volleying questions at God. He did not answer them directly, although Lady listened patiently. But those passing conversations with Mark and my teacher broke through my loneliness and connected me with the world around me again. I felt God had profoundly ministered to me through them.

Six weeks after Mom went into the mental ward, doctors let her come home for an evening with Dad. It was right around Valentine's Day. By this time Troy and I were spending some nights with Dad on Victory Road.

Troy and I came home from school that day to see something strange—the house was completely clean. Dad had picked everything up and even scrubbed the floors, the counters, and the table and vacuumed the carpet. For once our house looked fairly normal. I liked it.

Sitting in the center of the now-bare dining table were a stuffed bear, a box of candy, a flower, and a card. The envelope, in Dad's handwriting, was addressed, "To My Angel."

Troy and I went to Grandma and Grandpa's for the night.

Six weeks later, Mom came home for good. She had spent three months in the mental ward.

Dad sat us down before she arrived.

"Your mom's coming home," he said. "Things are going to be different. We're not going to give her as much guff. She is who she is. She's not going to change. The psychiatrists at the hospital are stupid. The counselors are stupid. The medical doctors are stupid. Dr. DeLasalle—what an idiot. What a waste of an education. They haven't been able to help her 'cause they don't even know what's wrong with her. So it's up to us. Lay off talking back to her. Quit fighting her on stuff. I will too."

Troy took this with a shrug. I took it as a potentially seismic shift in our family life.

Mom came home, happy and relieved.

"It's so good to see you boys!" she said, squeezing us. "Wow, look at this place."

Within a few hours our house seemed the way it was before Mom went to the hospital. Mom had brought a stack of coloring books with her. These joined her loom and the piles of Bibles and novels that quickly regathered around her chair. Among them were several by Janette Oke, who someone told us lived in Mishawaka and whose husband taught at the college on Miracle Lane, where Mom's accident had taken place. Dad made dinner that night and the next night and many nights from then on. The house slowly became cluttered again but not nearly as bad as before. Dad rallied Troy and me to help him straighten everything out. Now that we were old enough, it seemed easier.

Dr. DeLasalle, the psychiatrist, wanted Mom to see a psychologist regularly after she came home. On her second visit, the psychologist asked Dad to come as well. He complied.

"John, tell me about your childhood," the woman asked. Dad fumbled through an unwilling response. When the appointment was over, he and Mom walked back to the car, arm in arm.

"We are not going back," Dad said, shaking his head. "These people are crazy."

Mom agreed. She didn't like the experience either.

Back home, Dad took his own counsel, the same counsel he had given us. He gave in to Mom more often so their arguments wouldn't get out of hand, and instead of complaining, he simply worked around Mom's limitations or did things himself. Conflict didn't disappear completely, but it rarely rose to the level it had been at regularly before.

I noticed that the more Mom and Dad showed each other mercy and forgiveness, the more it created a healthy cycle for all of us. Mom still had outbursts, still cussed at us, and still threatened to divorce or kill Dad regularly. Dad still struggled with properly responding to Mom's outbursts. But something took root in Dad, some decision to be gracious moment by moment, not just at church but in our home. Troy and I caught on and tried to emulate him, however imperfectly. All of us seemed to improve enough to avoid another night like the one we had experienced, though our home was still anything but normal.

We had been through a kind of hell, and the worst seemed behind us.

CHAPTER 10

I WAS EIGHT YEARS OLD the first time I preached.

We were snowed in that Sunday morning, so I grabbed a fold-up metal music stand that I used when I practiced guitar and held a service of my own.

"Please stand for the opening hymn," I said, putting words in the mouth of my imaginary song leader. The "congregation" was an invisible group of people in our living room.

During the song, I sat in a chair positioned behind and to the left of the music stand as if I were sitting on the platform waiting to preach. There I sang from a hymnal with the rest of the congregation. Then I came to the pulpit with my Bible, directed the ushers to take an offering, gave announcements, and delivered my message. Dozens of invisible people were moved by my sermon and came forward to pray.

Every time we missed church due to weather, I brought out the music stand, a kitchen chair, my Bible, and a hymnal and eagerly led an hour-long service on my own.

"Shawn, take it to your bedroom," Dad said one Sunday, unwilling to endure another church service led by a grade-schooler.

Mom kept a baby book for me, noting things about my childhood periodically and sometimes randomly. When I was in kindergarten, she filled in the space that asked what I wanted to be when I grew up.

"A pastor, just like Pastor Jones," I had told her. Mom was supportive of the idea, even then.

• • •

A few months after Mom came home from the hospital, our church held its missions conference, an annual event that encouraged people to support missionary work around the world. It always started on Wednesday and culminated on Sunday night with a keynote speaker who rallied the church behind missions giving and missions work. That night we heard from a dynamic speaker named Donald Hurlbert.

At the end of his message he asked, "Is there anyone here who believes God is calling them to serve him vocationally? Any young person who is willing to say to God, 'Here is my life. Use it any way you want and anywhere you want'?" Then he said, "If so, I would like to ask you to stand."

My heart burned. *That's me,* I thought. The whole conference had captured my imagination. It felt purposeful, momentous, important. And now, on this last night, I believed God was calling me to a new level of commitment, even if I didn't fully understand it. I stood up.

"I see you, young man," Hurlbert said pointing to me. "And another—I see you, young lady. Three, four—five of you tonight."

This is huge, I thought. *I am pledging my life to a cause bigger than me.*

But what does that mean?

The next morning I didn't feel any different, but I knew the commitment I had made required me to do something. *I'd better start reading my Bible and praying more if I'm going to be serious about this,* I thought.

But I also wanted to get actively involved in ministry in some way. The first thing that came to mind was helping with Child Evangelism Fellowship, the ministry Mom had been involved with when she was young. Since I had attended a number of their ministries over the years, I knew the local ministry director. I called him and expressed my interest in helping.

That week I attended my first training session on Thursday night with seven other people, all adults. The CEF director taught us how to teach children the Bible effectively.

When I showed Mom my notes from class, her eyes sparkled.

"That's like what they taught us when I was working with Child Evangelism Fellowship," she said. "Go up into the attic and find my old materials. They are in an old box up there. I want to look at them with you."

Mom was so excited that she went with me to the next training session and to several more after that. A new and different bond was forming between us that helped make the chaos we had experienced together fade in significance.

Within a few months, I was teaching two CEF after-school Good News Clubs for elementary age kids. For a few summers I taught CEF 5-Day Clubs. Both the after-school and summer clubs met in homes in our community.

That same school year, I also plugged back into Awana at church. It had moved to Wednesday nights, and I was teaching and serving enthusiastically with the Sparks Club, which was for kindergarten through second grade.

Within months of standing up at the final service of the missions conference at church, I was teaching 100 to 150 kids each week—and having the time of my life. I moved the music stand—my childhood pulpit—permanently into my bedroom and spent hours practicing creative ways to convey Bible stories. My room, which had been at times a hideaway from the chaos of my home, became my place of preparation for the work I had been called to do.

• • •

Twin Branch Bible Church had gone through a couple of pastors since Pastor Jones left ten years before. Three months after the most recent pastor left, Pastor Jones returned. I was thrilled to have my early childhood hero back. Within a few weeks, Pastor Jones asked to meet with me.

"Shawn, I know you're teaching kids in Awana and else-where," he said. "How would you like to try preaching in a service?"

I was stunned. I had been preaching under Mark DeMateo, our youth pastor, at the nursing home, but since I was just sixteen, preaching at the church was more than I had hoped for.

"I'm scared, but I'd love to," I said.

Within weeks, Pastor Jones had me guest teach some adult Sunday school classes. Soon I had my first opportunity to preach in an evening service. It felt unreal to be facing the pews I had always sat in, but I was electrified by it.

I did my best to follow Mark's sermon preparation advice: find a passage of the Bible that speaks to you, discover its main idea, and meditate on it.

"Then comes the hard part," he had told me over dinner. "You have to live it out. That truth needs to come alive in you. You always preach to yourself first."

My message was from an Old Testament passage about God's people approaching him with humility. When I fin-ished preaching, I didn't know how well I had done until people started lining up to talk with me.

"You're a natural, Shawn!" said one woman who had been in the church my whole life. "You are going to become a fine preacher. Keep at it."

Another woman grasped my hand. "I remember when you stood at the missions conference," she said. "You're right on track."

A dozen others lined up to encourage me. They were like

family. Many had taught me over the years or had allowed me to serve with them. Their support buoyed my spirits.

And at the end of the line I saw Dad. When everyone else was gone, he came up. I held my breath waiting for his assessment.

"Well, it was a twenty-minute sermon, and you could have done it in ten," he said. That was it. Suddenly, the other comments dimmed by comparison.

"Okay, Dad," I said, reassuring myself that he just didn't know how to give compliments.

Dad had always been economical with his praise. He didn't like the idea of blowing hot air at someone, so he withheld compliments most of the time, trying instead to show love by his actions. But I was insecure, and I desperately needed his approval.

When Dad said something critical to me, as fathers inevitably do, and Dad did more than some, I was crushed. Sometimes I went to my room and cried. Troy seemed to take Dad's criticism in the same stride with which he took the chaos of our home, but Mom knew Dad's harsh words bothered me a lot.

One Sunday evening while driving home from church, Dad criticized the brief message I had preached in the service. Mom hit the roof.

"John, shut the f— up!" she said. "Leave the kid alone. You try and get up there and talk in front of people and do a better job than Shawn did."

I knew this would draw a response from Dad, and it did.

"Easy. I could do a better job than he did, anytime."

"No you can't!" Mom screamed.

Dad knew it was best not to push Mom, and I think he believed if he continued, it might hurt me. He seemed unaware that his words had already done their damage.

One day that summer I had to drive Dad to work in the morning so I could use our '79 Pinto throughout the day. Part of taking Dad to work involved picking up his coworker and carpool partner Arkie. Arkie was near retirement age. He was a heavy smoker with a deep Southern accent and had missing teeth and leathery skin.

We pulled up to Arkie's humble house, and Arkie came out the front door.

"Who's this?" he asked Dad, sticking his head in the backseat.

"This is Shawn, my oldest son," Dad said.

"Hi, Shawn!" Arkie said as he wedged himself in the back. He stuck his weathered old head between our seats, and I could smell cigarettes and chewing tobacco as if the odors were embedded in his very pores.

We drove for a few minutes with Dad and Arkie chatting about work-related things, forgetting I was in the car. Then Arkie leaned forward and stuck his head between the two front bucket seats again.

"So, you're Shawn. Your dad has told me a lot about you," he said. "He's so proud of you. You're the one that preaches a lot. He told me about that sermon you preached at your church recently, how the people loved it. He was so proud of you."

"Oh, Arkie, shut up. He doesn't want to hear any of that,"

Dad said, but a subtle smile spread across my face. I could hardly believe Dad had been bragging about me behind my back.

"No, I'm serious," Arkie said. "He talks about you all the time, and all the good stuff you do. We can't get him to shut up about you at work."

In the passenger seat, Dad fidgeted as Arkie kept talking.

"Your dad thinks the world of you," Arkie said as we approached the foundry. I almost wanted to take a longer route just to keep hearing him talk. "He's always telling us what you did lately. He has even quoted parts of your sermons to us."

"Cut it out, Arkie. We're sick of hearing it," Dad said, looking out his window.

I pulled the Pinto up to the factory, relishing every second before I stopped. Dad got out. Arkie got out and stuck his head back in the car.

"See you later, Shawn," he said. "Keep making your dad proud."

They both walked to the entrance. Dad was relieved to be free of the conversation. Arkie appeared to still be talking about me as Dad tried to ignore him. I put the Pinto in gear and drove off. I think my smile lasted for weeks.

• • •

Over time, Grandma and Grandpa Thornton's financial picture grew bleak. They hadn't saved any money for their later years. When the living was good, it was very good. For years, Grandpa ran the Bureau of Motor Vehicles, a patronage position appointed by the governor of Indiana. Grandpa bought the building next to the BMV in Mishawaka, and when a Republican governor was elected, Grandpa cut a hole in the wall and installed a door to his insurance office on the other side so he could go back and forth with ease. When a Democratic governor was elected, Grandpa bricked up the wall and stayed on his insurance business side, awaiting a fresh appointment from the next Republican governor.

But Grandpa's influence and income waned. The Thorntons' high-society lifestyle evaporated over time. With no money socked away to retire on, they sold their big house by the river and Grandpa's big black Cadillac and eventually ended up in nice but simple government housing for the elderly. We spent a lot of time in their little apartment.

Grandpa had always tried to teach me how to be successful. "Never wear a colored dress shirt," he said more than once. "Always wear a white shirt, a red tie, and a blue suit."

When he saw me one day wearing a suit with a light blue shirt, he looked at me and said, "No one's ever going to believe you."

When I picked up my chicken to eat it with my hands, he weighed in. "If you take a girl to the Lincoln Highway Inn, she's never going to marry you if you eat like that. You need to learn to eat your chicken with a fork and a knife. Be civilized."

Grandpa's ethics were very situational. He would bend basic values if he thought he could gain from others in such a way that it would not hurt them terribly. At Thanksgiving when our small extended family came to Grandma and Grandpa's apartment, everyone put their coats and purses on the bed in the spare bedroom. While the family was talking, I saw Grandpa slip away. He took a detour into the bedroom with the coats and purses. Moments later Dad, who had been using the bathroom, passed by. He poked his head in the guest room, and I heard his stern voice say to his own father, "Dad, get out of there. Get out of there."

Grandpa walked out and rejoined the group. I learned later that he had plopped down on the guest bed and was going through the coats and purses for cash with his one good hand. We caught him doing that on a number of occasions. Sometimes we just acted as if we didn't see him because we were too embarrassed. Maybe it shouldn't have surprised us that a guy who ran an illegal casino for the mob would steal from relatives.

For years we prayed for Grandma and Grandpa Thornton to come to faith in Christ, but as they entered their eighties, the possibility seemed increasingly remote. I had never seen them show any spiritual interest and hadn't seen them in church other than to visit Twin Branch to see Troy or me in a Christmas program. No prayer consumed me more during my childhood than the prayer that my grandparents would become Christians.

One day when I was in college, I was chatting with Dad over the phone and could tell he had something exciting to tell me.

"Guess what?" he said. "Your grandparents came to see the Christmas program your mother and brother were in.

The church sent a visitation team to their house afterward. Both of them came to Christ."

To say I was stunned would be an understatement. Grandpa was eighty-three, and Grandma was seventy-nine.

"Something clicked for them, I guess," Dad continued. "They listened really close and even ignored phone calls while the folks from the church were at the apartment."

It seemed too good to be true, but their commitment proved to be lasting. A member of the visitation team from Twin Branch Bible Church came by regularly to meet with them. Grandma and Grandpa had developed cataracts and couldn't read anymore, so they listened to the Bible on tape every day. When I visited them, our conversations were changed completely. Grandpa Thornton asked me questions about the Bible, some of them rather difficult. They attended Twin Branch Bible Church every Sunday after that and hardly ever missed.

A few years later, Grandpa Thornton's health deteriorated. Dave Childs, the pastor who had replaced Pastor Jones and had been instrumental in their coming to Christ, came by to visit him.

"Howard," he said, using Grandpa's first name, "they say it won't be long. You're about to come to the end of your journey on earth. Do you know where you're going when you step from this world into eternity?"

Grandpa smiled wryly, even in his weakened state. "I think so, Dave, unless you've been lying to me these last few years."

The next day Grandpa said good-bye to his beloved Mishawaka and became a permanent resident of heaven.

Grandpa didn't want a funeral, so our little extended family simply gathered for a meal to spend time together. With Grandpa's passing, I lost one of the key anchors of stability from the often stormy realities of my childhood.

CHAPTER 11

MOM APPEARED to age more rapidly than seemed natural. And although she was devoted to prayer and Bible study, she still had her typical outbursts and episodes of anger and depression. But she now had several means to help her remain calm. She kept crayons and coloring books around the house and colored carefully inside the lines with all seriousness. She also did word searches in an almost rhythmic fashion. When she found a word, she set the pencil on the first letter and slowly made a straight line through it, her hand continuing in the air after she had crossed it off. It was the same type of motion she made working her loom.

When she blew up or threw things or threatened Dad, we all handled it better. Troy and I were older and less shaken by Mom's instability. Our own lives were taking shape. Dad's choice to love Mom within her limitations had improved our home, and we followed his lead. While things were never completely peaceful, they were better than in earlier years.

One day I came home and found Lady lying listlessly on the living room floor. She didn't even raise her head when I came in. She had been ill for days.

Dad was in the kitchen.

"That dog isn't getting any better, and I'm not spending any money on medical bills for pets," he said. I knew what he meant: it was my task to have Lady put down.

I gave her one more night to recover, but she didn't. The next morning I lifted her into our car and put her in the front seat with the same care I used with Mom. Lady looked up at me, a small spark returning to her eyes amid the confusion and pain she seemed to be feeling.

As I drove to the vet, I leaned over and scratched her head.

"Thank you for letting me tell you my problems," I said. "Thank you for letting me cry. You were my friend in the darkest days of my life. I will never forget that."

She looked at me as if she had borne harder burdens. A number of times I wanted to turn the car around and give her another chance, but I knew it would only prolong the end.

I carried her in my arms into the veterinarian's office and filled out the necessary paperwork. The vet agreed it was time to put her down.

"Would you like to stay while the veterinarian administers the treatment?" the woman in the front office asked gently.

"I . . . I don't think so," I said. I walked out, knowing I

had said good-bye to one of the best friends I'd had in the toughest years of my life.

In those tough years, the thing I had wanted most was to be normal. As I grew up, I began to realize that the people I most wanted to be like were not as normal as I had thought.

A neighbor girl, whose family had a pristine lawn and a life I envied, followed her dream and went to Hollywood to be a TV star. She landed bit parts in shows and commercials but also got into drugs. One day our family received word that she had died in the home of one of the stars of a popular sitcom. The man was never charged. My view of TV families as perfect and stable was shattered, never to recover.

Broken lives began to emerge all around me. Maybe it was my age, but I began to notice that some neighbors, relatives, and friends whose lives had looked so ideal through the lens of my childhood now displayed obvious, sometimes tragic problems.

One relative lost a child to disease and became so distraught that he tried to kill himself in a violent way, leaving himself with life-threatening wounds. He survived, and Mom visited him in the hospital, relating to him the way she did to anyone in distress. He came to faith in Jesus, but his road remained tortured in many ways.

Another close relative tried to commit suicide several times and was repeatedly hospitalized. Other friends, relatives, and families from church dealt with bad relationships, divorce, wayward children, alcoholism, drug addiction, adultery, and mental illnesses of their own. As normal and enviable as their lives had seemed to me from my vantage point on Victory Road, they now began to crumble.

There was one boy I went to school with for years whose life always seemed perfect. When we were in high school, his dad bought him a brand-new Mustang that was the envy of all his friends. He roared around in it like a Roman soldier in his chariot, but he was already drinking heavily, and by the time he was seventeen, the state revoked his driver's license for repeated infractions.

By contrast, other friends and family members were an inspiration. Mom's sisters and their husbands grew in their commitment to Christ. The four young people who stood with me the night of the missions conference at Twin Branch Bible Church all went on to serve in ministry roles in churches and other Christian organizations.

I'm not sure when the shift happened, but about the time of Lady's death, I came to realize that I was no longer pursuing what would make me fit in. I was much less concerned with being normal and much more concerned with pursuing what God had called me to do.

And I received some confirmation of that call. Out of the blue I received a phone call from Brethren Christian Schools, which I hadn't attended for years. "We came across a plaque you never picked up," Nancy, the secretary, said. "The 1980 Christian Character Award. It has your name on it."

I went to the office and picked up the award. Nancy commented that it was odd they had held the award for so long. "God must want you to have it," she said.

I thanked her and walked back to the car holding the

simple award. Mom had ridden with me to the school. She pointed out that God may have had a hand in the delay and that now the Christian Character Award more accurately matched my reality. She was right. The award hadn't meant much to me the day Dr. Bowling announced it because I didn't feel I deserved it. But the award meant a lot to me now. God's timing meant a lot to me too.

•   •   •

At Penn High School, I joined the speech team. Several teachers who had heard me give speeches in class thought I would fit the team well. I also saw joining the team as a way to work on my ability to communicate persuasively. I specialized in an event called "extemporaneous speaking." I had half an hour to create a brief speech on a news topic using an article from a current events magazine. Dave Tygart and Harvey Hurst, teachers at Penn who served as speech team coaches, taught me the skill and art of creating an extemporaneous speech. The ingredients were simple: study the text, discover a main thought, decide how you want to persuade people, and develop an introduction, three points, and a conclusion. I prepared and delivered hundreds of those speeches during my high school years.

I lettered in speech and got the sweater and everything. I didn't care how geeky it seemed.

By the time I graduated from high school, I felt comfortable speaking in front of people, no matter who was in the group or how large the audience was. To continue my preparation for God's calling on my life, I enrolled at Appalachian Bible College in West Virginia. God used the faculty, staff, and fellow students at the college to shape me, my ministry skills, and my passion to share God's love with others.

My ministry education there and later at Capital Bible Seminary introduced me to a specific approach to counseling. This particular philosophy, or at least the way I perceived it, said that all of one's emotional or mental problems in life—every bad habit, every bad mood—are ultimately the direct result of sinful choices. And the only way to counsel someone toward freedom from their problems is to find and confront the sin. All problems are therefore spiritual problems.

"Mom, you don't have to be this way," I told her when I came back during my junior year for Christmas break. "Your problems are rooted in sin. If you'll confess your sin and repent, you'll be free of them."

"Well, I don't know what else to do," Mom said, shaking her head and gesturing with frustration. "I thought I gave God everything. I don't know what else to ask for."

"I'm saying if you read your Bible more and prayed more, then I'm sure God would free you from all this hardship," I responded.

"But I do those things!" she said and burst into tears.

That was about as tame and logical as our discussions on this topic got over the course of my next several college breaks. I was set on confronting and correcting Mom every time she yelled or cussed.

One day when Mom had an outburst of anger simply because she had tripped on a chair leg in the kitchen, I was ready.

"Mom, frivolous anger and cussing is sin!" I said, my voice rising in volume. "You will never be at peace, will never be happy. You will always be either depressed or angry unless you confess your sin and start living right!"

I was now yelling and pointing my finger at her.

Part of my motivation was to use the training I had gained at college, but a deeper part of me longed to find a cure for Mom. While her physical, mental, and emotional highs and lows had evened out some since her time in the hospital and Dad had learned not to match her hysterics as much as before, the situation at the house was still far from normal. I desperately wanted that to change, not just for me but for Mom, Dad, and Troy—for us as a family.

"You shut up!" Mom countered. "What do you know? Oh, you think you go to Bible college, and now you can come home and tell your mother how to live! Well, I've had it up to here. I'm the one who introduced you to Jesus. You are nothing but a little . . ."

And out came another four-letter word. That set me off.

"See, Mom, that's what I'm talking about!" I yelled back. "As long as you have sin in your life like cussing and irrational anger, throwing things and threatening to kill people, you will never be right! Never!"

Mom burst into tears, and before I knew it, Dad lunged into the kitchen, seemingly from nowhere. I felt his arm slam me in the chest, knocking me off balance.

"Enough!" he yelled. "You will not talk to my wife that way."

Like an idiot, I had an answer.

"But she's my mother."

"She's my wife first, your mother second," he said. "If you think this approach is going to help your mother, you're dumber than I thought you were. And you will never talk to your mother that way again. It's time you got off your high horse. You are not going to fix her with this stuff you're bringing back here. Now get out of here and never talk to her that way again."

I went out the back door and walked up Victory Road to cool down. Here I was at age twenty-one, walking down the same cinder road I had walked seven years earlier when God whispered to me about my own sin. Now he convicted me again, this time about my approach to Mom. God impressed on me that the issue was not just the combative spirit in which I approached her. It was that I was *wrong*. Confession and repentance would not "cure" Mom. Her problems were more complex than my simple formula.

I never did talk to her that way again.

Over the years, I quietly tried to fit Mom into the perspective of Christian counseling I was being taught. I was forced to ask myself whether all bad behavior was rooted in willful sin. Surely some bad behavior is directly connected to sin. Ultimately, I believed, all the problems and brokenness in our world go back to the Curse brought about by Adam and Eve's sin. But that didn't mean someone with Down syndrome, like Cheryl, was mentally disabled because of her sin or her parents' sin. And what about people like Mom?

On the spectrum ranging from "normal" to "disabled," wouldn't there be people like Mom who fell somewhere in the middle—people who were maybe difficult to diagnose and whose problems and behavior could not be explained in such a black-and-white way? For these people, maybe no amount of repentance would make their struggles and challenges go away. As I moved into pastoral ministry a few years later, this same conundrum presented itself with many families and individuals in the churches I served.

During one of my school breaks after the conflict with Mom and Dad, Dad called me into his bedroom.

"I want to show you something," he said in a hushed tone, pushing the bedroom door closed.

He opened the top drawer of his dresser. Dad's top dresser drawer was an expanded version of his wallet. Important papers and items that couldn't fit in his wallet or that he found unnecessary to carry with him ended up stashed under his socks and work bandannas. Dad pulled out a manila folder full of papers. He was not a file-keeping kind of guy, so it was strange to see him thumbing through the newspaper clippings and magazine articles he had gathered there.

"I think this is your mom," he said softly. "I think this is what happened to her."

One article was clipped from the *South Bend Tribune*, another from the *Wall Street Journal*. There were dozens. For the first time, in the text of those articles, I saw the term "traumatic brain injury" or "TBI." The term described people who were seemingly stable emotionally until they fell off a scaffolding or had a motorcycle accident or experienced some other serious blow to the head. Afterward, even with few obvious external injuries, they experienced significant personality changes, outbursts of anger, and volatile emotions.

That's Mom, I thought as I read about the different cases and what doctors had discovered about people in such situations. It seemed medical science was beginning to catch up with what we had been living for years.

"I've been collecting these articles for several years," Dad said. "It took me a while to figure it out, but with your Mom I think we're talking about a woman with a brain injury. That's what's causing it. It doesn't take much, and you don't have to be in a car accident. It can be almost any blow to the head."

He paused as I continued leafing through his private collection of articles. Dad impressed me when he did his own research. While not a great student in a formal setting, he had always been inquisitive and a lifelong learner.

"For years I thought your mother was supposed to be normal," he said. "That's what the doctors told us. We could see physically what the accident did; it just took me a while to see the emotional side of it. That's the reason she is the way she is. You can't resolve this kind of thing by getting her to change. It won't work. This is who she is. In the beginning I treated her as a normal person even though she wasn't normal, and I even *knew* she wasn't normal. Like that country singer—she's still around—she had a TV show with her sisters."

"Barbara Mandrell," I said.

"Barbara Mandrell. She got in a bad car accident some time ago. I read her story one time, and she was saying how her personality changed. Her husband was saying it too. You hear about football players, race-car drivers, and guys from Vietnam getting a concussion or being knocked out for a long time. Then later you hear they are different. They aren't reasonable with family. They have unexplainable emotional outbursts."

I could tell he had spent a good deal of time thinking and reading about the subject.

"Some people have a lot of issues, mentally," he continued. "They're not technically crazy, but they've got a temper. They have a hard time in school. Who's to say that half the people out there haven't had some kind of brain injury?"

He paused.

"Here's the weird thing," he said. "Your mom was very spiritual before. Then the accident happened, and her personality changed. It made her memory bad, and it has confused her a lot, but she can almost always remember Scripture and where a particular verse or story is in the Bible. She can't remember a lot of things, but everything she learned from the Bible before the accident never left her mind."

I knew what Dad was talking about. Years later when I was preaching regularly, I would call Mom when I couldn't remember where to find a passage in the Bible.

Dad continued. "What does that show? To me that shows that physically and mentally you can have something taken away, but spiritually—you can't lose that."

He sighed. Mom was in the other room watching TV.

"There's a lot of things we just don't know," he concluded. "That's the way God sometimes works."

I didn't know what to add, but it was a perspective-shifting conversation for me. After so many years of us wondering what had happened to Mom and searching for answers in so many directions, the answer now seemed clear: her brain had been injured, and that fact had shaped our lives. It was the beginning of my own research into TBI, what it looked like, and how it changed people. I handed Dad the file. He put it back in his drawer, and we walked out of the room.

When I was a senior in college, Troy came to Appalachian Bible College as a freshman, also pursuing a call he had received to pastoral ministry. I worked for the college as a traveling admissions representative the first year after graduating, and Troy and I lived together in a small trailer a family allowed us to live in rent-free.

During that year, Troy and I had a lot of long talks about our childhood. Gone were the days of throwing him from the roof with Lance. Our three-year age difference had become insignificant now that we were young adults. Dad had also shown Troy the file of articles about traumatic brain injuries, and we knew the file was still growing. We were even sending Dad articles we discovered. Having some explanation of Mom's intertwined physical, emotional, and mental challenges helped all three of us make sense of our life—what we often described as our "all but normal" life—on Victory Road.

"Things got a lot better after Mom came home from the psych ward at the hospital," Troy remarked one evening while we were making dinner. "I think she changed a little after that, but Dad changed a lot."

That comment was all it took to get us started. We spent dinnertime that evening swapping stories about growing up with Mom and Dad. We laughed so hard we cried. It felt good to talk openly about experiences that had once seemed so private.

Troy and I had responded in very different ways to our family chaos. My response as the elder brother was to internalize it all, blame myself, and ultimately develop low self-esteem and paralyzing insecurity. Troy instead looked at our parents, studied my response, and determined he would not let it get to him. He told himself he was better than that. By the time I left home, I had developed an unhealthily *deflated* view of myself. Troy, on the other hand, left home with an unhealthily *inflated* view of himself. College was good for both of us in correcting this.

Troy and I lived together for only that one year. But the bond between us, and eventually between our wives and families, never weakened. We had been through something together that most people wouldn't easily understand.

• • •

When my one-year commitment to work for the college ended, I married the woman of my dreams, Lesli Russell. She and I had met the second day of our freshman year at Appalachian Bible College and dated ever since. When I worked up the gumption to ask her out, I used a simple, direct line that may not work for everyone: "Have you ever thought of being a pastor's wife?"

Unbeknownst to me, during her teen years, Lesli had committed herself to ministry too.

"Um . . . a pastor's wife?" she responded. "Yes. Yes, I have."

She had me at "um."

Introducing Lesli to our life on Victory Road was not easy. I gave her plenty of preparation before her first visit to Indiana. She loved Mom right away. She and Dad got along so well that Dad warned if Lesli and I broke up, they would cut me out of the family and keep her. Of course, Lesli had a lot of adapting to do as time went on. While never the object of Mom's outbursts, she witnessed them at their worst.

After I completed a three-year master's degree at Capital Bible Seminary near Washington, DC, Lesli and I entered full-time ministry. We served in Limerick, Pennsylvania, near Philadelphia, then returned to our alma mater, Appalachian Bible College. There I served as a Bible and New Testament Greek instructor, while Lesli served as the dean of women.

Just a few years later, at age twenty-nine, I was called to serve as the senior pastor of Bible Center Church in Charleston, West Virginia. Bible Center was and is a well-respected, sizable church in that part of the country. Megan, our youngest child, was born then, joining siblings Jonathan and Katie. God continued to grow Bible Center Church, and I found great fulfillment in preaching week after week and leading the congregation through the pains and joys of growth. Often I thought back to the training I'd received as part of the speech team at Penn High School and the opportunities I'd been given at Twin Branch Bible Church. I realized that all those experiences had prepared me well.

But more than that, to my surprise, my experiences of growing up on Victory Road gave me special insights into the hurting, the poor, the marginalized, and the forgotten.

"No one is normal!" Mom often shouted in frustration during her outbursts.

In many ways she was right. Even the wealthiest had their own kind of crazy, and just because they had money didn't mean they weren't marginalized or held in the grip of life-controlling emotional pain. I encountered all sorts of people in my pastoral ministry who felt that the world didn't treat them as normal—families of children with special needs, elderly folks who felt life had passed them by, people with social quirks, individuals with mental illness or emotional problems, people experiencing the breakup of a marriage or other family trauma, others grieving the loss of someone dear to them, still others struggling to make ends meet.

My college and seminary training helped me minister to them, but only to an extent. In reality, God used Victory Road Seminary to shape my heart for people who looked like they had it all together but were going through private pain. As a pastor, I found I could empathize with them from personal experience. I might not have experienced precisely the same circumstances, but I knew the acute pain they were feeling. I was keenly aware of the isolation and hollowness of living with unspoken suffering.

Over the years as Mom visited Troy and me, she was drawn to the most marginalized in the churches we served.

She loved everyone, but her comments always focused on people I knew were hurting badly.

"Oh, I met Virginia today after the first service," Mom said during one Sunday visit. "She seems like such a nice, sweet elderly lady, but boy does she miss Ralph."

I knew Virginia so missed Ralph that she struggled to keep going. They had been married for nearly six decades.

"Pastor, when will your mother be in town again?" Virginia asked me a few months after Mom's visit. "I told her she should come over to my house for an afternoon next time so we can continue our conversation from the church lobby during her last visit."

Mom had so impacted one marginalized life in a brief foyer conversation that Virginia wanted to renew the connection in her home. As someone who worked hard to help people through their difficult times, I was impressed.

"Diana needs some help, Shawn," Mom said during our Sunday lunch on another visit. "I met her in the ladies' room before the service, and she is struggling with depression right now. You know she is a single mom and life is hard for her."

"Okay, Mom. I'll check on her or have another pastor check on her," I responded.

Mom continued, "The sun sets earlier now that it's fall, so her depression is getting worse. Don't forget to have someone reach out and help her. Her situation makes me so sad."

Mom could quickly learn about hurting people in seemingly casual conversations. During her visits, she identified many in our church whom I knew—and some I didn't know—were experiencing deep pain or feeling marginalized.

Over the years, as we watched Mom struggle with her passion to live for God and cope with the torment of traumatic brain injury, she inadvertently poured that same perspective for the marginalized into Troy and me. That gift from Mom greatly impacted our ministries.

Before taking the pulpit on Sundays, I often found myself imagining who was sitting in the congregation that day and what they were struggling with. I visualized wealthy people who had family members held captive by alcohol or drugs. I pictured poor people who had just heard they had cancer and had no way to pay for treatment. I thought of grandparents whose grandkids didn't visit anymore, men who had lost their jobs, kids who were lonely. Hundreds of scenarios played through my head, and I felt the pain of each of them. More than that, I saw the potential victories on the other side.

I realized our family possessed something in our little house on Victory Road that many people simply didn't have: the love and the purpose of God in the midst of seeming chaos. Even in the noise of our brokenness, God had whispered hope to us as we leaned on him. No matter how bad or broken life seemed, God met us with hope. The insight this gave me into people's lives and situations was almost like a sixth sense. I could never have learned it in a classroom. It came from living with Mom. It came from watching Dad try to cope with Mom's challenges. And it gave me deep compassion and motivation to comfort others with the comfort I had received from God.

Somehow in the context of craziness and pain, God had given Troy and me each a pastor's heart.

CHAPTER 12

"Shawn, this is your mother."

It was 2 a.m., and Mom was angry.

"Your father is an idiot, and I am not going to take this anymore. I've already got the phone book out, and I'm calling lawyers in the morning."

I held the phone to my ear, my head resting on the pillow, and just listened. Mom had mellowed somewhat, but her volatile emotions still flared up regularly.

"What's the problem, Mom?" I asked.

"I can't stand this mop I'm using," she said. "I want a new mop, but he won't take me to get one."

I knew at this point that I was getting a fragment of the story and that Dad probably had his own explanation.

Sometimes Mom insisted on something and then forgot about it the next day. Of course, sometimes Dad was just as obstinate as Mom.

"How about I call him tomorrow and suggest he get you a new mop?" I said.

"He's asleep," she said, uttering obscenities.

"You should be too," I said. "Can I pray with you? Because then I'm going to go back to sleep myself."

"I know. I'm sorry I woke you up."

We prayed together, and Mom calmed down. It was perhaps not the perfect dynamic for me to act as her counselor, but it was better than my criticizing her for not getting her life together.

The next day I called Mom, and Dad tried to hand her the phone.

"Tell him to go to hell," she replied.

"Did you hear that?" Dad said.

"Yeah, I heard it," I said. Just like old times. Later she called back, completely normal, and we solved the mop problem.

Mom also began to call my uncle Mark. Mark had been through his own emotional highs and lows, and Mom recognized him as another person who knew what it meant to hurt. Mark listened to Mom and let her release steam. And to his credit, he challenged Mom to be true to her convictions in Christ as a wife and as a mother.

Dad and Mom joined a weekly ministry of Twin Branch Bible Church at a nursing home in the area. Dad eventually led the ministry, and he and Mom recruited others to work with them in loving the elderly people there. Mom and Dad had a special heart for those who were becoming more limited mentally, physically, and emotionally by age. Like Mom's visits to the nursing home when I was a boy, this ministry seemed a natural outgrowth of love and compassion from the brokenness Mom and Dad were keenly aware of in their own lives.

One time Dad put Mom on a train to visit us in West Virginia. At our house she played on the floor for hours with our young children and sat and read with them in a chair. She loved being a grandmother, and her childlike streak made her great fun. Our kids loved her visits and couldn't believe they had found such a willing playmate in their grandma. Dad couldn't make the trip because he was still working at the factory.

During the visit, my phone rang at 3 a.m. one night.

"Hello?"

"Hey, what are you doing?" Dad asked. From his tone I pictured him grinning on the other end.

"Dad, what are you calling this late for?" I asked.

"Your mother called me," he said. "She has a toothache that's killing her. She needs to get to the dentist."

Mom was staying in the guest bedroom on the lower level of our two-story house. I was puzzled.

"Mom called you? When?"

"About two minutes ago. I just hung up with her."

"But she's downstairs."

"I know."

"So why'd she call you?"

"I don't know, but can you take her to the dentist in the morning?"

"Of course," I said. We hung up, and I went down and knocked on Mom's door.

"Come in," I heard.

I opened the door, and there she was, sitting on the end of her bed, already wearing normal clothes like she was going somewhere.

"Mom, do you have a toothache?" I asked, ignoring how surreal it all felt at such an hour.

"Yes," she said. "I'm going to have to take a walk or something. It hurts so bad."

"Why did you call Dad in Indiana?" I asked as innocently as I could. "He has to get up and go to work soon. You could have just come up to me or talked through the speaker."

We had bought a baby monitor, so all she had to do was push a button, and it would buzz me upstairs. She usually had no problem going up and down the stairs on her own. And I knew she had no problem yelling.

She shrugged in response, as if it were all perfectly natural.

"I just decided to call your dad because I know he cares and would try to help me somehow," she said.

I wouldn't have preferred any other answer.

Mom could still lose control easily. I took her to the mall one day and didn't realize I was walking too fast for her. As always, she had her arm hooked in mine for stability.

Suddenly I felt her fingernails dig into my arm with alarming strength.

"Stop. Walking. So. Fast!" she said in a deep, menacing, staccato voice.

"Ow, ow, Mom, okay! I'll slow down. Let go, let go!"

I pried her fingers off and cut my pace in half.

The next day we were in the car together with my son, Jonathan, who was a toddler. He was in the backseat, fussing and working himself into a fit as I drove the car down our street just after pulling out of our driveway. Mom instantly became upset.

"You're going to have to tell him to be quiet," she said. Then moments later, "You've got to shut that kid up."

I knew Jonathan needed a nap, and I hoped the car ride would put him to sleep. But it wasn't soon enough for Mom. I could tell she was beginning to have an outburst and lose control of her emotions. Finally she turned around in her seat, stared at Jonathan, and spoke in an all-too-familiar, guttural voice. "Shut up, you little s—!"

Her words rang in the car and in my ears as if they had come from twenty years earlier. I suddenly stopped the car, put it in park, and looked at Mom.

"You are not going to call my son that," I said. "You are welcome to stay with us, but if you are going to talk to my son like that, you had better just go home, because that will never happen again."

There was an anger in me I did not recognize. Raising my voice a bit, I continued, "You can get out and walk back up the hill to our house if you can't control yourself."

In that moment I drew a line in the sand. Verbal abuse had been part of my childhood, but I was determined it would not be part of the childhood my kids knew.

Mom's eyes welled up, and she began crying. She sensed my seriousness.

"I'm sorry," she said. "I'm sorry. I was wrong to do that. Please forgive me."

I knew she meant it. I also knew it could very well happen again, and there was little any of us could do about it.

• • •

One afternoon Dad drove home from the factory listening to Paul Harvey's *The Rest of the Story*. As usual, he arrived home before the story ended, so he turned off the car and sat in our gravel driveway near the end of Victory Road to hear the last couple of minutes. When the program was over, he swung the car door open and walked into the house through the back door.

The TV was on. The kitchen was empty. He glanced left and saw that the shower curtain in the bathroom was down.

"What the heck now?" he said to himself.

He walked back to see what had happened. Mom was lying in the bathtub. She was wearing her nightgown and her watch and lying on her back. The tub was partly filled, and water covered her face. Dad reached in and grabbed her arm to pull her up, wondering if she had fallen asleep.

"Wake up," he said. "Wake up, Bev."

A chill went through him as she didn't respond. Clearly she had pulled the shower curtain down and perhaps fallen into the tub. He hit the drain lever, thinking that maybe if he got rid of the water, she would be all right.

The water drained out. Mom still didn't move.

It's over, Dad thought instinctively. *That's it. It's done.*

He walked out, picked up the phone, and called my house.

"Hello?" Lesli answered.

"This is John," Dad said. "Is Shawn there?"

"No, he's not," she said.

"Okay. I found Bev," he said. "She was lying in the tub with water on her face. I don't know what to do."

"You'd better call 911 before you call anyone else," Lesli said.

"That's a good idea," Dad said. "She appears to be dead."

"Call 911," Lesli said again.

He hung up and called 911, then called Nana, who called Aunt Gail and Twin Branch's newest pastor, Daniel Boes, who asked a woman from the church to call Troy and me.

Then Dad waited. Fire trucks and police cars pulled up in a flurry of lights and professional haste. The medics came in, shoved the kitchen table out of the way, marched into the bathroom, picked up Mom, and brought her out. They worked on her for a moment, but it was clear she was dead. Aunt Gail and then Pastor Boes arrived.

"What happened?" Aunt Gail asked.

"I don't know. It looks like she fell in the shower," Dad said.

They waited for the coroner to come.

I was sitting in a doctor's office in Charleston, about to get a shot of strong antibiotic for a bad case of strep throat. It was Wednesday, April 19, 2000, just a few days before Easter. The shot, I hoped, would restore my voice enough to allow me to preach for the biggest Sunday of the year. When my cell phone rang, I saw it was Lesli.

"Go head, answer it. I can wait," the doctor said with syringe in hand and my arm in position.

"No, that's okay," I said. "It's my wife. I'll call her right back when we're done. She'll understand."

I had no idea it was urgent until my phone rang again just as the doctor stuck the needle in. I didn't recognize the number but knew the area code was Northern Indiana.

Wonder what's going on? I thought. *Maybe it's a relative calling about Grandma or Nana.*

Rolling my sleeve down, I was able to catch the call just before it stopped ringing.

"Hello?" I said hoarsely.

"Shawn," came a woman's voice, "this is Luanna Randolph from Twin Branch Bible Church. I know we haven't talked in a long time, and I hate to make this call, but I am calling to tell you that your mother was found in the bathtub at her home, and it appears she may have died."

The words almost didn't register. I couldn't move. Even if it was real, this was such a strange way to find out.

"Your dad went to the factory this morning," she continued. "It looks like your mom did her normal routine and got in the shower, but she lost her balance, tried to grab the curtain, and fell, hitting her head. Your dad came home and found her in the water."

It was thirty-eight years since the car accident on Miracle Lane. Now an accidental injury of exactly the same type—a harsh blow to the head—had taken her life.

"Thank you, Luanna," I said. "I will call Troy."

"You guys and your dad are in our prayers," she said.

I immediately called Troy. He, too, was stunned. The next day Lesli and I and our three preschool-age children flew home to Mishawaka.

Driving from the airport to Grandma's, where Dad and Troy's family were waiting for us, my main thought was, *Should I hug them?* I knew this would be an emotional meeting for all of us, but I couldn't remember a time I had ever hugged Troy other than wrestling on the floor as kids. Dad and I had not hugged since I was a very young boy. It wasn't because of any unresolved tension. We loved each other. We just showed our love in other ways.

As I walked into Grandma's little apartment, I gave my father and brother a firm handshake and an awkward half-hug. In some ways, that exchange described many of our family interactions better than words could.

Mom's visitation was held at Hahn Funeral Home in Mishawaka with an open casket. For the Gilvin side of my family, this new grief was added to previous ones. We had lost Papaw two years earlier, and before that Aunt Sue and Uncle Chuck's oldest daughter, Teri, died of a rare form of cystic fibrosis. That pain was felt again as we mourned the loss of Mom.

To my surprise, hundreds of people from near and far came to pay their respects to her and to us. So many people told me how Mom had touched their lives, either directly or by example. Some knew a little of our family situation; most did not. Some were from church and the factory; some were old friends and family; some were people I didn't even know.

Our neighbors came, and since they were from the only

other two homes on our dead-end street, that meant our whole neighborhood was there. I always suspected that over the years they heard more and saw more than they let on, but I so appreciated their coming to honor Mom.

Pastor Jones and his wife walked in about an hour into the visitation time. Seeing them brought tears to my eyes. I hadn't expected them to come. They had been gone from Twin Branch for some time, were elderly, and lived several hours away.

"Your mom was one of a kind, guys," Pastor Jones said, shaking our hands and looking us right in the eyes. "She loved the Lord and is home now with him."

Pastor Jones was one of the few who really knew the depths of Mom's challenges. His words were some of the most comforting I heard that night.

"Thank you for coming," Troy said. "It means a lot."

Others came to share their thoughts and sympathy with us.

"We all respected Bev because she was bright, caring, loved Jesus, and knew the Bible better than anyone," a woman from our church said.

"When you walked into the church foyer, Bev was an unassigned greeter. She would grab your hand and not let it go until she heard how your life was going," another woman shared, coming to tears. "She would say, 'It will be all right. It will be okay. Can we pray about that?' She was an encourager."

Another woman told us, "When someone said, 'Bill might lose his job at the factory,' Bev would say, 'God will take care of you. The Bible says God will take care of his children. He will take care of you and Bill. I'm sure he will get another job.'"

"Mrs. Thornton led me to the Lord," one young man simply said. "She was a spiritual leader to me. And I remember all the prizes she gave out."

After the visitation I cried from the overwhelming outpouring of others, not just over Mom's death.

The next day, Troy and I led the funeral service together. Lesli and our children, Jonathan, Katie, and Megan, were there, along with Troy's wife, Stephanie, and their children, Caleb and Kyleigh. I told how Mom was instrumental in leading me to Christ and how she gave Troy and me a godly example to follow. Then I imagined what Mom was experiencing now.

"She's probably running, no longer cursed with the emotions that got so quickly beyond her control. She was one of the spiritual giants and mentors in my life and taught me so much about the Word of God and caring for overlooked people."

As Troy spoke about the hope we have as Christians that Mom is in heaven, I scanned the crowd gathered in the sanctuary of Twin Branch Bible Church. Grandma Thornton was crying and leaning on my dad's sister, Aunt Donna. Nana and Mom's sisters sobbed and handed fresh tissues to one another and my cousins.

Every time I glanced at Dad in the front row, I saw tears dropping from his cheeks. I had never seen him cry before—not once. Wordlessly, he wiped them all away as they continued to come.

Our trip to the cemetery for the burial was difficult. As a pastor I had led many graveside services, but when it was for my own mother, the service seemed to extend the sorrow needlessly.

The next week, Lesli, Troy, Stephanie, and I went to the house to clean it up. Aunts Connie and Gail helped too. It took days of hard work to finish the task. Each item, every purse, every romance novel, every crayon, every needle in the carpet brought back memories. We found at least twenty-five of Mom's Bibles, some missing covers, many looking like they came from garage sales. They were stashed all over the house.

My personal tears over losing Mom didn't really arrive until later. Around the first anniversary of Mom's death, I took my family to Indiana to visit Dad at the house. In the middle of the night, I got up to use the bathroom. For some reason, that's when it hit me.

This is the room where Mom died, in that kidney-shaped tub where we washed dishes for so many years, where Troy and I took a thousand baths.

The dam of emotions broke. I leaned on the wall, stared into the empty tub, and cried. I cried harder than I can remember ever crying. Questions returned that had buzzed around the back of my mind.

What were Mom's last moments like? Did she know she was dying? Did she try to get up? Was she unconscious right away?

Lesli heard me sobbing and knocked on the bathroom door. It hadn't latched completely for years, so she gently pushed it open.

"Are you okay?"

I followed her back to my old bedroom and bawled for an hour.

She's gone, I kept thinking. *Mom is gone.*

In the weeks after Mom's death, Dad visited Nana several times. They shared an unspoken bond, unique to the two of them, of a sense of responsibility for the accident that caused Mom's traumatic brain injury. During these visits, they seemed to grieve together in a way only they could.

Nana replaced Mom as the greatest cheerleader and champion for my ministry. She shared tapes and CDs of my sermons with others. Even though Nana's upbringing in a children's home had warped her sense of familial love in some ways, she loved Mom. She loved her daughters, sons-in-law, and grandchildren. My kids came to love her deeply, for which I was glad, because they were too young to remember Mom. Before her death, Nana came to visit us a few times. Odd as it sounds, her visits were precious to me because they were like visits from Mom.

• • •

Statistics say that most men between ages forty and sixty who lose a spouse remarry relatively quickly. Dad joined that category. Less than six months after Mom's sudden passing, Dad married a friend of our family. While Troy and I were happy Dad had found companionship, we made it clear we thought this was too soon. But we indicated we would support him and his decision. He and his fiancée planned a quiet ceremony before a justice of the peace, and I flew home to be there. My flight was delayed and then rerouted into Kalamazoo, so I rented a car and drove down to Mishawaka. I arrived at the house on Victory Road at 2 a.m. and crawled into my old bed.

At 5 a.m. I heard Dad get up to leave for work. His routine seemed strangely one-sided. Mom wasn't there to yell at him or to put cookies in a baggie or coffee in his Thermos. The radio wasn't even on, though I did hear the drip of the coffee maker.

Dad walked into my room with a cup of coffee in hand and sat next to me on the bed. I rolled over and squinted at him.

"Hi, Dad," I said groggily.

"You want to know if I love her, don't you?" he said.

I sat up, still yawning.

I wasn't really in the mood to discuss Dad's soon-to-be wife. "Dad, I really don't. It's okay with me."

"But you are wondering," he said.

"Look, I don't want to have this conversation," I said. "As I told you when you said you were getting married, I'm not your pastor. I'm not your counselor. You're on your own, but I will support you in this."

"You know, the problem with your generation is you get married out of emotional love," he said. "Your generation has the cart before the horse. My idea of love has a lot of duty in it. It's not just about fleeting romance. Love is not this affection, this feeling. Today people marry out of quick love, and if duty doesn't follow, they give up. They think emotional feelings for each other on their wedding day will somehow magically become a deep sense of practical duty to each other for years. But it doesn't work that way. Hard stuff comes at you fast, and the emotions fade long before there is any sense of duty."

He stopped, looked at me, and shook the bed. "Are you listening?" he asked.

"Yes, Dad, I'm listening," I answered, and I was, but I was also yawning and somewhat taken aback at how openly he was speaking.

"I believe the day you say 'I do,' love is commitment," he continued. "You commit to stay with that person for the rest of your life, no matter what. Even when it gets really hard, you find a way to make it work. Here's the key that your generation misses. When you do that out of commitment, over time devotion grows. As the years pass, the commitment that kept your love together transforms into a deep emotional bond—devotion—and love that grows from commitment to devotion is the strongest and deepest love."

He paused to drink his coffee and to reflect.

"Shawn, I couldn't leave your mother behind in the condition she was in after the accident. I've always asked myself if I married her out of a sense of duty because of my responsibility in the accident or out of devotion because we had so much fun together. I learned that real love is deep and develops over time as you give yourself to someone else. We had that. I had a deep affection for Bev, your mom."

He continued after another sip, his mind seemingly in a past era.

"Plus, I was seventeen. She was fourteen. My hormones were going pretty good."

"Hey, Dad, where is this going?" I interrupted, fearing he was heading in a direction I did not want to go. He ignored my question and kept talking.

"After the accident I asked, 'Now what am I supposed to do? Just walk away from this situation? Should I try to hang around and see if I want to be with this girl? I have to make a decision,'" he said. "After we got married, I just tried to use the brain God gave me. And I struggled, but I tried to grow over time—did what I felt was best, loved your mom, helped you kids grow in the Lord, used my head. Then you see the world around you having success, and you feel like, 'Am I doing the right thing, or is this a bunch of hooey?' Everyone seemed successful. It was all about the world, all about today. Nice homes, jobs, going here, doing that. And to tell the truth, I saw Lance's family and your aunts and uncles and thought, *What if?* I often thought life would be better with a wife who could cook, clean, drive, get a job, do the grocery shopping."

Another sip of coffee.

"But I was committed to your mom and to you boys, to giving you the best life I could with the resources I had. To me it was putting a roof over our heads, making sure there was food on the table, getting us to church where we could grow, coping with your mom, and eventually trying to send you guys off into life—maybe even college. I think I did that. Maybe not well. But we made it. Why else would I spend almost forty years working eight hours a day at a hot, awful factory with a bunch of idiots?"

He smiled and threw back the last of his coffee. I could hardly believe we were having this conversation, or mono-logue, or whatever it was. But he wasn't done.

"Looking at it spiritually, you have to ask—why? From God's standpoint, why did all this happen?" he said. "What was gained by all of it? What did I do that caused it or did not cause it? But I've decided that as long as you hang in there, no matter how bad you screw it up, God turns it around and makes it something. You look back, and you can see where God's in there, pulling your butt out of the fire, as usual. I bet he gets tired of that."

He chuckled, then shook his head.

"I always wondered, if I died first, would Bev be taken care of?" he said. "I didn't have much, just a little bit. I fig-ured she'd live with one of you boys."

He looked at me with uncharacteristic candor.

"Shawn, I loved your mother," he said.

He got up from the bed, went outside, and drove to work another day at the foundry. He was married that evening in a simple civil ceremony at the Mishawaka courthouse. Grandma Thornton and I were the only ones there from Dad's family. We joked that she was the flower girl and I was the ring bearer. I threw the wedding reception for the four of us at TGI Fridays.

Dad sold the house on Victory Road a few months later.

• • •

Troy and I often talked and laughed about our upbringing. He was much more stoic and dismissive about it than I was.

"Everybody has bad lives," he said. "God is good. We all survived."

Troy served in the military. I kidded him that the first place he learned survival tactics was in our own home. Even while serving in the armed forces, Troy pursued his call to ministry and transitioned to pastoral work. In between pastoral positions he worked in the marketplace. That time only added strength to his ability to minister as a pastor.

I was offered the great privilege of serving on the board of Awana Clubs International and helping lead one of the largest children's ministries in the world. For someone whose life was greatly shaped and directed by Awana, I couldn't think of a higher honor.

Eight years after Mom's passing, Lesli and I, along with our three children, answered the call to serve at Calvary Community Church in Westlake Village, California. Calvary is a megachurch in Southern California—quite a different setting from the Bible Belt of West Virginia. But the assignment is always the same no matter where you are geographically: to extend the heart and hope of Christ to hurting people and their families, no matter how poor or wealthy, how broken or seemingly whole.

The day I arrived in my new office at Calvary, in the barrenness of its empty shelves and tables, I found a personal note neatly placed in the center of my desk. It was from someone who had been a friend of Calvary for years and whose ministry headquarters sat right down the road.

"Ken and I are praying for you! You are God's answer to

our prayers for Calvary. Welcome and we look forward to meeting you in person. —Joni Eareckson Tada."

The author of the book that had so impacted my mother's life was within walking distance of my new office. *If Mom could only see this*, I thought. Soon Joni and Ken became dear friends and ministry partners. I was asked to serve on the board of the Joni and Friends Foundation.

Our church and Joni and Friends partnered together to serve people with special needs. At Christmastime we brought in ninety-five tons of snow and created a sledding hill in front of the church. Many kids in Southern California have never even touched snow. Everyone dressed up in their winter gear and mittens, which sit in closets most of the year. We even served hot chocolate and pretended the weather was really cold.

The best part was that an hour before the event began, we opened the hill for families whose children have special needs. They got to enjoy the snow at its fluffiest and best.

I was watching these children slide down the snow when a woman came up to me.

"Pastor Shawn," she said, her voice thick with emotion and her eyes dampening, "no one has ever treated my autistic son with this kind of dignity. Instead of letting us use the hill after everyone else was done, your church let us use it first. Thank you."

She gave me a hug and rejoined her family for the fun.

You can feel it when the heart of God is being expressed through a group of people, especially when they treat the least of these as the most important people in the world. Many people, those being served and those serving, had stories much more difficult and challenging than mine. God was doing what he always does—using the comfort they had received to comfort and support others. That's how compassion and mercy spread.

In that moment and many other similar moments, I thought of Mom and everything she had been through. My heart for those who are often overlooked came from her. Her stature had only grown in my heart since her death, and I knew I would never have a greater spiritual hero.

I'm not sure if there are street addresses in heaven, but I know where Mom lives today.

She lives on Victory Road.

Afterword

My friend Shawn Thornton has reminded us that often the "broken" people in our lives need fixing the least. Now that you have completed Shawn's memoir, *All But Normal: Life on Victory Road*, I am sure you have been reminded of the broken people from your own past or in your life today. Maybe you even recognize your own brokenness more clearly.

Maybe with all of her struggles, Beverly Thornton needed fixing the least. Maybe the "normal" people in her life needed to be repaired more than she did. I, for one, can testify to the fact that God uses broken people. I was born without arms or legs. Sounds pretty broken to most people. I have experienced the bleakest depths of despair and the darkest shadows of fear due to my own struggle to cope with my disabilities.

Yes, life without limbs can be as overwhelming as it sounds. Coping with a mother with the lasting effects of traumatic brain injury can be enough to crush a child. Your past may not be described by either of these scenarios, but you, too, know that life can be challenging. No matter what trauma or struggles shape our stories, we all fall into the category of "broken" people.

Maybe you are like me, and Shawn's story connected to your heart. His story made you think of your own story. You were reminded of the wounds of your past or the brokenness of your life today. All that the Thornton family experienced on Victory Road had a purpose—it was a part of God's plan. Shawn can now look back over his life and see that. I can see how God has used my life without limbs to accomplish his eternal plan in me and in others. The reality is that God did not allow anything to happen in Shawn's past, my past, or even your past that was not designed for our good and the good of others.

When speaking to his disciples as to the reason why a man was born blind, "broken" by the standard of that day, Jesus simply told them it was "that the work of God might be displayed in his life." Truly the work of God has been displayed in Shawn. Others have shared with me that they have seen God's work displayed in me. God also wants to redeem the brokenness and pain of your past to allow your life to display his work in you. Growing up in the chaotic setting of that little house on Victory Road taught Shawn to depend on God. He learned to be sensitive to the emotions, needs, whims, and moods of others. God grew in him a heart that cares for the private pain of others. Along with our wounds come blessings, skills, and gifts that God gives us to come alongside others who are wounded. If God doesn't give you a miracle, he can still use you to be a miracle in someone else's life.

I was struck by Beverly Thornton's determination to speak into the lives of some of the most marginalized. She treated an odd woman with smeared-on lipstick the same way she treated the pastor of her church. She talked to people because they were people. She laughed with those overlooked because they needed to laugh. Bev was drawn to those others avoided. Bev had some extreme challenges, but she did not use her physical or mental disabilities as an excuse to stop teaching Sunday school, to stop talking to the fringe of society, or to stop reaching out to God.

Because of my brokenness, God has given me a broad platform to share his hope with others. It has not always been easy, but I thank God for this unique gift. Frankly, I would not have it if I had limbs. Bev would not have been able to connect with the marginalized without her traumatic brain injury. She would not have been able to share with them a simple laugh, a kind word, or a brief prayer in the way she did, if the accident of 1962 had never occurred.

Life can be hard. We carry wounds from the past. We cope with the challenges of today. God is looking to use more people like Beverly to bring hope to the overlooked and hurting. After reading *All But Normal: Life on Victory Road*, I am even more determined to be someone who loves like God and who points to the hope that only he can offer in the middle of life's darkest hours.

It's possible that the challenges of your story are not in your past—you are currently in the middle of some deep waters and are facing some ongoing storms. Maybe you have felt like you are trapped in your current circumstances with no way out. I encourage you to accept that you might not be able to see a path right now, but that does not mean it's not there. Remember that just because you cannot understand God's plan, it does not mean he is not with you. Shawn found God in some of his most hopeless moments. God spoke into my life when I was ready to end my life at eight years old. God intervenes when we least expect it and when we need it the most!

Join me in noticing those near us who go unnoticed and who are being overwhelmed with their circumstances. Before we ask God to fix us, let's see if we are some of those broken people who need fixing the least. Let's share the hope of God with families who, like the Thorntons, cope with private pain every day. Let's do what Bev did and spread the love and hope of God to others no matter what challenges we face in life!

Nick Vujicic
Life Without Limbs
Westlake Village, CA

Acknowledgments

WRITING THIS MEMOIR HAS NOT BEEN EASY. For the first fifty years of my life I have kept my "all but normal" childhood on a shelf, sharing it with my wife and few others. This project has taken nearly four years to complete because it has at times been extremely uncomfortable to see my own story on the printed page.

I knew my story had impacted who I have become, but I didn't realize it might help anyone else deal with the wounds of their past. God used some incredible people to encourage and complete the writing of this book.

Joni Eareckson Tada encouraged me to share my story publicly for the first time in the fall of 2012. Pastor Max Lucado was in the audience when I did. That day both of them insisted that I write a memoir. They told me my story could help so many others with similar wounds. Thank you both for pushing me to do it!

My wife, Lesli, and my kids—Jonathan, Katie, and Megan—have been nothing but supportive in this journey.

Their loving response to the initial draft kept me going when I was having doubts. Lesli, I love you more than life itself! Jon, Katie, and Megan, I am so proud of the young adults you have become and love you each so much! Thank you all for holding my hand through this process.

Joel Kilpatrick, my cowriter, is a master at his craft. He once told me that he seeks to love on people as he tells their stories. Joel, thank you not only for bringing your expertise to this endeavor, but also for loving me, my mom, and my family in how you guided the journey of writing the book.

Of course a huge thank-you to my dad (John Thornton) and my brother, Troy. Your input on *All But Normal* was invaluable. I know it wasn't easy for you to allow me to share some of the most emotional and private stories of our lives. I love and admire you both more than you can imagine.

To my mother's sisters, my aunts Sue, Connie, Gail, and April, thank you for being cheerleaders in my life and ministry—and specifically in this project. Thank you for trusting me to honor your sister even as I told the tough challenges of her life. You are each special to me, and I love you!

To my administrative assistant Jennifer Ziegler, thank you for managing the daily complexity of my life and ministry. You are a Godsend.

To our agent, Scott Miller at Trident Media Group, thank you for believing in the importance of this book and for working out a great partnership with Tyndale.

The team at Tyndale House Publishers has been such a hardworking and enjoyable group to work with. Thank you Carol Traver, Jonathan Schindler, Kristen Magnesen, Alyssa

Anderson, and the rest of the Tyndale team. If I ever write another book, I can't imagine I would enjoy working with any other team more than I have this one!

And thank you, reader, for reading my story. If your heart has connected to my story, may you find the hope I have found—Jesus Christ. Reach out to me through AllButNormal.com for further help in your journey or to learn more about my journey and ministry.

Ultimately, I am thankful to God for his sovereignty in all aspects of my story. Challenges that seemed insurmountable he continues to use for my good and his glory.

Finally, Mom, you showed me how to live and love like Jesus no matter what challenges you faced. I look forward to walking with you on heaven's Victory Road someday.

About the Authors

SHAWN THORNTON serves as senior pastor of Calvary Community Church in Westlake Village, California. He is also the Bible-teaching voice heard daily across America on the half-hour radio program *All Things New*. Shawn has the honor of serving on the board of directors of Awana Clubs International and on the board of directors of the Joni and Friends Foundation. He blogs regularly at PastorShawn.com. Shawn and his wife, Lesli, have three young adult children— Jonathan, Katie, and Megan.

JOEL KILPATRICK is an award-winning journalist and author whose work has been featured in *Time* magazine, the *Washington Post*, *USA Today*, CBS Radio, the *Dallas Morning News*, and many other newspapers and magazines. He lives in Southern California with his wife and children.

"A touching memoir.... Immensely inspiring."
KIRKUS REVIEWS

the tank man's son
A MEMOIR

MARK BOUMAN
WITH D. R. JACOBSEN

The time Mom met Hitler,
Frost came to dinner, and
I heard the Greatest Story ever told

a memoir

DIKKON EBERHART

SAVING
MY
ASSASSIN

A MEMOIR
VIRGINIA PRODAN

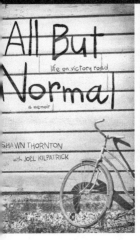

All But
life on victory road
Normal
a memoir

SHAWN THORNTON
with JOEL KILPATRICK

Ruined

RUTH EVERHART
(a memoir)

RAY & BETTY WHIPPS
WITH CRAIG BORLASE

'TIL
WE MEET
AGAIN
A MEMOIR OF LOVE AND WAR

Memoir
ADDICT

CP1065

Love memoirs?

Find your next great read at
MemoirAddict.com!

At Memoir Addict, we find ordinary people
with extraordinary stories.

Explore:

- updates on new releases
- additional stories from your
  favorite authors
- FREE first-chapter downloads
- discussion guides
- author videos and book trailers

- inspirational quotes to share
  on Pinterest, Twitter,
  and Facebook
- book reviews
- and so much more!

While you're there, check out our blog, featuring unique perspectives
on memoirs from all facets of the publishing industry. From authors
to acquisition directors to editors, we share our passion for story-
telling. You'll get an insider's look at the craft of shaping a story into
a captivating memoir.

Are you a memoir addict? Follow us on Twitter @MemoirAddict and
on Facebook for updates on your favorite authors, free e-book promo-
tions, contests, and more!

Plus, visit BookClubHub.net to

- download free discussion guides
- get book club recommendations
- sign up for Tyndale's book club
  and e-newsletters

MemoirAddict.com:
ordinary people,
extraordinary
stories!

Online Discussion *guide*

TAKE *your* TYNDALE READING
EXPERIENCE *to the* NEXT LEVEL

A FREE discussion guide for this book
is available at bookclubhub.net, perfect
for sparking conversations in your book
group or for digging deeper into the text
on your own.

www.bookclubhub.net

TYNDALE

*You'll also find free discussion guides for
other Tyndale books, e-newsletters, e-mail
devotionals, virtual book tours, and more!*

CP0071

RESOURCES FOR YOUR JOURNEY

The online resources below provide you with an opportunity to follow the life and ministry of *All But Normal* author Shawn Thornton. Through these resources you will be able to connect with Shawn via social media, follow his blog, learn more about his story, and discover resources to help you in your own journey.

→ **AllButNormal.com**

This is a comprehensive site with resources related to Shawn's memoir. The site includes videos of Shawn and his brother, Troy, chatting about the book and sharing more stories about their childhood. You will also find discussion questions for book clubs, sermons from Shawn, and links to organizations and support groups related to traumatic brain injury, mental illness, and special needs.

→ **PastorShawn.com**

PastorShawn.com is a great place to find resources to help you discover the hope God offers you in your journey and to help you grow in that hope. You will find helpful podcasts, blog posts, videos, and much more. Much of the site is dedicated to *All Things New Radio*—Shawn's half-hour Bible-teaching broadcast heard across the United States daily Monday through Friday. PastorShawn.com contains links and information to help you find radio stations and broadcast times in your area, gives access to each day's program as a podcast, and will direct you to the *All Things New Radio* free app for your smart phone or tablet.

→ **Calvary101.com**

Calvary101.com provides you all things related to the congregation Shawn leads in Southern California. This site will give you service times, ministries offered, and more sermons with life-changing content to help you in your daily walk. Shawn and his congregation would love to have you worship with the Calvary Community Church family when you are in the greater Los Angeles area.

 @shawnthornton | pastorthornton | pastorshawn

CP1121